RXpert SERIES
Student's Companion

Biopharmaceutics and Pharmacokinetics

Revised Edition

Rxpert SERIES
Student's Companion

Biopharmaceutics and Pharmacokinetics

Revised Edition

Kamla Pathak
M.Pharma (Pharmaceutics), Ph.D.
Professor and Dean,
Pharmacy College Saifai,
Uttar Pradesh University of Medical Sciences,
Saifai, Etawah, Uttar Pradesh.

Ravi Shankar
Associate Professor,
TRC Mahavidyalaya,
Department of Pharmacy,
Barabanki, Uttar Pradesh.

Monika Joshi
Assistant Professor,
Faculty of Pharmacy,
Maharshi University of Information Technology,
Noida.

TM
PharmaMed Press
An imprint of BSP Books Pvt. Ltd.
4-4-309/316, Giriraj Lane,
Sultan Bazar, Hyderabad - 500 001.

Biopharmaceutics and Pharmacokinetics, *Revised Edition*
***by* Kamla Pathak, Ravi Shankar and Monika Joshi**

Published by

Pharma Med PRESS
An Imprint of
BSP Books Pvt. Ltd.

™ **PharmaMed Press**
An imprint of BSP Books Pvt. Ltd.
4-4-309/316, Giriraj Lane, Sultan Bazar, Hyderabad - 500 001.
Phone: 040-23445688
E-mail: info@pharmamedpress.net
www.bspbooks.net/www.pharmamedpress.net

ISBN: 978-93-48734-77-8 (Hardback)

Preface

The subject Biopharmaceutics and Pharmacokinetics are twin disciplines that arequantitative in nature. The mathematical description of the drug's biofate is primarily deduced with the help of these disciplines that is useful both from formulation development and in clinical settings. Though several books are available on the subject,the contents of the present book are in accordance to the prescribed PCI syllabus. Utmostcare has been taken to incorporate all the elements describe in the syllabus. Additionally, some newer concepts have been introduced taking care of the changing times, the language is kept as simple as possible and illustrations have been used liberally for easy grasp of the subject. The pharmacokinetics part has been in particularly elaborated especially the stepwise derivations of mathematical expressions. Additionally, some practice problems, definitions and explanation of certain terms in Boxes are highlight of the compilation. At the end of each chapter MCQs, short answer questions and long answer questions have been included that would help the students in evaluating their knowledge.

We hope that this book will not only be a valuable addition to the libraries and an important guide for succeeding in examination but also will serve as basic research foundation for students pursuing postgraduate courses.

Particular efforts have been made to avoid mistakes, but if found and brought to our notice, will be corrected in next edition.

Happy read.

Prof. Kamla Pathak
Ravi Shankar
Monika Joshi

Contents

Introduction

CHAPTER 1

Learning Objectives

- Introduction to biopharmaceutics
- Aim and scope of Biopharmaceutics
- Understanding the concept of pharmacokinetics
- Applications and applied fields of pharmacokinetics

Biopharmaceutics

"Pharmaceutics" is a field of science that involves the preparation, use, or dispensing of medicines. Addition of the prefix "bio-" coming from the Greek "bios," relating to living organisms or tissues, expands this field into the science of preparing, using, and administering drugs to living organisms or tissues. Inherently biopharmaceutics is the interdependence of biological aspects of the living organism (the patient) and the physicochemical principles that govern the preparation and behavior of the medicinal agent or drug product. This philosophy was introduced in the mid-twentieth century by the biopharmaceutical scientists who recognized the importance of absorption, distribution, metabolism, and elimination (ADME) on the clinical performance of medicinal agents as well as the impact of the physicochemical properties of the materials on their *in vivo* performance. As a result, biopharmaceutics has evolved into a discipline that encompasses fundamental principles from basic scientific and related disciplines, including chemistry, physiology, physics, statistics, engineering, mathematics, microbiology, enzymology, and cell biology. The biopharmaceutical scientist, therefore, must have sufficient understanding of all of these scientific fields in order to be most effective in a drug development role. One should also be well versed with interrelated specialty disciplines including formulation, pharmacokinetics, cell-based transport, drug delivery, or physical pharmacy as these are significant for the drug development (design) process.

A drug is designed as dosage form with the aim to deliver the drug to produce desired therapeutic effect. Additionally, the dosage form is expected to meet the patient's needs including elegance, safety, convenience and favourable organoleptic properties. The focus primarily is to achieve desired clinical effect that entirely relies on how the dosage form (drug product) performs in the body. Hence, the onus lies on the release of the drug substance from the drug product either for local drug action or for absorption of drug into the blood for systemic action. The release of drug from the dosage form is dependent on the physicochemical properties of the drug, its formulation strategy and route of administration.

Biopharmaceutics evaluates the interrelationship of the various factors namely, the physicochemical properties of the drug, its dosage form characteristics and the route of administration of the dosage form on the rate and extent of systemic drug absorption. The dosage form when administered is subjected to various processes that play a key role in drug absorption, in addition to the physicochemical properties of drug. Absorption followed by *in vivo drug* distribution to the site of action, elicits the therapeutic response. A general scheme describing the events is illustrated in Fig. 1.1.

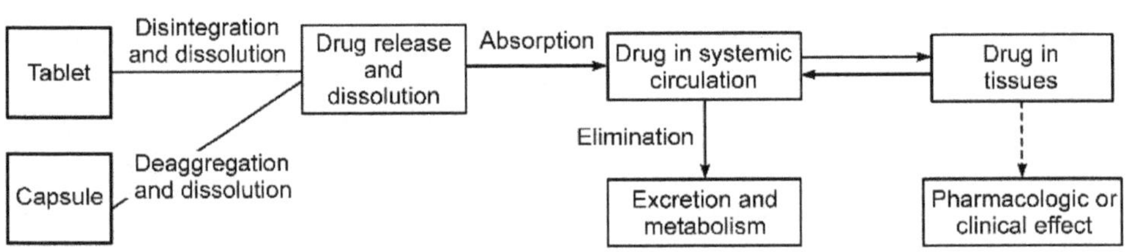

Fig 1.1 Scheme depicting the fate of oral dosage form of a drug and its therapeutic effect.

The drug in its dosage form is administered to the patient by a specific route (oral/ parenteral) depending on the dosage form. This is followed by drug release from the dosage form in a predictable manner. Thereafter, a fraction of the drug is absorbed either into the blood or the adjacent tissue /organ, or both. Next, the drug reaches the site of action and the pharmacological/ clinical effect is observed when the drug approaches a concentration equal to or more than *minimum effective concentration* (MEC). It is important to predetermine the dosing regimen, including the initial dose, maintenance dose, and the dosing interval, through clinical trials to achieve drug concentration(s) that are clinically effective in large number of patients. The efficacy and safety of drug are primarily dependent on the dosing regimen. Different drugs have different optimal dosage and dosing intervals. Furthermore, for a given drug, the optimal dosage and dosing intervals can vary widely between the patients.

Historically, the pharmaceutical researchers have assessed the relative drug availability *in vivo* after administering a drug product via different routes to either animals or humans, followed by comparing a specific pharmacological, clinical, or potential toxic responses. For example, isoproterenol administration results in an increase in heart rate when given by intravenous route, however, no such effect on the heart is observed when the drug is given orally. Thus development of biopharmaceutical principles allow for rational design of drug products, which would enhance the delivery of active drug, and optimize the therapeutic efficacy of the drug in the patient. Box 1 highlights the biopharmaceutical principles.

Box 1

Biopharmaceutics is

- Study of the effect of formulation factors on therapeutic activity of a drug product.
- Study evaluates the relationship between the physical, chemical and biological sciences as applied to drug, its dosage form(s), and to the drug action.
- Modern biopharmaceutics studies the interrelationship of the physicochemical properties and *in vitro* behavior of the drug and its product on administration of the drug to the body under normal or pathological conditions.

Biopharmaceutical studies involve both *in vitro* and *in vivo* methods. The *in vitro* methods use laboratory test apparatus without involving test animals and humans. For e.g. disintegration test, dissolution test, etc. The in *vivo* test involves measurement of systemic drug availability (bioavailability) after administering a drug product to test animals or human volunteers. The ultimate aim is to achieve effective therapeutics. Box 2 summarizes the aims of biopharmaceutical studies.

Box 2

Aims:

- The aim of biopharmaceutics is to adjust the delivery of drug to the general circulation in such a manner as to provide optimal therapeutic activity for the patient.
- Some drugs are intended for topical or local therapeutic action at the site of administration. For these drugs, systemic absorption is undesirable.
- Drugs intended for local activity generally have a direct pharmacodynamic action without affecting other body organs. These drugs may be applied topically to the skin, nose, eyes, mucous membranes, buccal cavity, throat and rectum.

Each product is a formulation unique unto itself. Biopharmaceutical considerations often determine the ultimate dose and dosage form of a drug product. For example, the dosage for a drug intended for local activity, such as a topical dosage form, is often expressed in concentration or as percent of the active drug in the formulation. The amount of drug is not specified because it is the concentration of the drug at the active site that relates to the pharmacodynamic action. Biopharmaceutical studies must be performed to ensure that the dosage form does not irritate, cause an allergic response or allow systemic drug absorption. The dosage of a drug intended for systemic absorption is given on the basis of absolute amount, such as mg or g.

Secondly, each route of drug application presents special biopharmaceutical considerations in drug product design. By carefully choosing the route of drug administration and properly designing the drug product, the bioavailability of the active drug can vary from rapid and complete absorption to a slow, sustained rate of absorption or even virtually no absorption, depending on the therapeutic objective. For e.g.: The design of a vaginal tablet formulation for the treatment of a fungal infection must consider ingredients compatible with vaginal anatomy and physiology. An eye medication may require specific biopharmaceutical considerations including appropriate pH, isotonicity, local irritation to the cornea, draining by tears, and concern for systemic drug absorption.

A primary concern in biopharmaceutics is the bioavailability of drugs. Bioavailability refers to the measurement of the rate and extent of active drug that reaches the systemic circulation. It means access of drug to the bloodstream (Figure 1.2). The pharmaceutical factors affecting drug bioavailability are (i) type of the drug product, (ii) nature of excipients in the drug product, (iii) physicochemical properties of the drug, and (iv) measurable characteristics by which a drug interacts with other systems.

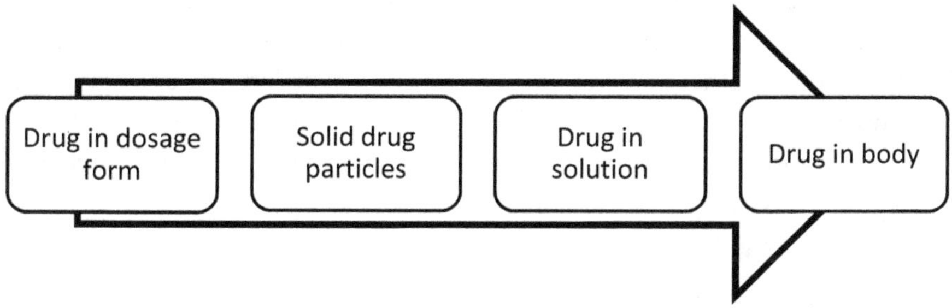

Fig. 1.2 Schematic representation of drug bioavailability process.

Scope of Biopharmaceutics

1. Encompasses all possible effects observed following the administration of the drug in various dosage forms.
2. Encompasses all possible effects of various dosage forms on biological response.
3. Encompasses all possible physiological factors which may affect the drug in various dosage forms.

Applications of Biopharmaceutics

1. A company is going to market a new dosage form of a certain drug (the dose is known). When this dosage is administered to a healthy human, there are two possibilities: (i) the drug may not be release quickly and hence the action of drug will be delayed, (ii) the drug may be released quickly and hence the duration of action will be very short. With the knowledge of biopharmaceutics we can change various formulation factors to obtain optimum onset of action and duration of action.

2. A company is marketing tablets of certain drug. Now it wants to change a few ingredients or some formulation factors. Whether or not the new tablets will behave in a manner similar to the previous one; bioavailability studies are done. So the bioavailability of the newer tablets is compared with the old tablets. If it is found that the bioavailability of the newer tablets is equivalent (i.e. bioequivalent) to that of older tablets then the new tablets will be permitted to be marketed.
3. A company is marketing the tablets of a certain drug. Now they have planned to make transdermal dosage form of the same drug. To establish its efficacy the bioavailability of the transdermal dosage form is compared to that of the established tablet dosage form. If both are found to be close then the transdermal dosage form will be accepted by the FDA.

Pharmacokinetics

Knowing what the drug does to the body is just not sufficient; it is also extremely important to know what the body does to the drug. Thus knowledge of both the pharmacodynamic and pharmacokinetic aspects of the drug and its metabolites in animals and humans is significantly important for adjusting drug dosing. The final aim of a drug is to achieve optimal therapy and to attain this aim:

1. The drug is first developed into a suitable dosage form which is administered in to the body through a suitable route of administration.
2. The drug is released at the site of absorption at a certain rate.
3. The drug is then absorbed from the site of absorption into the systemic circulation.
4. The drug is carried to various tissues through blood for distribution to the extravascular tissues. Distribution is a reversible process and hence the drug returns back to systemic circulation.
5. The drug produces its action at the site of action: extravascular/ intravascular.
6. The drug is metabolized in liver/tissues.
7. Finally the drug is eliminated from the body.

The events have been illustrated in Fig 1.3 for quick understanding. All the processes occur at a certain rate. In pharmacokinetics we study those rates and pharmacokinetic equations are used to predict these rates. Pharmacokinetics is the study of the time course of a drug in the body (extent and duration of systemic exposure) and it also encompasses the study of the rate processes involved in *absorption*, *distribution, metabolism* and *excretion* (ADME).

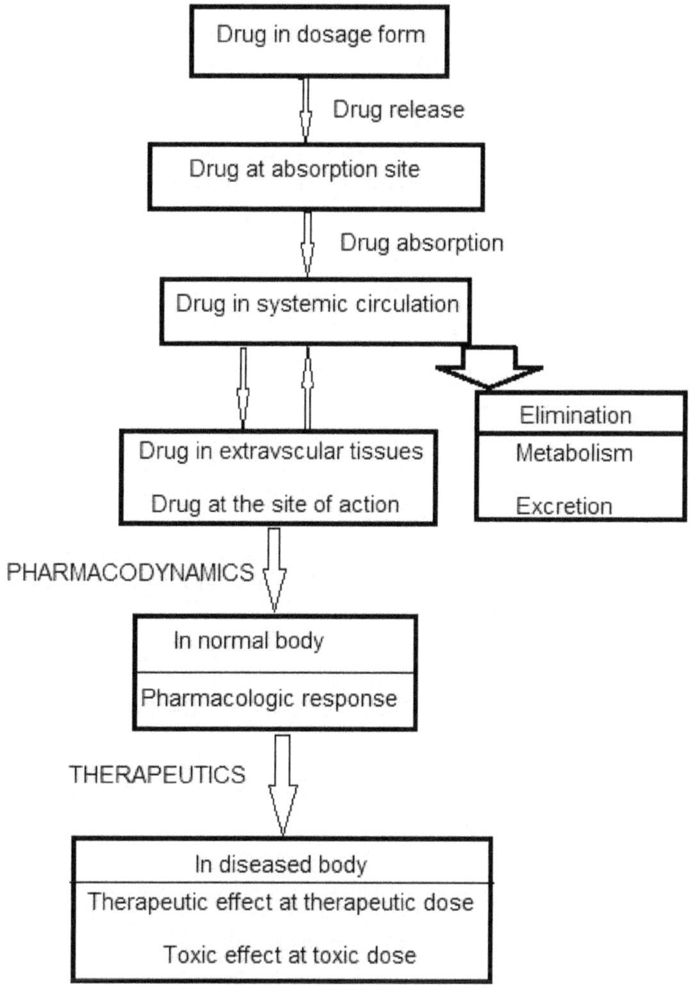

Fig. 1.3 Schematic representation of the processes involved in drug therapeutics.

The plasma drug concentration is the primary fundamental of pharmacokinetics. Furthermore, the plasma drug concentration is in equilibrium with certain tissues in the body. In case the drug binds to plasma proteins, the concentration of free drug available in the systemic circulation influences the dose calculations. In general, the pharmacokinetic parameters of a drug are derived from the measurement of the drug concentration(s) in either blood or plasma. The goal is to quantitatively account for the amount which has entered the body (bioavailable dose) from the time of administration until it has been completely cleared. The mathematical descriptions that have emerged have proven valuable for both drug research and drug therapy.

The study of pharmacokinetics involves both experimental and theoretical approaches. The experimental approach involves development of biological sampling techniques, analytical method development for measurement of drug(s) and metabolites, and procedures for data collection and interpretation. The theoretical aspect of pharmacokinetics involves the development of pharmacokinetic models that predict drug disposition after drug administration. The application of statistics is an integral part of pharmacokinetic models to determine data errors, deviation in models and correlation.

Application of Pharmacokinetics

1. The bioavailability of a dosage form is calculated by pharmacokinetic equations.
2. The frequency of dosing is calculated from pharmacokinetic equations.
3. The equations also assist in calculation of dose for controlled release formulations.
4. In case of patients with kidney/ liver failure the dose of a drug should be calculated very cautiously. If the rate of absorption of drug is greater than the elimination rate of the drug, then the drug will be accumulated in the body in such patients and may show toxic effects. The rate of elimination of a drug from the body is calculated with the help of pharmacokinetic equations.
5. When a potent anticancer drug is administered to a patient the plasma concentration of the drug must be very close to minimum effective concentration. Since the therapeutic index of the drug is very narrow in

case of potent drugs, so rate of administration must also be very slow. This rate of administration is calculated by pharmacokinetic principles.

6. Antagonism or potentiation of the effects of one drug by another has a pharmacokinetic basis and not pharmacological basis. ADME may be affected by concomitant administration of second drug leading to clinical differences.
7. Selecting or modifying dosage regimen requires an understanding of clinical pharmacokinetics. For e.g. higher dose of theophylline is required for children and smokers, and lower dose for patients with congestive heart failure.

Fields in Pharmacokinetics

Based on the variety of applications of pharmacokinetics, various specialized fields have emerged.

1. **Clinical pharmacokinetics** is the application of the pharmacokinetic methods in drug therapy. It is a multidisciplinary approach where the dose of a drug is optimized for a specific patient depending on the disease state, age and sex of the patient. This subject requires information from medical and pharmaceutical research.
2. **Population pharmacokinetics** is the study of pharmacokinetic differences of drug in various population groups.
3. **Pharmacodynamics** deals with the relationship between the drug concentration at the site of action (receptor) and pharmacological response, including biochemical and physiological effects that influence the interaction of drug with the receptor.
4. **Toxicokinetics** refers to the application of pharmacokinetic principles to the design, conduct and interpret the drug safety and is also used in validating dose related toxicity in animals. Toxicokinetic studies are conducted in animals and the result obtained is used to interpret possible toxic reactions in humans.

Therapeutic Drug monitoring: When drug with narrow therapeutic indices are used in patients, it is necessary to monitor plasma drug concentration closely by taking periodic blood samples. Some drugs that are frequently monitored are aminoglycoside antibiotics, anticonvulsants and anticancer drugs in order to minimize adverse effects.

Pharmacokinetic studies date back to 1924 when Widmark and Tandberg published two theoretical papers on the one-compartment open model followed by additional two papers by Teorell in 1937. The work was largely disregarded owing to complexity of the equations and lack of analytical tools. However, with the advent of computers and proliferation sophisticated analytical tools pharmacokinetics has emerged as a significant branch with numerous applications.

Questions

Multiple Choice Questions

1. The release of drug from the dosage form is not dependent on
   (a) The physicochemical properties of the drug
   (b) Route of administration
   (c) Its formulation strategy
   (d) Pharmacodynamic property
2. Systemic absorption is desirable for
   (a) Nasal preparation
   (b) Otic formulation
   (c) Opthalmic preparation
   (d) SR formulation
3. The strength of topical dosage form is expressed as
   (a) Amount of drug
   (b) Percent of drug
   (c) Volume of drug
   (d) Moles of drug
4. Pick the odd one. Biopharmaceutical studies on topical dosage form must be performed to ensure that the dosage form does not
   (a) Irritate
   (b) Allow systemic drug absorption
   (c) Cause an allergic response
   (d) Have foul odor
5. Select the wrong one. The pharmacokinetic parameters are derived from the measurement of drug concentration(s) in
   (a) Blood (b) Urine (c) Plasma (d) Lymph

6. Pharmacokinetic models are used to predict
   (a) Drug disposition after drug administration
   (b) Physicochemical properties of drug
   (c) Bioavailability
   (d) Presystemic metabolism
7. Statistics, an integral part of pharmacokinetic models is not used to determine
   (a) Data errors
   (b) Correlation
   (c) Deviation in models
   (d) Frequency

Descriptive Questions

1. Define biopharmaceutics. What are its aims and scope?
2. Explain the applications of biopharmaceutics.
3. Define pharmacokinetics. Highlight various fields of pharmacokinetics.
4. With the help of diagram explain the events of drug release and ADME.
5. Enlist the applications of pharmacokinetics.

Absorption of Drugs

CHAPTER
2

LEARNING OBJECTIVES

- Understanding the concept of absorption
- Impact of routes of administration on absorption
- Mechanisms of absorption
- Understanding the factors affecting absorption

The primary step in pharmacokinetics is the absorption of the drug from the administered dosage form. Absorption describes the movement of drug molecules (unchanged) from the site of administration via dosage form, to the blood stream. Absorption is the mandatory requirement for the drug to exert its therapeutic effect. Blood mainly consist of red blood cells, liquid called plasma and few white blood cells. White blood cells make up a very small portion of the blood. Since, it is easy to measure the concentration of drug in plasma and also there exist a direct correlation between the concentration of the drug in blood and plasma. Therefore, absorption can also be defined as the transfer of drug molecules from the site of administration to the site of

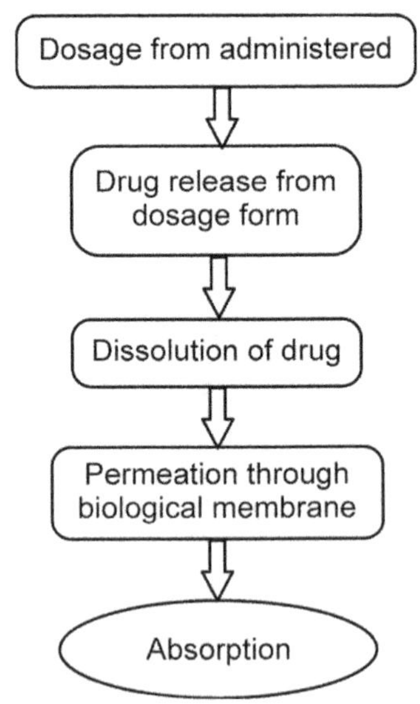

Fig. 2.1 Steps of drug release till absorption.

measurement (blood/ plasma). When the dosage form is administered the drug must be released from the dosage form (disintegration should take place), followed by dissolution of the released drug, afterwards permeation through biological membrane is required for efficient absorption (Fig. 2.1).

The extent and rate of absorption both determines the therapeutic efficacy of drug. This chapter will cover the description of various routes for absorption of drug. Since oral route is the major route of absorption therefore mechanism of absorption through gastrointestinal tract (GIT) is discussed in detail, followed by factors affecting drug absorption through GIT. At last the brief description of various non-per oral extra vascular route has been covered.

Routes of Administration

For the drugs to be clinically or therapeutically effective, they must be absorbed. There are several routes by which drug can be administered to accomplish absorption. These routes of administration were majorly divided into four sections:

1. **Enteral route:** This includes oral (most common route of administration), sublingual or buccal and rectal routes (e.g. suppositories).
2. **Parenteral route:** Intravenous injections, intra-arterial injections, intrathecal injection, subcutaneous injection and intramuscular injections are covered under parenteral routes. If the drug is administered intravenously, it directly enters to systemic circulation i.e. blood stream and need for absorption is bypassed entirely.
3. **Topical route:** Application of drug topically to skin, eye or some specific membrane minimizes the systemic exposure. Various medicated creams, gels, ointments are applied topically for local effect.
4. **Other routes:** Transdermal, ocular and inhalation routes.

Table 2.1 lists the advantages and disadvantages of various routes of administration

Table 2.1 Various routes of drug administration.

Route of adminis-tration	Advantages	Disadvantages	Bioavailability	Examples
Enteral route				
Buccal or sublingual (SL)	- No first pass effect. - In buccal route drug may be	Drug may be swallowed.	Rapid absorption of lipid soluble drugs	Isosorbide dinitrate tablet (Isordil),
	in buccal mucosa for local prolonged action. - In sublingual route the dosage form is placed under tongue	Not suitable for drugs with high doses		Buprenorphine hydrochloride +Naloxone film (subozone)
Oral (p.o.)	- Easiest route of administration offering high patient compliance - Suitable for both immediate and sustained release formulations	- Presystemic metabolism of drugs - Some drugs may have erratic absorption - May be unstable in GIT	-Variable absorption. Slower absorption rate when compared to IV bolus and IM injection	Paracetamol and ibuprofen (Diclofenac)
Rectal	- Useful for pediatric and geriatric patients who have problem in swallowing of drugs - Used for local and systemic effects	- Absorption may be erratic - Suppository may migrate to different position - Patient unaccep-tability	- Variable absorption from suppository - More reliable absorption from enema (solution)	- Bisacodyl tablet (Bisa-lax) - Indomethacin (Indocin)

Contd...

Route of adminis-tration	Advantages	Disadvantages	Bioavailability	Examples
Parenteral route				
Intravenous (IV)	- Drug is given for immediate effect - Dose can be accurately titrated against response	- Increased chance of adverse reaction - Possible anaphylaxis - Expensive and labour intensive than other routes	- Complete (100%) systemic absorption	Heparin Na (Heprin), Paclitaxel-lypophilized powder for injectable suspension (Abraxane)
Intramuscular (IM) route	- Easier to inject as compare to intravenous - Larger volume may be used compare to subcutaneous injections	- Irritating drugs may be painful - Absorption rate may vary depending on muscle group injected and blood flow	- Rapid absorption from aqueous solution - Slow absorption from oily solutions	Streptomycin inj. Fluvestrant inj. (Faslodex)
Subcutaneous injection	- Less painful than other parenteral routes - Generally used for vaccines and drug not absorbed orally e.g. insulin	- Volume limitation (<1-2 ml) - Irritant drug may cause local tissue damage	Rapid absorption from aqueous solutions and slow from depot formulations	Insulin (Levemir flexPen), Adalimumab (plamumab)
Intrathecal injection	Drug is directly injected into cerebrospinal fluid for direct uptake into brain	- Requires skilled personnel	- Complete absorption	Baclofen injection (Lioresal)
Intra arterial injection	Used in chemotherapy to target drug to organ	Drug may distribute to other tissues or organs in the body	- Complete absorption	Epirubicin HCl (Pharmorubicin RD)

Contd...

Route of adminis-tration	Advantages	Disadvantages	Bioavailability	Examples
Topical route	- Easy to apply - Non-invasive - High level of patient acceptance	- Most drugs have a high molecular weight and are poorly lipid soluble, so are not absorbed via skin or mucous membranes	- Very slow / poor absorption	Estradiol cream, Diclofenac sodium topical gel
Other routes				
Transdermal	- First-pass effect is avoided, thus minimizing drug input. - Drugs with narrow therapeutic range can be delivered. - Better control of blood levels for potent drugs is possible.	- Drug permeation may vary with age, gender and disease condition - Not useful when required to deliver large doses of drug(s),	- Variable absorption rate - Slow absorption	Nicotine (Nicotinol), Scopolamine (Transderm-scop)
	- Patient compliance can be increased. - Therapy can be terminated by simple removal of the delivery system	- Not useful when the drug or the formulation is skin sensitizing or irritating.		
Inhalational and intranasal	Can be used for local or systemic effect	- Particle size of drug determines placement in the respiratory tract - May stimulate cough reflex	- Instant absorption	- Salbutamol sulfate (Asmalin)

Oral administration and Subsequent Absorption of Drugs

Most of the drugs are administered orally due to the high degree of patient compliance and these drugs will show their therapeutic activity only when they reaches to blood stream. Therefore oral administration generally gives systemic effect rather than local effect. Before a drug can be absorbed it has to pass through several stages as illustrated in Fig 2.1. Further, presystemic metabolism will affect their absorption. Absorption takes place in different part of alimentary canal like mouth, stomach, small intestine and large intestine. However, due to the large surface area of small intestine, it is the major site of absorption. Two fundamental processes that are involved in oral absorption are dissolution of drug in GIT and permeation of dissolved drug through intestinal wall into the systemic circulation. The drug for permeation has to cross the biological cell membrane and therefore the brief description of cell membrane structure and physiology is required.

Structure and Composition of Cell Membrane

For absorption of orally administered drug passage across cell membrane is a perquisite step. The phospholipid bilayer is the common feature of the cell membrane. Phospholipids make up of 75 % of the membrane. Other components of the membrane are cholesterol (20%) that provides fluidity to the membrane and glycolipid (5 %). A single phospholipid molecule has phosphate group that forms the head hydrophilic portion on one end and two chains of fatty acids that form the lipid tail. The polar head faces extracellular fluid outside and cytoplasm inside, the membrane sandwich like structure is formed where the hydrophilic heads from both sides surrounds the central lipophilic chains (Fig. 2.2). The membrane is thus termed as amphipathic membrane. Cholesterol molecules are interdispersed between the lipidic tails of both the membrane. Tiny –OH group of cholesterol form hydrogen bond with polar head of phospholipid and glycolipid. Glycolipid is only present in the membrane that faces the extracellular fluid. This membrane is embedded with proteins that are attached to outer and inner leaflets. Two different types of proteins integral and peripheral are associated with the membrane. Integral protein is embedded in the fatty acid tail of bilayer. Integral protein may serves as ion channels, transporters, enzymes, receptors or linkers. Peripheral proteins are mainly attached to the polar head of the membrane or with integral protein to inner and outer surface of membrane. Many membrane proteins are glycoproteins to which carbohydrate group is attached to the end that protrude into the extracellular fluid. Glycoprotein mostly functions as cells identify markers that help to distinguish between the internal and foreign cells. Since the lipid and proteins are not fixed or locked in a place and therefore the cell membrane is also described as fluid mosaic model.

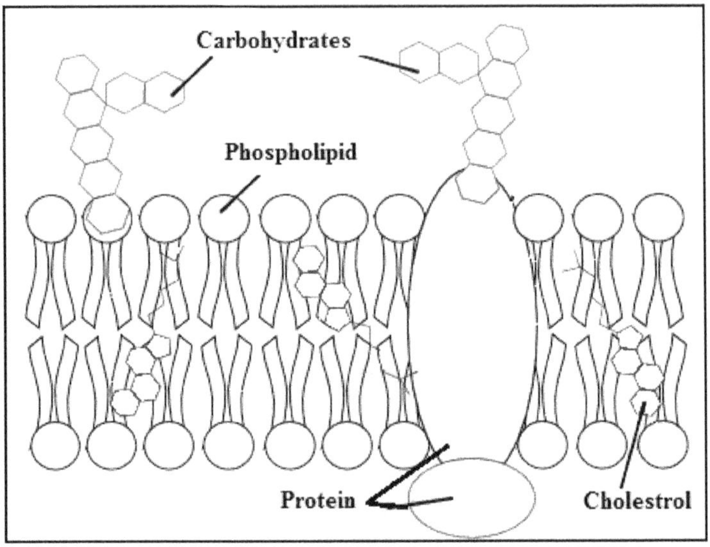

Fig. 2.2 Structure of cell membrane (fluid mosaic model).

Mechanism of Drug Absorption through Gastrointestinal Tract

The cell membrane acts as a semi permeable membrane that selectively allows certain substances to pass through it. The drugs with low molecular weight and having lipid solubility are allowed to pass through the lipid bilayer. This lipid bilayer limits the passage of water soluble materials like glucose and electrolytes and therefore these materials need some assistance to cross the barrier. The mechanism for transport of drug across membrane is mainly described by passive (no energy required) or active transport (energy required from adenosine tri phosphate, ATP).

1. **Passive transport:** The transport of drug molecules from a region of high concentration to lower concentration under the influence of concentration gradient, without expenditure of energy is termed as passive transport. Passive transport comprises of two pathways:
   (a) ***Paracellular pathway:*** In this transport of drug molecules through aqueous pore at tight junction between the GI epithelium takes place. The small drug molecules are either absorbed by diffusion or hydrostatic pressure.

(b) ***Transcellular pathway:*** This is the major route of drug absorption in which transport across the lipid cell membrane of GI epithelium takes place. Generally the drug molecules absorbed through this pathway are unionized and lipophilic in nature.

Mechanisms Involved in Passive Transport of Drug

(a) **Simple diffusion:** This movement of molecule from region of higher concentration to lower concentration is known as **simple diffusion** and is a part of passive transport. Most of drugs are absorbed through passive diffusion. Molecules always tend to diffuse towards the concentration gradient until the concentration on both the sides becomes equal (Fig 2.3). One of the examples is the concentration of oxygen which is higher outside the cell than inside therefore it generally diffuses into the cell. The concentration of drug at blood initially will be lower than concentration at absorption site because after the administration of drug when it reaches into the blood it rapidly distributes into the large volume. For a drug which is administered orally concentration of drug at gastrointestinal tract will be greater than concentration of drug at plasma ($C_{GIT} >> C_p$), thus driving the drug molecule from GIT to plasma.

Fick's first law of diffusion states that the movement of drug occurs along the concentration gradient until equilibrium is achieved and is expressed mathematically as

$$\frac{dQ}{dt} = DAK_{m/w}\frac{C_{GIT} - C}{h} \qquad .....(2.1)$$

where dQ/dt = rate of diffusion (amount/time), D = diffusion coefficient of the drug,

A = surface area of absorbing membrane for diffusion, $K_{m/w}$ = partition coefficient of drug between lipoidal membrane and aqueous GI fluid, (C_{GIT} - C) = difference in concentration of drug in GI fluids and the plasma (concentration gradient) and h = thickness of membrane.

This equation clearly implies that the rate of drug diffusion across biological membrane is directly proportional to the concentration gradient (Fig. 2.3). The concentration gradient should be maintained for continuous transport of drug across membrane and through other side of the membrane the drug is distributed to tissue or organ so that this gradient is maintained. This condition is called sink and it is the mandatory requirement while performing dissolution testing procedure.

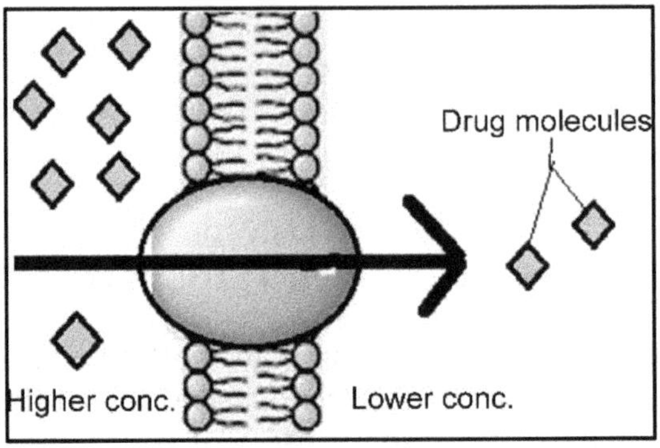

Fig. 2.3 Simple diffusion towards the concentration gradient.

(b) Pore or convective transport or filtration: This is the mass transport of molecules due to bulk flow of fluid. In such case hydrostatic or the osmotic pressure is the driving force for the transport of drug molecules across membrane. Very small water soluble molecule of molecular weight less than 250 Da (example urea, water and sugar) can transport towards concentration gradient through the protein channels and pores present in the membrane.

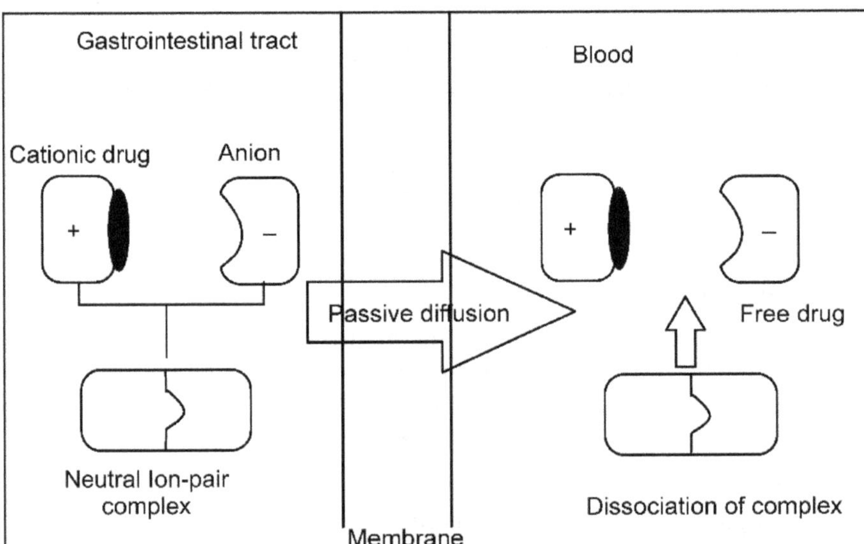

Fig. 2.4 Transport of cationic drug by forming neutral complex with endogenous anion.

(c) **Ion pair transport:** Strong electrolytes like quaternary ammonium compounds and sulphonic acid that maintain their charge at all physiological pH are unable to cross the membrane. In such case the ionized molecule is linked with oppositely charged ion to form ion pair complex where the overall charge of complex is neutral. This neutral drug complex is able to penetrate the drug easily through passive diffusion (Fig. 2.4). Example, propanolol a basic drug forms ion pair complex with oleic acid, and quinine forms ion pair complex with hexylsalicylate that make it to diffuse more easily across the membrane.

(d) **Facilitated diffusion:** Large polar and ionic molecule however cannot transport across the membrane by simple diffusion. Such molecules can move either through protein channels or using some specialized transport mechanism. The process is named as **facilitated diffusion.** It is a carrier mediated transport where a carrier binds reversibly to the drug molecule to be transported and form drug-carrier complex. The carrier then cross the membrane and release the drug molecule over other. The carrier then returns to its original site to accept the fresh molecule of drug. Transport of glucose which is both large and polar across the membrane using specialized carrier protein called the glucose transporter (GLUT1 and GLUT5) is an example of facilitated diffusion. Since facilitated diffusion does not require the expenditure of energy it is a passive process. Another example is the transport of vitamin B12 which forms complex with the glycoprotein produced by the gastric parietal cell. Vitamin B12 is then transported across the intestinal membrane.

2. **Active transport:** Active transport requires energy from ATP to transport the molecules across the membrane, often with the help of protein carriers (Fig. 2.5). Active transport generally occurs against the concentration gradient. Active transport is classified into two types:

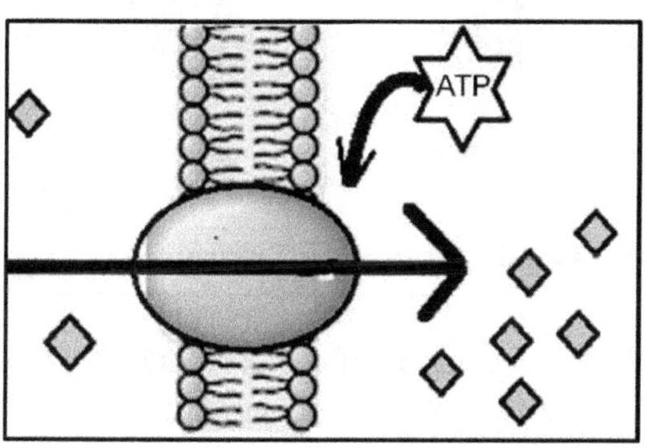

Fig. 2.5 Active transport through expenditure of energy (ATP).

(a) **Primary active transport:** It involves the direct use of energy to mediate the transport. Sodium potassium pump (Na^+/K^+ ATPase) is an ion pump which is abundant in the nerve cells. The pump transports sodium out of the cell, while potassium to inside of the cell to maintain electrical gradient across the membrane. Each Na^+/K^+ pump moves three Na^+ ions out of the cell and two K^+ ions into the cell for each ATP molecule that is used to maintain negative electrical gradient of -70 mV inside the cell. Because the transport process uses ATP as an energy source, it is considered an example of primary active transport.

(b) **Secondary active transport:** Active transport can also work together with other active or passive transport. For example the in case of Na^+/K^+ pump, the concentration of sodium is higher outside and whenever the cell need sodium ion it will open its sodium pump and ion will transfer across the concentration gradient. Thus active transport (sodium-potassium pump) supports the passive transport of sodium ions across the gradient. This is called secondary active transport. Secondary active transport is further classified as **symporters** and **antiporters** (Fig. 2.6).

I. ***Symporters*** are the secondary active transporters that transfer two molecules in the same direction. Example is transport of glucose molecule via sodium ions into the cells.

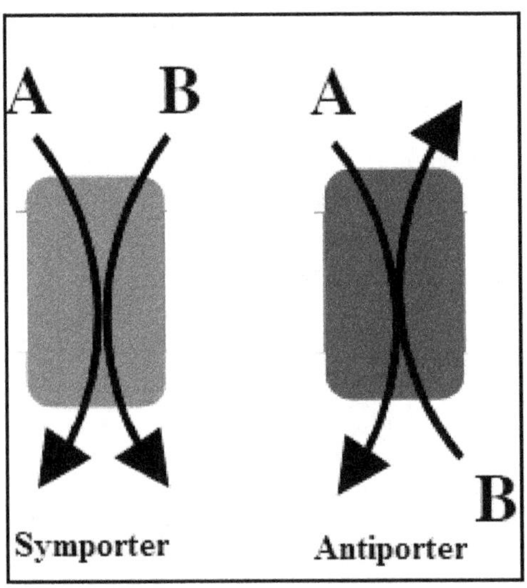

Fig. 2.6 Secondary active transport via Symporter (in same direction) and Antiporter (in opposite direction).

II. ***Antiporters*** are the secondary active transporters that transfer the molecules in opposite direction. For example, the sodium-hydrogen ion antiporter uses the energy from the inward flood of sodium ions to move hydrogen ions (H+) out of the cell.

3. **Vesicular transport:** The weak association of phospholipid fatty acid tails provide the membrane fluidity and flexibility for which phospholipid can move around to some extent. As a result of which larger materials can enter and leave the cell without crossing the membrane due to the process of spontaneous breaking and reforming of bilayers. This process requires ATP hydrolysis and therefore is a part of active process.

   (a) **Endocytosis** (bringing into the cell) is the form of active transport in which the cell engulfs foreign materials using its cell membrane. It consists of two steps (1) Substance ingestion by engulfing it in a portion of cell, (2) Grasping off that portion of the membrane. More often endocytosis brings the substance that needs to be digested or broken down. Endocytosis includes two processes of phagocytosis and pinocytosis. ***Phagocytosis (cell eating)*** is the engulfment of large particles. Many invading pathogens as a process of phagocytosis are engulfed by the immune cells. On other hand ***Pinocytosis (cell drinking)*** is the engulfment of fluid containing dissolved substances into the cell through vesicles (Fig. 2.7).

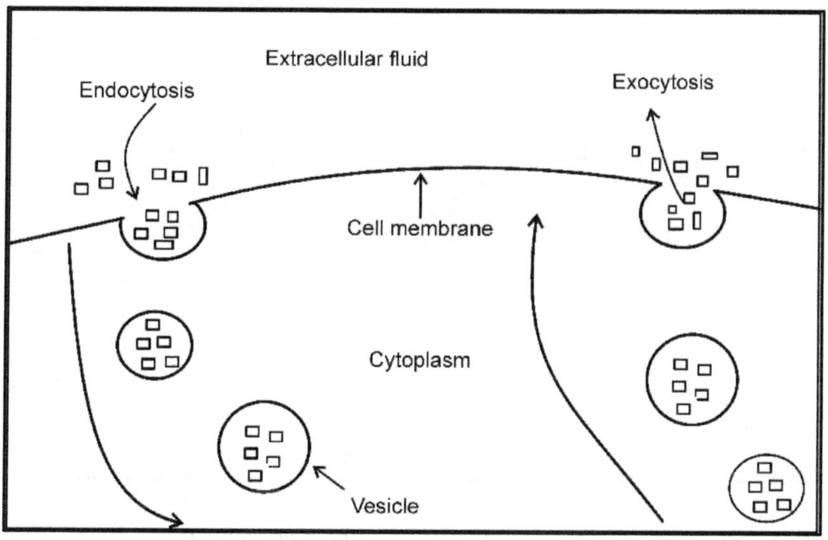

Fig. 2.7 Vesicular transport of drug molecules inside (endocytosis) and outside (exocytosis) the cell membrane.

(b) Exocytosis (taking out of the cell) is the process of expelling materials using vesicular transport. Cells of the stomach and pancreas produce and secrete digestive enzymes through exocytosis. An example is the transport of insulin from pancreatic cells into the extracellular space. Insulin molecule remains entrapped in the intercellular vesicle which afterwards fuses with the plasma membrane releasing insulin to outside of the cell (Fig. 2.8).

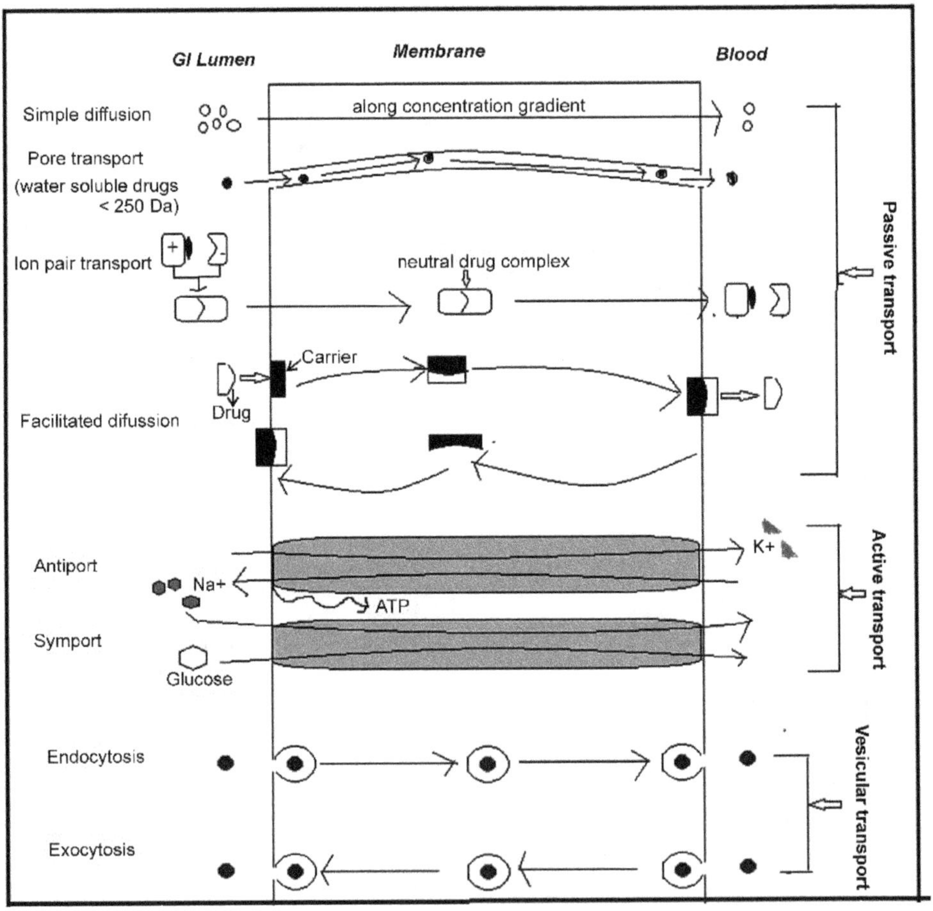

Fig. 2.8 Summary of various absorption mechanisms.

Factors Influencing Absorption of Drug in the Gastrointestinal Tract

The study of parameters such as permeability, solubility and their effect on drug absorption is mandatory in order to achieve acceptable oral bioavailability while manufacturing any dosage form. Other factors like dose, nature of dosage form, drug stability etc that effect the oral absorption of drug must also be considered. The factors affecting drug absorption are listed in Table 2.2 and discussed in detail thereafter.

Table 2.2 Factors affecting drug absorption.

Physicochemical properties of drug substances	Formulation factors	Patient related factors
1. Drug solubility and dissolution rate 2. Particle size and effective surface area 3. Polymorphism and amorphism 4. Solvate/hydrate form of drug 5. Salt form of the drug 6. Effect of drug's pKa and GI pH 7. Lipophilicity of drug 8. Drug stability 9. Stereochemical property of the drug	1. Disintegration time 2. Dissolution characteristics 3. Manufacturing variables a. Method of granulation b. Compression force 4. Nature and type of dosage forms 5. Excipients or adjuvants used in dosage forms 6. Product age and storage conditions	1. Age 2. Gastric emptying rate 3. Intestinal motility 4. Perfusion through GIT 5. Effect of food, food drug interaction and fluid 6. Gastrointestinal pH and surface area of GIT 7. Disease state 8. Presystemic metabolism

A. Physicochemical properties of drug substances

1. **Drug solubility and dissolution rate:** Solubility is the phenomenon of dissolution of solute in solvent to give a homogenous system. A drug must be in solution form in order to being absorbed. The variation in solubility of various dosage forms could be arranged as follows-

   Solution > Suspension > capsule > compressed tablet > coated tablet

   Absolute or intrinsic solubility can be defined as the maximum amount of solute dissolved in the given solution under the standard conditions of temperature, pressure and pH. The drug must have minimum aqueous solubility of 1% in order to avoid bioavailability problems. The rate determining step(s) in absorption of orally administered drugs are:

1. Rate of dissolution
2. Rate of drug permeation through the biological membrane

As per Biopharmaceutics Classification System (BCS), based on the dissolution and permeability, the drugs have been divided into four classes as Table 2.3.

Table 2.3 Biopharmaceutical classification of drug.

BCS class of drug	Drug solubility and permeability	Examples
Class I	Highly soluble and highly permeable	Propanolol, verapamil, metoprolol
Class II	Low soluble and highly permeable	Ketoprofen, naproxen, carbamazepine
Class III	Highly soluble and low permeable	Rantidine, cimetidine, vancomycin
Class IV	Low soluble and low permeable	Furosemide, taxol. Hydrochlorthiazide

Dissolution is the rate limiting step for poorly water soluble drugs (lipophilic) like griseofulvin and spironolatone while permeability is the rate limiting step for highly water soluble drugs (hydrophilic) like neomycin and cromolyn sodium. Dissolution rate is defined as the amount of solid substance that enters into the solution per unit time. Solubility is the thermodynamic process that tells us the extent to which a solute will be dissolved in solution however dissolution rate is the kinetic process that describes how quickly the solute will reach to its respective solubility units. Dissolution rate can be expressed using Noyes Whitney equation (Eq. 2.2),

$$\frac{dm}{dt} = K\ (C_s - C) \qquad .....(2.2)$$

where dm/dt is rate of dissolution of drug particles, K is dissolution rate constant (first order), C_s is the maximum drug solubility expressed as concentration of drug in stagnant layer and C is the concentration of drug in the bulk solution.

Theories of Dissolution

Dissolution of a solid takes place in two steps: Step 1 is when solid state drug molecules become solvated; followed by Step 2 that involves transport of these dissolved molecules into the bulk solution. Furthermore, three theories has been proposed to explain the mechanism of dissolution, that are

1. Diffusion layer model (Film theory)
2. Danckwert's model (Penetration or Surface renewal theory)
3. Interfacial barrier model (Double barrier mechanism OR Limited solvation theory)

Diffusion Layer Model

This model assumes that a layer of solution of solute is formed at the solid/liquid interface and the layer remains stagnant as the bulk liquid passes over the solid surface at certain velocity. This occurs instantaneously resulting in formation of saturated solution. Thereafter, diffusion of the solute from this stagnant layer to the bulk of solution, takes place (Fig. 2.9). As this is the slowest step therefore it governs the rate of dissolution.

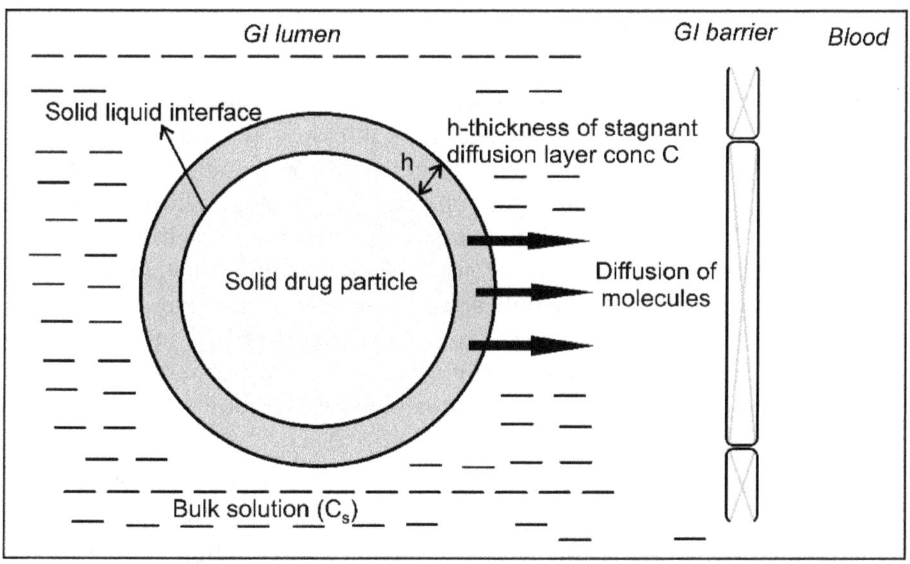

Fig. 2.9 Diagrammatic representation of diffusion layer model.

Nernst and Brunner modified the Noyes Whitney equation to explain the dissolution of solute molecules (Eq. 2.3).

$$\frac{dm}{dt} = DAK_{w/o}\frac{C_S - C}{Vh} \qquad .....(2.3)$$

where, D is the diffusion coefficient of the drug particles, A is the effective surface area of the drug particles in contact with bulk solution, h is the thickness of the diffusion layer around each drug particles, $K_{w/o}$ is intrinsic dissolution rate constant or water/oil coefficient of the drug and V is volume of dissolution medium.

Intrinsic dissolution rate (IDR)

- IDR is rate of mass transfer per unit area of dissolving surface. Expressed as $mgcm^{-2}min^{-1}$
- Independent of boundary layer thickness (h) and volume of liquid (v), IDR = KCs
- Measures intrinsic properties of drug only as a function of dissolution media
- Conditions such as stirring speed, temperature, pH, ionic strength and surface area are kept constant

The factors that are directly proportional to dissolution rate will enhance it for their greater value however with more thickness (h) the dissolution will decrease. As per modified Noyes Whitney equation the rate of dissolution is dependent on concentration gradient (C_s – C), thus follows first order kinetics. In the *in vitro* dissolution where the dissolution medium is limited, the dissolution is said to be under non sink condition. Dissolution will slow down as concentration of the bulk solution increases. However, in the *in vivo* condition the as the drug dissolves, it will be absorbed in the systemic circulation and therefore concentration in bulk will not increase and sink conditions (C_s >>C) will always be maintained. Dissolution in such a case follows zero order kinetics.

In vitro dissolution under sink conditions can be maintained either by increasing the volume of dissolution fluid, adding adsorbent to remove dissolved drug, adding water miscible solvent to dissolution medium so that a good *in vitro in vivo* correlation (IVIVC) can be established.

As per Noyes-Whitney equation the surface area of solute should remain constant but this is practically not possible as dissolution of solute will definitely change its surface area. The Hixon and Crowell cubic root law dissolution is used to account for change in surface area (Eq. 2.4)

$$W_0^{1/3} - W^{1/3} = Kt \qquad .....(2.4)$$

where, Wo = initial mass of the drug; W = remaining mass of drug, t = time, and K = dissolution rate constant.

Danckwert's Model or Surface Renewal Theory

Danckwert after five years of research claimed that the conditions to maintain the stagnant layer in stirred or agitated system is not possible and he suggested existence of turbulent liquid characterized by bursting movement of eddies. Danckwert proposed that the surface of agitated or stirred liquid composed of eddies or packets that reach the solid liquid interface absorb the solute by diffusion and then carry it to the bulk of the solution. Each time eddies (packets) are replaced by the fresh liquid that comes from bulk solution and therefore the theory is termed as surface renewal theory. The concentration of solute at bulk solution (C_s) will always be less than the concentration of solute at solid liquid interface (C). The model is expressed mathematically by equation 2.5.

$$\frac{V\,dC}{dt} = \frac{dm}{dt} = A\,\frac{C_{GIT} - C}{\sqrt{\gamma}\,D} \quad \text{.....(2.5)}$$

where, m = mass of solid dissolved and γ = rate of surface renewal

Interfacial Barrier Model

As per the interfacial barrier model the dissolution of drug is considered to be as crystal dissolution in which hydration of drug occurs initially and this process is not instantaneous. An intermediate concentration that exists between the solid liquid interfaces is due to solvation mechanism rather than diffusion of dissolved molecules. Therefore, the rate of solubility of solid in liquid film becomes rate limiting step. During dissolution of crystal each face of the crystal will have different interfacial barrier. This theory is explained mathematically as (equation 2.6)

$$\frac{dm}{dt} = K_i\,(C_s - C) \quad \text{.....(2.6)}$$

where, K_i is the effective interfacial transport rate constant.

2. **Particle size and effective surface area:** The solubility of the drug and hence the absorption is also related to the particle size. With decrease in particle size, the interaction of solute with solvent increases and consequently the solubility increases. Two terms related to surface area need to be emphasized: (i) Total surface area, and (ii) effective surface area. Total surface area of the solid is termed as specific surface area or absolute surface area. Effective surface area is the area of solid which is exposed to the dissolution medium. As per Noyes-Whitney equation with increase in effective surface area the dissolution rate is increased. With decrease in

particle size, the effective surface area of any material increases. Additionally with decrease in particle size the thickness of diffusion layer around each particle decreases, resulting in an increase in concentration gradient. The concentration gradient is directly related to the dissolution rate. Thus to increase the dissolution rate particle size should be reduced.

Several methods have been developed to reduce the particle size of the drug. Milling is the oldest technique that reduces the particle size. Micronization is another technique that converts coarse powder into ultrafine powder with mean particle size range 2-5 μm, thus increasing the effective surface area and the dissolution rate. Furthermore, nanosizing of drugs in form of nanoparticles, nanocrystals or nanosuspensions can reduce the particle size to nano range and hence enhance dissolution rate and hence the absorption.

3. **Polymorphism and amorphism:** When a substance exists in more than one crystalline form, such crystalline forms are named as polymorph and the phenomenon is known as polymorphism. Chloramphenicol palmitate (I,II,III), methyl prednisolone (I and II), cortisone acetate (I,II,III,IV and V), chlortetracyclines (alpha and beta form) , furosemide (I and II), paracetamol (I and II), amobarbitol (I and II) are some of the drugs that exhibit polymorphism. The polymorphs differ from each other in terms of their melting point, solubility, dissolution rate and other physical properties. The crystalline form of the polymorph that shows highly stable and organized structure at a given temperature is referred to as stable form while the one that exhibits poorly organized and weakly bonded structure is referred to as metastable forms (Table 2.4).

Table 2.4 Differences between metastable and stable form.

Stable form	Metastable form
Highly organized and strongly bonded crystals	Poorly organized or weakly bonded crystals
More energy required to break bonds	Less energy required to break bond
High melting point	Low melting point
Low solubility and dissolution rate	High solubility and dissolution rate

Due to the favorable pharmaceutical attributes, the metastable form of polymorphic drug is always considered and recommended over the stable form. For example chloramphenicol palmitate exhibits the stable and metastable forms. The metastable form of the drug if formulated as a suspension will show higher solubility, dissolution rate and absorption as compared to the stable form. Another example is of methyl prednisolone that exists as polymorphs and has both metastable and stable polymorphs. If the drug is formulated as a suspension for subcutaneous injection containing the a blend of both the two crystalline forms, then that means metastable form which is highly soluble can provide the rapid initial dose (rapid dissolution) while the stable form that will dissolve slowly will provide the prolonged or sustained action dose called the maintenance dose. Thus the metastable form presents favourable properties to a pharmaceutical formulator. However, due to its poor thermodynamic stability, on storage the metastable form may convert to stable form which is less soluble. For example more soluble crystalline form of cortisone acetate in an aqueous suspension converts to less soluble form resulting in caking of solid. This can be prevented by taking into account some measures like dehydrating the molecule environment or by adding viscosity modifying agents like polyvinyl pyrrolidone, pectin or gelatin that adsorb to the surface of crystal and thus inhibits conversion.

In addition to different polymorphic forms some drugs may also exist in non-crystalline or poorly crystallized form. This is known as amorphous form of the drug. The amorphous form exhibits higher dissolution rate and absorption rate when compared to its crystalline form and thus will have shorter duration of action. Novobiocin, chloramphenicol acetate and insulin are the examples in which amorphous form have high absorption values while crystalline forms show poor absorption. The dissolution and absorption of different solid forms follows the order

amorphous > metastable > stable.

4. **Hydrate/solvate:** At the time of crystallization, the drug crystals may incorporate one or more molecules of solvent into the internal structure or crystal lattice and are called **solvates**. These solvates can exist in different crystalline forms and are called pseudopolymorphs and the phenomenon is known as pseudopolymorphism. When the incorporated solvent is water then drug crystals are referred as hydrates. Solvate term is used when it is any other organic solvent. The term asolvate means no solvent molecule has been trapped in the drug molecule crystal. The dissolution and hence the absorption of these forms were described while considering two conditions:

   1. When water is used as solvent the anhydrous form (asolvate) shows higher solubility and thus higher absorption than already hydrated form (solvate) as the already hydrated form will already have level of water saturation and thus will not extensively react with water while anhydrous form will interact with water more extensively. The drugs like caffeine, theophylline and glutethimide show higher dissolution and absorption for anhydrous form when compared to the hydrous one.

2. On the other hand when solvent other than water is used (organic solvate) the solvate form exhibit higher absorption than asolvate form. The proposed reason is the higher lipophilicity (partition coefficient) will increase the permeation of solvate by gastrointestinal tract. For example, the ethanol and acetone solvates of hydrocortisone and prednisolone show higher absorption rates than the non-solvated forms.

5. **Salt form of the drug:** Most of the approved drugs are either weak acid or weak base. Weak acid on dissociation will release protons to the medium, further decreasing the pH of the microenvironment while weak base will accept the hydrogen ion that will increase the pH of the diffusion layer. Thus, for weak acid, due to dissociation, the pH in the diffusion layer will be lower than the bulk pH. On the other hand for weak base the diffusion layer pH will be more as compared to the bulk pH. This difference in pH of diffusion layer and bulk solution will affect the drug solubility. In pharmaceutical industry salt formation of weak acid or weak base is the most important strategy to increase aqueous solubility and hence absorption. The process of salt formation is simple and is represented diagrammatically in Fig. 2.10.

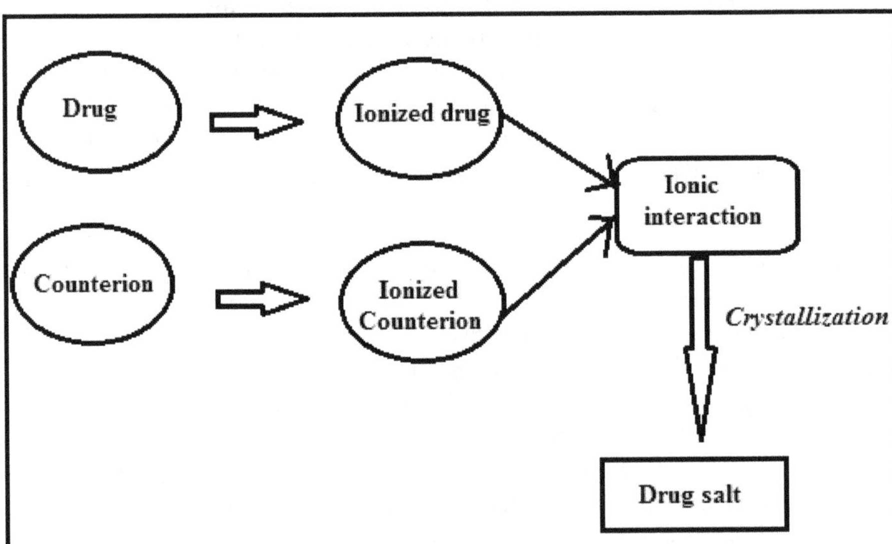

Fig. 2.10 Schematic diagram for salt formation process.

Salt form of the weak acid at gastric pH, will alter the pH of the diffusion layer (pH 5-6) than pH of gastric fluid (pH 1-3). As higher pH favors the solubility of weak acid, therefore the solubility of weak acid will be promoted in this diffusion layer. Once the drug diffuses out, the salt form will transform into free acid that will be precipitate as fine particles. The precipitates will have higher surface area that will promote its re-dissolution and absorption across gastrointestinal tract (Fig. 2.11). Conversely, when the salt of weak base reaches the intestine, the pH of diffusion layer will decrease resulting in increased dissolution and absorption. Therefore, the drug salt form increases the dissolution rate by altering the pH of diffusion layer formed at solid liquid interface. For example theophylline which is weakly acidic in nature, when converted into salt form, results in increase in the pH of diffusion layer and thus promotes greater *in vitro* dissolution rate.

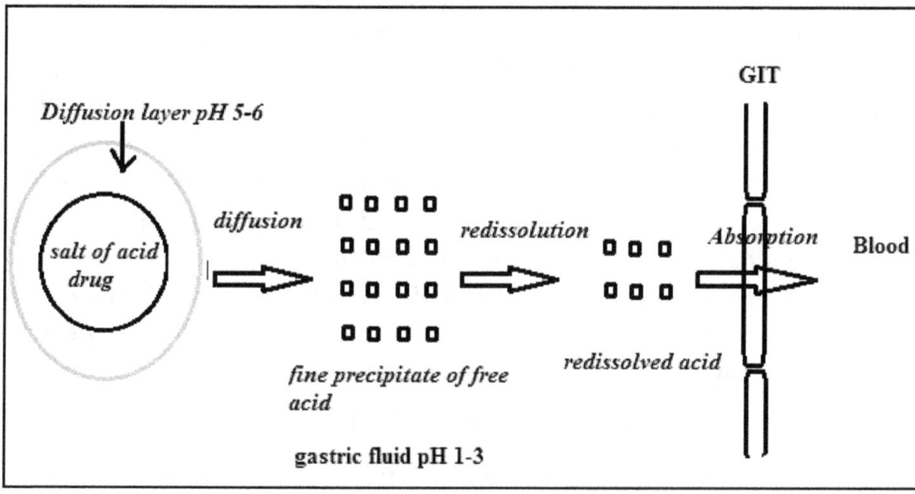

Fig. 2.11 Dissolution of salt form of acid in gastric fluid.

Another example is the sodium salt form of tolbutamide (an oral hypoglycaemic agent) that dissolves 5,000 times faster in acidic media when compared to the free acid. Similarly, the sodium salt of a non-steroidal anti-inflammatory drug naproxen has a better solubility when compared with the free acid form and as a result the salt form is absorbed faster. Whereas, strongly acidic salt forms of weakly basic drugs such as chlorpromazine and ranitidine as hydrochloride (s) have enhanced dissolution in gastric and intestinal media when compared to the free base forms.

Relation between drug pKa, gastrointestinal pH and log P

A drug, for absorption, must have sufficient lipophilicity to cross the cell membrane and also the drug must have adequate aqueous solubility to come out of the membrane. In other terms a perfect Hydrophylic Lipophilic Balance (HLB) is required for the optimum bioavailability. As stated before, most of the drugs are either weak acids or weak bases for which the pKa of drug, GI pH and pH of blood stream will control the solubility and hence the absorption through the membrane lining the GI tract.

Brodie proposed the pH-partition theory that states for drug having molecular weight greater than 100 and are transported across membrane primarily by passive diffusion. The absorption is governed by three parameters: (i) pKa (dissociation constant) of the drug; (ii) Partition coefficient (log P) or lipophilicity of the drug, and (iii) pH of the gastrointestinal tract. Brodie reasoned that when a drug is ionized it will not be able to get through the lipid membrane, but when the drug is non-ionized or unionized it has higher lipid solubility than the ionized form and it will be able to cross the biological membrane. This theory indicates that the dissociation constant of the drug is dependent on pH of the medium and both these parameters will influence the concentration of the unionized form and this in turn will control the degree of partitioning and hence effect the amount of drug absorbed and the total bioavailability.

6. **Effect of drug pKa and gastrointestinal pH**

The amount of drug that exists in unionized and ionized state depends on the pKa of drug and pH of fluid at the absorption site. The fraction of unionized and ionized drug can be determined using Henderson-Hasselbach equation. For monobasic drug the fraction of the unionized form can be calculated using following equation

$$\text{pH} = pKa + log\frac{(unionized\ concentration)}{(ionized\ concentration)} \qquad .....(2.7)$$

For monoacidic drug the fraction of the unionized form can be calculated by eq. 2.8.

$$\text{pH} = pKa + log\frac{(ionized\ concentration)}{(unionized\ concentration)} \qquad .....(2.8)$$

pKa is defined as the pH were a drug exists as 50% ionized and 50% unionized. If pKa – pH = 0, then 50% of drug is ionized and 50% is unionized. The relevant interpretation of pKa in reference to the drugs is tabulated below.

For acids	For bases
1. High pKa means the species is predominantly unionized, is a bad proton donor, and a weak acid. 2. Low pKa means the species is predominantly ionized, is a good proton donor, and a strong acid	1. High pKa means the species is predominantly ionized, is a good proton acceptor, and a strong base. 2. Low pKa means the species is predominantly unionized, is a bad proton acceptor, and a weak base.

Table 2.5 Examples the absorption sites of drug based on the pKa values.

Drugs	pKa	pH/site of absorption
Very weak acids e.g. pentobarbital, hexobarbital	>8	• Unionized at all pH values; • Absorbed along the entire length of GIT
Moderately weak acids e.g. Aspirin, ibuprofen	2.5 – 7.5	• Unionized in gastric pH & ionized in intestinal pH • Better absorption from stomach
Strong acids e.g. Disodium cromogylate	< 2.0	• Ionized at all pH values; • Poorly absorbed from GIT
Very weak bases e.g. Theophylline, caffeine	< 5.0	• Unionized at all pH values; • Absorbed along entire GIT
Moderately weak bases e.g. Codeine	5 – 11	• Ionized at gastric pH, unionized at intestinal pH • Better absorption from intestine.
Strong bases e.g. Guanethidine	> 11	• Ionized at all pH values; • Poorly absorbed from GIT

7. **Effect of lipophilicity:** Lipophilicity measures the affinity of the drug for lipid environment and is important parameter for drug absorption. If a drug is unionized but has poor lipophilicity, it will not be able to cross the cell membrane and thus hinder its absorption. A direct relation exists between drug lipophilicity and its absorption. Lipophilicity can be measured by the

distribution of a drug between the organic phase (generally n-octanol) and the aqueous phase, which is generally water. The partition coefficient (P) is the ratio of the equilibrium concentrations (Ci) of a dissolved compound in a two-phase system consisting of n-octanol and water. The partition coefficient (P) is usually given in the form of its logarithm to base 10 (log P)

$$P = \frac{concentration\ of\ drug\ in\ organic\ phase\ (n{=}octanol)}{concentration\ of\ drug\ in\ aqueous\ phase\ (water)} \qquad .....(2.9)$$

$$\text{Log P} = \log \frac{concentration\ in\ n{-}octanol}{concentration\ in\ water} \qquad .....(2.10)$$

8. **Drug stability:** Drug stability refers to the extent to which a pharmaceutical dosage form retains its properties and characteristics, same as that at the time of manufacture during the time of storage and usage by patient. Expiry date on the other hand means that the drug contained in the dosage form is not to be used after this date as the concentration of drug will be reduced and become lower than therapeutic concentration. Also some drug degradation products may be harmful or toxic to the patients. Several factors such as temperature, moisture, light, interaction with other component of dosage form, oxygen etc affects drug stability. Drug will not be able to reach its therapeutic level due to decomposition, instability of drug and that will further decrease the bioavailability of the drug.

9. **Stereochemical nature of the drug:** Drugs containing one or more chiral centres exist in stereoisomeric molecular forms. Most commonly, drugs containing a single asymmetric carbon atom exists in two enantiomeric forms, designated as eutomer (the more potent) and distomer (the less potent). Enantiomers possess identical physical and chemical properties but have different spatial configuration. Majority of the racemic drugs absorption appears to be through passive diffusion, with no selectivity for one isomer over the other. On the other hand, in case of carrier mediated transport, stereoselective intestinal transporter is the main cause of variation in oral absorption of enantiomer. For example, L-methotrexate has 40 fold higher bioavailability than D-methotrexate. Also the process like stereoselective plasma protein binding may influence distribution and elimination of drug as the enantiomers possess different magnitude of stereoselectivity for different proteins found in the plasma. For example R-propanolol binding to albumin is greater than S-propanolol.

B. Formulation factors

1. **Disintegration time:** Disintegration refers to the breakdown of tablet or capsule into granules that will further break into the fine particles. The time taken by the tablet to disintegrate is known as disintegration time. *In vitro* disintegration test is performed to determine the disintegration time. Wetting and then subsequent disintegration is the first step of absorption. Without disintegration, only the active ingredient near the surface of the drug will be able to dissolve. Therefore, full disintegration of the tablet on exposure to dissolution medium is important to achieve the desired bioavailability. If the disintegration is faster than dissolution is also faster and thus a drug can be absorbed at a faster rate. The disintegration time of different dosage forms as per pharmacopoeial standards is listed in Table 2.6.

Table 2.6 Pharmacopoeial limits of disintegration time for various dosage forms.

Type of dosage form	Disintegration time (min)		
	USP	IP	BP
Uncoated tablet	5	15	15
Film coated tablet	30	30	30
Sugar coated tablet	60	60	60
Dispersible tablet	3	3	3
Enteric coated	60	60	60

The disintegration time is directly proportional to the hardness and amount of binder present in any formulation. Further to facilitate the disintegration and to achieve the desired disintegration time various disintegrants/ superdisintegrants like starch, microcrystalline cellulose, cross linked polyvinylpyrrolidone, sodium croscarmellose, may be incorporated in the solid dosage forms.

2. **Dissolution time:** Disintegration time tells us about the time taken by tablet to break up into fine particles; however it does not give any assurance that the particles will release the drug into the medium. For this dissolution test is performed. The rate of dissolution influences the onset, rate and extent of absorption. *In vitro* dissolution test is performed to determine the amount of drug available for absorption from any dosage form.

3. **Manufacturing variable:** The manufacturing process used to design solid dosage form affects its physiochemical properties like dissolution and absorption. The two processes that primarily affect absorption of solid dosage form like tablet are

   (a) Method of granulation, and (b) Compression force.

   (a) Method of granulation: Granulation is a technique used to form sphere like or regularly shaped aggregates of powder called granules that improve flow property of powdered material carried out to improve the uniformity of active ingredient in the dosage form. During granulation many variables like concentration of excipient(s) like binder and disintegrant, drying time and drying rate will affect the dissolution and absorption of the dosage form. For example the presence of binder in the dosage form will lower its disintegration time followed by dissolution and absorption. Conversely, higher concentration of disintegrant in the formulation will promote dissolution. On the other hand prolonged drying will produce brittle tablets leading to faster dissolution and absorption.

   (b) Compression force: Increase in compression force during tablet manufacturing lowers the rate of dissolution. The following reasons may be accounted for its slow dissolution.

   1. Due to the increased hardness of the tablet resulting from high compact arrangement of the granules in the tablet, the tablet requires more time and effort to get dissoluted in the dissolution medium.
   2. As the compression force increases, surface area of the tablet that is exposed to the dissolution medium will be decreased/reduced, hence the dissolution rate will be minimized.
   3. The wettability of the tablet decreases in the dissolution medium hindering the penetrability of the dissolution medium into the tablet core thereby slowing slows down the dissolution of the tablet.
   4. Nature and type of dosage form

Active ingredient cannot be administered in their pure state and hence are converted into suitable formulation or dosage form so that it remains stable and convenient to use. The nature and type of dosage form seems to alter the physiochemical properties of the drug. For example a drug in liquid dosage form like suspension and emulsion will have higher dissolution rate when compared to the solid dosage forms like tablet and capsule. The reason accounted for it is the more number of steps involved in the release and subsequent absorption of the drug from solid dosage forms. The steps followed by various conventional dosage forms for release of drug are depicted in Fig. 2.12.

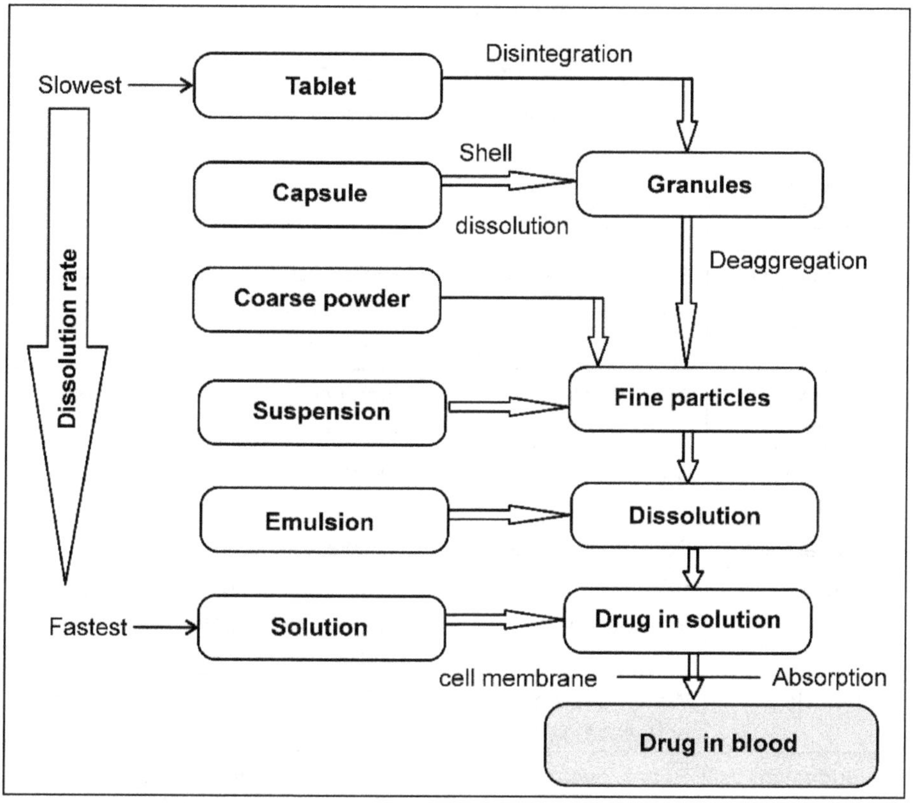

Fig. 2.12 Dissolution steps for conventional dosage forms after oral administration.

The nature of the dosage form will depend on the excipients present in it. For example, prolonged release dosage form may contain the polymer that will release the drug for longer period of time whereas the presence of superdisintegrants in orodispersible tablet will make it to disintegrate within minutes in the mouth. The effect of several other excipients on drug absorption has been discussed in the next section.

5. **Excipients or adjuvants used in dosage forms:** Excipients are the inactive ingredients that are added to formulation to provide certain kind of characteristics. Some of the characteristics include increase in stability of drug, prevention from gastric degradation, improvement in elegancy; control the rate of absorption, increased absorption etc. The various excipients used in oral dosage forms are summarized in Table 2.7.

Table 2.7 List of excipients used in oral dosage forms along with their example and function.

Excipient	Example	Function
Diluent	Starch, lactose	Provide bulk in solid dosage form
Disintegrant	Starch, microcrystalline cellulose	Rapid breakdown into fine particles in solid dosage form
Lubricant	Magnesium stearate	Reduce friction
Binding agent	Acacia, gelatin, PVP	Impart cohesiveness to powder or granules
Coloring agent	Brilliant blue	Improve elegance
Sweetener	Sorbitol, sucrose	As sweetening agent
Coating agent	Shellac, methylcellulose	Mask taste, sustain release, avoid chemical incompatibility, protection of drug etc
Vehicle	Water, glycerol, propylene glycol	Major component of liquid dosage form
Surfactant	Spans, tweens	Wetting, solubilizers or emulsifiers, used in liquid dosage form
Preservative	Methyl paraben, propyl paraben	Prevent microbial growth, mainly used on aqueous liquid dosage form
Suspending agent	Carboxymethylcellulose	Reduce rate of particle settling in liquid dosage form

Excipients may also affect the dissolution of drug in dosage form in either of the two ways-

1. Alter the pH of the medium in which drug is dissolved e.g. buffers

2. May react with the drug e.g. tetracycline forms insoluble complex with calcium carbonate and thus decreases dissolution rate.

A suspending agent tends to increase the viscosity of the vehicle in liquid dosage form and thus decrease the rate of drug dissolution resulting in low absorption. The most commonly used lubricant; magnesium stearate inhibits penetration of water into tablet and thus increases the disintegration time followed by decrease in dissolution and absorption. Surfactants have unpredictable action. In low concentration it increases the dissolution rate by lowering the surface tension while in high concentration they tend to form micelles with drug and thus decrease the rate of dissolution. Excipient like sodium bicarbonate alters the dissolution rate by changing the pH of the dissolving medium. Binders in large concentration tend to increase the hardness of the formulation and thus decrease dissolution and absorption. The disintegrants as already discussed, exert positive effect on dissolution. Coating agents used in the formulation retard the dissolution rate in following order:

Enteric coat > sugar coat > non-enteric coat

6. **Product age and storage conditions:** For most of the pharmaceutical products the USP requires that drug must retain its 90% of potency till expiration date. On aging the active ingredient(s) in the pharmaceutical products may deteriorate or convert into inactive form. This may alter the dissolution and absorption of the drug and thus decrease its therapeutic usefulness. Further agglomeration of particles may occur in suspension leading to increase in particle size and decreased dissolution. On aging the conversion of metastable to poorly soluble stable form may occur in liquid dosage form. The physical and chemical properties of the drug can be influenced by storage conditions like temperature, light, air and humidity. As a general rule, an increase in solubility may be observed with rise in temperature. The photosensitive drugs may undergo degradation in the presence of light. Therefore, proper protection of the dosage form is required from high temperature and humidity to maintain the physical integrity and stability of the product within the stipulated shelf life.

C. Patient related factors

1. **Age:** In older patients, loss of mucosal intestinal surface, decrease in gastrointestinal blood flow and reduced gastric acidity results in a decrease in absorption of drugs. Similarly in infants the reduced intestinal surface and blood flow to GIT, presence of drug metabolizing enzymes in intestine result in reduced absorption.

2. **Gastric emptying rate:** Gastric emptying is the passage of drug from stomach to small intestine. The major site for the absorption of most of the drugs is intestine due to its large surface area. Thus ethanol and acidic drugs such as aspirin, paracetamol, warfarin and barbiturates are absorbed much more rapidly from the intestine than from the stomach. The rate of gastric emptying can be expressed as the milliliter of content that reaches into intestine per minute. As a general statement increase in gastric emptying rate will increase absorption. Exceptionally, the absorption will reduce if the drug is unstable in basic pH. The factors affecting the gastric emptying are tabulated below in Table 2.8.

Table 2.8 Factors affecting the gastric emptying.

Factor	Effect on gastric emptying rate
Volume of meal	Larger the volume, longer the gastric emptying rate.
Composition of meal	The presence of meal in the stomach delays the gastric emptying rate in order carbohydrate > protein > fat
Osmotic pressure	Increase in concentration of salt and non-electrolytes lowers gastric emptying rate or vice versa.
Viscosity of meal	Viscous meals take time to empty while non viscous empty at faster rate.
Gastrointestinal pH	Higher or alkaline pH of stomach promotes gastric emptying
Exercise	Vigorous exercise retards gastric emptying rate
Body posture	Gastric emptying is favored for the person lying on right side.
Drugs	Some drugs like anticholinergic (eg atropine), narcotics (morphine) and tricyclic antidepressant (amitriptyline) delay gastric emptying rate. Conversely, prokinetic drug like metaclopromide enhances gastric emptying.
Disease state	Disease like diabetes, hypothyroidism, duodenal or pyloric ulcers, Parkinson disease and multiple sclerosis reduces gastric emptying while hyperthyroidism increases gastric emptying.

3. **Intestinal motility:** During normal peristaltic movement, the contents of the duodenum mix together and bring the drug particles into close contact with intestinal mucosal cell for absorption. For optimum absorption a drug must reside in the absorption site for longer period of time. Since intestine is the

absorption site for most of the drugs, long residence time in intestine is required. Disease condition like diarrhea increases the peristaltic movement in intestine that leads to less residence time in stomach and inadequate absorption.

4. **Perfusion through GIT:** Good flow of blood through GIT is important for transporting the drug to systemic circulation for optimum absorption. In GIT a large number of capillaries and lymphatic vessels lead to high absorption. A drug after absorption through small intestine goes to mesenteric vessel and thus reaches the hepatic portal vein and liver. In case of the disease condition like congestive heart failure, the blood flow through mesenteric vessel decreases that will reduce the transport of drug thereby minimizing the availability of drug for absorption. Drugs are also absorbed through the lymphatic vessel by microvilli present in intestine. The drugs that are absorbed through lymphatic system do not enter the hepatic portal vein and thus bypass first pass metabolism. The dietary lipids are absorbed through the lymphatic system. Some lipophilic drugs may dissolve in chylomicron and can be absorbed through lymphatic system.
5. **Effect of food, food-drug interaction and fluid:** As a general statement the drugs are better absorbed in empty stomach. However, the presence of food in the stomach can have marked effect in drug absorption. Food can increase, decrease or delay the absorption of drugs or it may not have any effect in the drug absorption. The examples of drugs falling into these categories are listed in Table 2.9.

Table 2.9 Impact of food on absorption of certain drugs.

Increased Absorption	Decreased Absorption	Delay in Absorption	No effect
Griseofulvin	Penicillin	Aspirin	Glibenclamide
Phenytoin	Amoxicillin	Acetaminophen	Glipizide
Propanolol	Tetracycline	Sulfadiazine	Metronidazole
Metaxalone	Levodopa	Nitrofurantoin	Theophylline
Hydrochlorthiazide	Aspirin	Sulfanilamide	Chlorpropamide

The increase in drug absorption after food intake may be due to the digestion that tends to increase splanchnic blood flow. Prolonged residence time in the stomach favors absorption of basic drugs as the acidic pH of stomach favors drug dissolution and that will increase the amount of drug that reaches the intestine which tends to increase absorption. On the other hand retention of acidic drugs in stomach will result in decreased dissolution and absorption. The decrease in intestinal motility, chelation of drug by metal ion present in food, inability of drug to reach gastrointestinal lining may be accounted for decrease in drug absorption. These may be due to delay in gastric emptying, change in pH of GI tract, physiochemical interaction of drug with food or increase in blood flow. The effect of food is highest when the medicine is taken just after the intake of meal. Therefore, patient must be advised to take medicine either 1 or 2 hr after the meal.

Most of the drugs are absorbed rapidly when taken with concentrated fluid. However, more rapid emptying of dilute solutions from the stomach may be accounted for increase in absorption of some drugs as the drug is being exposed to greater surface area of intestine. The fluid volume also influences the drug absorption. Intake of large volumes of fluid with solid dosage form facilitates the dissolution of drug and hence favors absorption. For example erythromycin when taken in empty stomach with a glass of water shows enhanced absorption.

6. **GI pH and surface area effect on absorption:** The pH of gastrointestinal tract increases while moving downwards from stomach to colon. Also the surface area of small intestine is much larger as compared to stomach and large intestine.

The role of pH and surface area on absorption after oral administration of drug is mentioned in the Table 2.10.

Table 2.10 Effect of pH and surface area on oral drug absorption.

Organ	pH and surface area effect	Effect
Stomach	pH 1-3, surface area is much less than intestine	Lipophilic, neutral and acidic drugs are absorbed but to a lesser extent than intestine
Small intestine	pH 5-7.5, Very large surface area	All types of drugs are absorbed, major site of drug absorption
Large intestine	pH 7.9-8, small surface area	All type of drugs are absorbed but to lesser extent.
*Bile secreted by liver has pH between 7.8-8.6 that promotes absorption of lipophilic drugs		

5. **Disease state:** Several diseases that influence GI motility, GI pH, blood flow to GIT, bile secretion, gastric emptying rate or digestive enzyme secretion

also influence the drug absorption. Liver disorder like hepatic cirrhosis enhances the drug absorption of drug like propanolol that undergo first pass metabolism. Patients in advanced stage of Parkinsonism show decreased GI motility and thus delay in the absorption of drug like levodopa. Congestive heart failure patients with persistent edema have reduced splanchic blood blow and GI motility resulting in reduced absorption. For example furosemide, a loop diuretic when given to patient of CHF shows reduced absorption and delay in onset of action. Gastrointestinal diseases like diarrhea and achlorhydria influence drug absorption. Disease conditions such achlorhydria (reduced acidic production in stomach) leads to decrease in absorption of basic drugs like dapsone, itraconazole and ketoconazole.

6. **Drug-drug interaction affecting absorption:** Anticholinergic drugs reduce acid production in the stomach. Propanthelin bromide slows down stomach emptying rate and thus delays the absorption. Tricyclic antidepressants exert anticholinergic side effects, reduce emptying rate of stomach and thus delay absorption.

   Proton pump inhibitors reduce acid secretion in stomach that also affects absorption of acidic and basic drugs. Prokinetic drug like metaclopromide reduces intestinal motility and thus results in reduced peak drug concentration along with the time to reach peak drug concentration thus affecting the effective drug absorption. For example metaclopromide reduces the absorption of digoxin from tablet.

   Antacid drugs that contain calcium, magnesium or aluminium, may form complex with tetracycline, ciprofloxacin, and indinavir resulting in reduced absorption. Antihyperlipedimic drugs like cholestyramine adsorb warfarin, thyroxin and loperamide, which results in reduced absorption of drugs. Calcium absorption is known to be facilitated by vitamin D. The reason accounted for this is an increase in calcium binding protein after vitamin D intake that binds calcium in the intestinal cell and thus transfers it to blood.

7. **Presystemic metabolism:** After oral administration the loss of fraction of drug through metabolism by liver or gut wall before it reaches systemic circulation is known as first pass or presystemic metabolism (Fig. 2.13). Low absorption of orally administered drug is mainly due to low permeability, low solubility or poor gastrointestinal stability. The enzymes of the gastrointestinal lumen, gut wall enzymes and hepatic enzymes affect first pass metabolism of a drug.

   (a) ***Luminal enzymes*:** This includes digestive and bacterial enzymes. Digestive enzymes are present in GI fluids and also include the enzymes from pancreatic and intestinal secretions. Examples are peptidase and esterase. Insulin and calcitonin are the examples of drug degraded by proteolytic enzymes present in GI tract and therefore poor absorption. The GI microflora abundant in colon causes hydroxylation of sulfasalizine to sulphapyridine and 5-amino salicylic acid.

(b) ***Gut wall enzymes*:** These enzymes are present mainly in intestine, stomach and colon. For example alcohol dehydrogenase is the enzyme present in stomach that inactivates ethanol. Intestinal and colonic mucosa contains both Phase I and Phase II enzymes. Phase II enzymes are predominant enzymes. Example of Phase II reaction is metabolism of sulfasalazine by N-acetyl transferase and of 6-mercaptopurine by thiopurine methyl transferase.

(c) ***Hepatic enzymes*:** Several drugs like propanolol, nitrolglycerine, diltiazem, morphine isoprenalin etc undergo first pass hepatic metabolism. Aspartate aminotransferase and alanine aminotransferase are the examples of enzymes present in liver that cause metabolism of drugs.

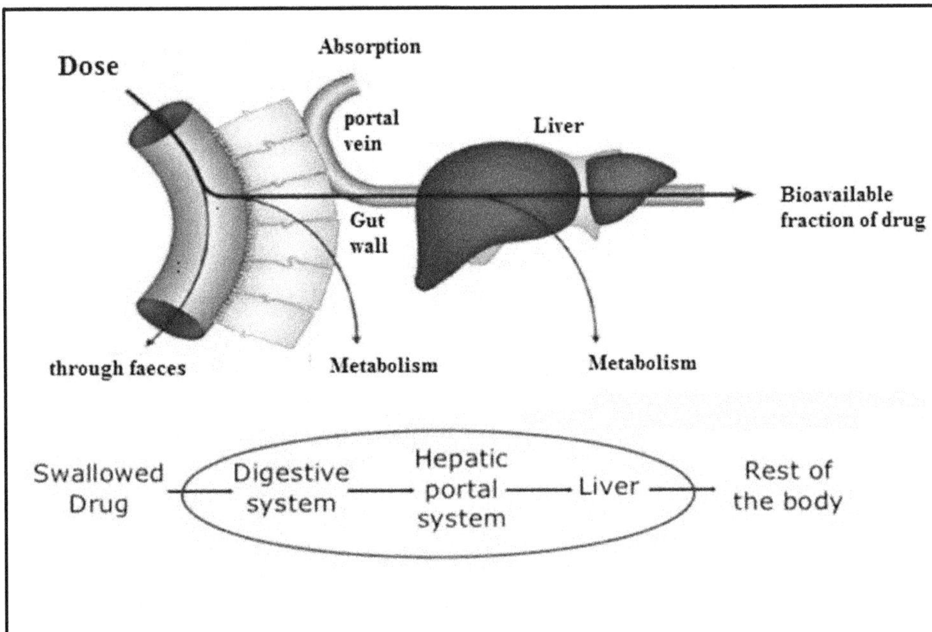

Fig. 2.13 Diagrammatic representation of presystemic metabolism.

Non-peroral Extravascular Routes

Non-peroral route means that the drug is administered other than oral route which bypasses GIT and reaches into systemic circulation. Oral route is the easiest and safest route for administration of drugs. However oral route is not suitable for some drugs that are bitter in taste, unstable in GIT and undergo first pass metabolism. In that case the administration route other than oral is preferable. Buccal and sublingual, topical, rectal, vaginal, transdermal, nasal and inhalational are some of the non-peroral extravascular routes of administration. Inhalational and topical drug delivery system can also be used for local effect.

Buccal and sublingual route

Buccal route involves the placement of drug in between the gums and cheeks where it dissolves and is absorbed into the blood whereas in sublingual route the drug is placed under the tongue where it dissolves and passes through mucosal membrane for absorption. Cheeks and the area beneath tongue possess many capillaries or tiny blood vessels and are more permeable. Therefore, this area is preferred for application of dosage form in oral cavity. Drug from sublingual route is rapidly absorbed and this therefore appropriate for immediate release dosage forms. For example sublingual tablet of nitroglycerin, erythrityl tetranitrate, isoproterenol and isosorbide dinitrate usually dissolve rapidly. Buccal dosage form may release drug rapidly or may be designed to produce sustained or prolonged effect. For example buccoadhesive or mucoadhesive dosage forms are designed so that these interact with buccal mucus and adhere to the mucosal lining. For example acyclovir tablet is used for labial herpes and miconazole for orophangeal candidiasis.

The major advantages of this route are (1) Rapid effect can be obtained and therefore can be used in emergency condition, (2) avoidance of hepatic first pass metabolism, (3) pH in mouth is relatively neutral and thus drugs are more stable, and (4) easy administration and removal of dosage form.

Topical route

Dosage forms for delivery through topical route are applied to the skin or mucous membrane mainly for local effect, and systemic absorption is minimal. Based on surface for application these are classified in to two types:

External application: The formulation is spread or dispersed on the skin surface covering affected area.

Internal application: The formulation is applied to mucosal membrane of eye, ear, nasal, oropharyngeal or vaginal region for local action.

These formulations may be powder, lotion, cream, ointment, paste etc. The principal route of absorption for formulations for external use may either be transepidermal (diffusion through skin) or transfollicular (permeation through hair follicles, sweat gland or sebaceous gland). Transepidermal route includes two pathway for diffusion of drug namely transcellular and/or intercellular.

The major advantages of this route are (1) avoidance of first pass metabolism and systemic side effects of drug, (2) easy application and termination of medicine, when required, (3) large area available for application, (4) suitable for self medication and improved patient compliance, and (5) avoidance of GI incompatibility.

Transdermal route

The drug given through transdermal route is absorbed through skin or mucous membrane. It mainly produces systemic effect. Here the drug penetrates through the various layers of skin to exert its effect on deeper or more distant tissue. Transdermal route of drug delivery system offers several advantages like,

1. Reduced dosing frequency and improved patient compliance
2. No presystemic metabolism
3. Effective use of drug with short biological half life
4. Administration of drug with narrow therapeutic window as drug is maintained within the therapeutic window for prolonged period of time.

The examples of transdermal systems include the development of scopolamine patch for motion sickness and nitroglycerin patch for angina pectoris.

Vaginal and rectal route

Rectal route is used for local or systemic effect. Drugs in solid forms such as suppositories or in liquid forms such as enema are given by this route. The rectal route is used for systemic absorption if patient is suffering from nausea or vomiting, is unconscious, drug is of bitter taste or other conditions where the drug cannot be given orally. In this the drug is mixed with a waxy substance that tends to melt or liquefy when inserted into the rectum in suppository form. The rectum wall is thin and rich in blood supply that leads to absorption of drug. Examples of drugs administered as suppositories include acetaminophen (for fever), diazepam (for seizures), and laxatives (for constipation). Irritating drugs are not suitable for suppository formulation.

Some drugs may be inserted vaginally as a solution, tablet, cream, gel, suppository, or ring. Vaginal route is mainly for local effect, but some systemic absorption may take place. Vaginal route allows women to self administer the drug. The dosage form can be designed such that medication may be released continuously for several weeks or month after single application, thus producing prolonged effect. Sodium salicylate, quinine hydrochloride, and various hormones including insulin, estrogens, progestens, androgens, and prostaglandins are the example of drugs that can be administered through vaginal route.

Nasal route

Rich supply of blood vessels in nasal region makes it a suitable delivery system for systemic drug delivery. However, the route can also be used for local delivery in conditions like nasal congestion and rhinitis. The examples of drugs for local action include oxymetazoline, azelatine, budesonide and fluticasone. The surface area of nasal mucosa is 150 cm^2 that provides rapid onset of therapeutic effect, potential to deliver drug direct to central nervous system, avoidance of first pass metabolism and non-invasiveness. This route bypasses the GI system and therefore can be used for delivery of peptide hormones. This system is of extreme importance if fast relief is required and patient is not in a condition to deal with injections. Intranasal triptanes for migraine treatment, fentanyl to stop cancer breakthrough pain and ondansetrone to relieve nausea are examples that can be delivered through this route. The drugs that are lipophilic in nature of molecular weight up to 600 daltons can be absorbed satisfactorily by diffusion. Surfactant can be used to increase the permeation of drug for systemic absorption. Hydrophilic drugs up to 200 daltons are able to cross the nasal mucosa.

Inhalational route

This route can be used for either systemic or local action. The drug is mainly administered through nose and mouth. The surface area of alveoli is 70 m^2; much larger when compared to small intestine or nasal passage thus the effect produced after inhalation is as rapid as that of i.v. injection. This route is mainly used for drugs in gaseous form or that can be dispersed in aerosol form. Only the 10% of the administered dose is absorbed if the drug is in solid and liquid form and has particle size greater than 20 micron. As this route delivers the drug directly to the site of action is thus convenient for patient with respiratory problems like asthma and chronic obstructive pulmonary disorder thus minimizing systemic side effects and producing local effect. However, this route can be used to produce systemic effect (such as general anesthesia).

Questions

Multiple Choice Questions

1. For a drug to be available from tablet dosage forms, it must first undergo-
   (a) Dissolution (b) Disintegration
   (c) Ionization (d) None of the above
2. According to pH partition theory, a weakly basic drug will be absorbed from small intestine because-
   (a) Weak base are more soluble in basic intestinal fluids
   (b) Weak base exists in the unionized more lipid soluble form
   (c) Weak base will further increase the GIT pH
   (d) The ionic form of basic drugs is absorbed more rapidly from intestine
3. The absorption of the drug is not required when it is given by-
   (a) Oral route (b) Intramuscular
   (c) Intravenous (d) Subcutaneous
4. If a drug is absorbed rapidly and completely from a solution dosage form than from a capsule dosage form, it means absorption is rate limited by-
   (a) Dissolution (b) Disintegration
   (c) Ionization (d) None of the above
5. Which of the following is not the characteristic of carrier mediated transport system?
   (a) Energy dependent (b) Metabolically inhibited
   (c) Structure specific and saturable (d) Reach equilibrium

6. Rapid gastric emptying is desirable when-
   (a) Rapid onset of action is desirable
   (b) Dissolution of drug occurs in intestine
   (c) Gastric fluid affects the drug stability
   (d) All of the above
7. Which of the following is not the characteristic of facilitated diffusion?
   (a) Carrier mediated transport
   (b) Concentration gradient is required
   (c) Structural specificity
   (d) Non-saturable
8. The rate of drug dissolution from dosage form follows following order-
   (a) Uncoated tablet > capsule > solution > enteric coated
   (b) Solution > Uncoated tablet > capsule > enteric coated
   (c) Solution > Uncoated tablet > enteric coated > capsule
   (d) Capsule > Uncoated tablet > enteric coated > solution
9. Transdermal drug administration
   (a) Is most suitable for highly polar drugs
   (b) Is not subject to hepatic first pass metabolism
   (c) Provide rapid and complete absorption
   (d) Is only used for localized effect
10. Which one of these is not absorption mechanism?
    (a) Endocytosis (b) Electrochemical diffusion
    (c) Facilitated active transport (d) Ionic pore transport
11. Passive diffusion follows
    (a) Noyes Whitney equation (b) Fick's first law
    (c) Fick's second law (d) none of the above
12. The first step of pharmacokinetic process is-
    (a) Absorption (b) Distribution
    (c) Metabolism (d) Excretion
13. Which of the following statement is correct?
    (a) Unionized form of the drug is readily absorbed because it is more water soluble than ionized form

(b) Ionized form of the drug is readily absorbed because it is more lipid soluble than ionized form

(c) Unionized form of the drug is readily absorbed because it is more lipid soluble than ionized form

(d) None of the above

14. Absorption can be defined as-

(a) Movement of unchanged drug from site of administration to blood stream

(b) Movement of unchanged drug from site of administration to target tissue

(c) Movement of only ionized drug from site of administration to blood stream

(d) None of the above

15. Following route of administration is not a part of enteral route-

(a) Oral (b) Sublingual

(c) Transdermal (d) Rectal

16. Hydrostatic pressure is driving force for transport of drug molecules in case of-

(a) Ion-pair transport (b) Pore transport

(c) Endocytosis (d) Exocytosis

17. Which of the following is a carrier mediated transport?

(a) Simple diffusion (b) Facilitated diffusion

(c) Ion-pair transport (d) Pore transport

18. The main mechanism of most drugs absorption in GI tract is:

(a) Active transport (carrier-mediated diffusion)

(b) Filtration (aqueous diffusion)

(c) Endocytosis and exocytosis

(d) Passive diffusion (lipid diffusion)

19. What is implied by «active transport»?

(a) Transport of drugs trough a membrane by means of diffusion

(b) Transport without energy consumption

(c) Engulfment of drug by a cell membrane with a new vesicle formation

(d) Transport against concentration gradient

20. Which route of drug administration is most likely to lead to the first-pass effect?
    - (a) Sublingual
    - (b) Oral
    - (c) Intravenous
    - (d) Intramuscular
21. What are the features of class II Biopharmaceutics classification system?
    - (a) High solubility low permeability
    - (b) low solubility and high permeability
    - (c) High permeability and high solubility
    - (d) Low solubility and low permeability
22. Which of the following explains dissolution rate by mechanism of diffusion?
    - (a) Fick's first law
    - (b) Henderson Hasselbach equation
    - (c) Noyes Whitney equation
    - (d) None of the above
23. Diffusion layer model is based on-
    - (a) Formation of stagnant layer
    - (b) Existence of turbulence
    - (c) Solvation mechanism
    - (d) All of the above
24. The dissolution and absorption of solid solute will follow following order-
    - (a) Amorphous > Stable > Metastable
    - (b) Amorphous > Metastable > stable
    - (c) Metastable > stable > Amorphous
    - (d) Metastable > Amorphous > Stable
25. In a pregnant women the transfer of antibodies across placenta to fetal circulation is based on which transport mechanism
    - (a) Endocytosis
    - (b) Exocytosis
    - (c) Transcytosis
    - (d) All of the above
26. For a poorly water soluble drug like griseofulvin the rate limiting step is
    - (a) Permeation
    - (b) Dissolution
    - (c) Both a and b
    - (d) None of the above
27. Amount of solid substance that goes into solution per unit time is-
    - (a) Dissolution
    - (b) Dissolution rate
    - (c) Disintegration
    - (d) Absorption

28. The minimum solubility requirement to avoid absorption problem is
    (a) 5% (b) 10% (c) 2.5% (d) 1%
29. The major site for drug absorption is
    (a) Stomach (b) Liver
    (c) Large intestine (d) Small intestine
30. With an increase in gastric emptying rate, the absorption will
    (a) Increase (b) Decrease
    (c) No change (d) Delayed
31. Dankwerts model theory is the related to-
    (a) Drug disintegration (b) Drug dissolution
    (c) Both of the above (d) None of the above
32. The cell membrane model of which globular proteins are embedded in lipid layer matrix-
    (a) Fluid mosaic model (b) Lipid protein layer
    (c) Mayonnaise model (d) None of the above
33. The dissolution of drug under sink condition follows which type of kinetics-
    (a) Zero order kinetics (b) Dissolution of tablet in blood
    (c) Pseudo first order kinetics (d) Second order kinetics

Long Questions

1. Define absorption. Explain the various routes of absorption.
2. Explain the various mechanisms for transport of drug across biological membrane.
3. What are the various formulation related factors that affect the absorption of drug?
4. Detail the various theories for dissolution of drug.
5. How is the change in pH of diffusion layer by salt formation effect the solubility of weak acid or weak base?
6. How does facilitated diffusion differ from simple passive diffusion?
7. Why is intestine the major site of absorption? Explain
8. Discuss briefly the patient related factors affecting drug absorption.

9. What are the advantages of administering drug using non per oral extravascular route? Enlist the name of such routes.
10. Explain the effect of nature and type of dosage form in drug absorption.
11. How will you account for dissolution of hydrate and solvate in aqueous or organic solvent?
12. What is the effect of increase in surface area in absorption? Describe the various methods to increase surface area of drug.
13. What is the influence of various excipients on bioavailability of drug?
14. Name the various orally administered dosage form in order of their decreasing absorption. Detail the steps followed by them for absorption.
15. What is pre systemic metabolism? Explain its influence in absorption.

CHAPTER 3

Distribution of Drugs

LEARNING OBJECTIVES

- Understand the concept of distribution
- Learning apparent volume of distribution and its applications
- Understanding the factors affecting drug distribution

Introduction

Once drug is absorbed into the blood stream, it circulates through the body in a very less time of around one minute. After which the drug recirculates and moves from blood stream to the body tissue filled with interstitial fluid. The interstitial fluid together with plasma water is termed as extra cellular fluid as this fluid resides outside the cell. ***This reversible movement of drug between blood and extravascular fluids and tissues is known as distribution***. As stated in definition, distribution is reversible process, as with time due to elimination the drug is removed from the blood and therefore a reverse concentration gradient is established between blood and tissue resulting in back movement of the drug from tissue to blood. The driving force here is passive diffusion; however transporters may be involved in certain tissues such as brain. For a drug to produce its effect it must reach at site of action (receptor) at adequate concentration and this concentration at site of action depends on the ability of drug to distribute and pass through various membranes and tissue. The drug may be distributed to other tissues (non-receptor site) as well as where side effects or adverse reactions may occur. The process of distribution is described in Fig. 3.1

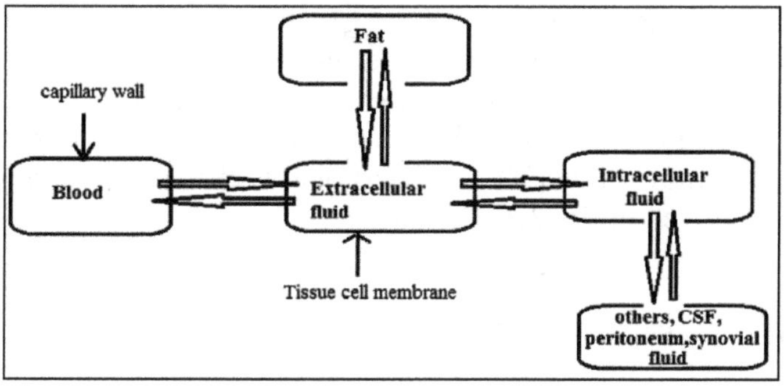

Fig. 3.1 Process of drug distribution.

Distribution of drugs takes place in two steps: (1) *Permeation of unbound (free) drug through capillary wall of blood capillaries to interstitial or extracellular fluid* (as some or virtually all molecule of drug may remain bound to protein making drug inactive, blood protein gradually releases the drug bound to them) and then (2) *permeation of drug from the extracellular fluid through tissue cell membrane to intracellular fluid.* With respect to distribution, the drugs can be divided into two categories namely,

1. **Permeability-limited drugs:** For such drugs the rate limiting step is the ability to cross biological membranes.
2. **Perfusion-limited drugs:** For such drugs the rate limiting step is access to the tissue or the blood flow to that tissue.

Apparent Volume of Distribution

The volume of distribution (V_d) provides a measure of the location of the drug, whether the drug is located in the blood, extracellular space, or out in the tissues. ***By definition, volume of distribution is the apparent volume which is required to evenly distribute the drug in the body at a concentration equal to that in the plasma***. The term apparent is used as the volume is purely theoretical which can substantially exceed the total body volume, or potentially even be infinite in size. High molecular weight drugs having low lipid solubility that does not cross capillary wall, will remain confined intravascularly and have a small volume of distribution (approximately equal to intravascular volume), whereas highly lipophilic drugs that distribute to tissues all around have a large volume of distribution. For example some drugs (e.g. tolbutamide, phenytoin, gentamicin, warfarin) are known to have small volumes of distribution (0.1–1 L/kg) while others (e.g. meperidine, propranolol, digoxin) are known to have large volumes of distribution (1–10 L/kg). If volume is constant then the amount of drug in the body will be linearly proportional to the drug concentration. The volume of distribution is a proportionality factor that relates the amount of drug in the body to the measured plasma drug concentration. The amount of drug in the body (X) is proportional to the concentration of drug in plasma (Cp) as given in Eq. 3.1.

$$X = V_d * Cp \qquad .....(3.1)$$

Thus V_d can be calculated as

$$V_d\,(L) = X\,(mg) / Cp\,(mg/L) \qquad .....(3.2)$$

where X is amount of drug in the body at particular time and Cp is concentration of drug in plasma. It is not a real volume, therefore called as apparent volume of distribution. The determinants of V_d are

(i) pKa of the drug
(ii) Plasma protein binding
(iii) Partition coefficient of drug in fatty tissue
(iv) Difference in regional blood flow
(v) Degree of binding to other tissues

Significance of V_d

(i) ***In designing dosage regimen***: V_d can be used in determining loading dose. If the V_d of a drug is 20 L (in a 70 kg man) and desired plasma concentration is 10 mg/L.

Then, loading dose = V_d × Desired concentration (C)

$$20 \times 10 = 200 \text{ mg}$$

Thus 200 mg has to be given as loading dose (iv) to achieve quickly a concentration of 10 mg/L. The speed at which this loading dose is given will depend on the therapeutic index of the drug. For a drug with a narrow therapeutic index, loading dose will be given slowly, example: for over 24 hours for digoxin and over 30 min for theophylline (wide therapeutic index). Loading dose can be given iv or orally depending upon the urgency of onset of action. When given orally, the bioavailability of the drug should be taken into account i.e.

$$\text{Loading dose (p. o.)} = \frac{V_d \text{ X Desired concentration (C)}}{\text{Oral bioavailability (F)}} \qquad .....(3.3)$$

(ii) *Heamodialysis in drug toxicity*

Another significance of V_d is in predicting the usefulness of heamodialysis in cases of drug toxicity due to overdose. A drug with small V_d implies the most of the drug present in the body is in plasma or blood. Hence, in overdose with such a drug (e.g., salicylates), heamodialysis would be useful for eliminating quickly the excess drug present in the body. On the other hand, a drug with large V_d e.g. imipramine, gets widely distributed in the body. In overdose with such a drug, dialysis is not of much use therefore not advised.

The apparent volume of distribution has no direct relationship with the real volume of distribution. The real body water has physiological significance and is related to body water. The total body water varies from 50-70% of body weight. The body water is mainly divided into four compartments: (i) extracellular fluid comprising blood plasma (about 5% of the body weight or 3.5 L for average body weight of 70 kg) and interstitial fluid (16% or 11 L); (ii) intracellular fluid (35% or 25 L) is the sum of the fluid content of all the cells in the body; (iii) Blood cell (7% or 5L); and (iv) Fat comprises the 20% of body weight. If the drug is not able to cross capillary membrane, its V_d will be equal to that of plasma volume i.e. 3 L. The V_d of certain drugs is exemplified in Table 3.1.

Table 3.1 Drugs exemplified according to the volume of distribution in various compartments.

Compartment	Volume of distribution	Examples of drugs
Plasma	Less than 5L	Heparin, insulin, warfarin, sulfamethoxazole
Extracellular fluid	Approx 15 L	Tubocurarine, theophylline
Total body water	More than 20 L	Ethanol, methotrexate, paracetamol, morphine, propanolol, digoxin, nortriptyline, imipramine

- Drugs that have a volume of distribution 4 L or less are thought to be confined to the plasma, or liquid part of the blood.
- If the volume is between 4 and 7 L, the drug is thought to be distributed throughout the blood (plasma and red blood cells).
- If the volume of distribution is larger than 42 L, the drug is thought to be distributed to all tissues in the body, especially the fatty tissue.

- Some drugs have volume of distribution values greater than 10,000 L. This means that most of the drug is in the tissue, and very little is in the plasma circulating.
- The larger the volume of distribution, the more likely that the drug is found in the tissues of the body. The smaller the volume of distribution, the more likely that the drug is confined to the circulatory system.

The distribution of administered drugs is non-uniform throughout the body as different body tissues receive the drug from plasma at different rates and to varying extent. Various factors are responsible for varied distribution and are summarized in Table 3.2. The factors are discussed in the preceding text.

Table 3.2 Factors influencing distribution of drugs in the body.

<table>
<tr><th>1.Tissue permeability of drugs</th><th>2. Physiological factors</th><th>3. Miscellaneous factors</th></tr>
<tr><td>a) Physiochemical properties of drugs:
• Molecular size,
• lipid solubility and
• degree of ionization</td><td>a) Cardiac output and rate of blood flow to different organs/tissue size</td><td rowspan="2">a) Age and fat deposition
b) Pregnancy
c) Disease state</td></tr>
<tr><td>b) Anatomical barriers
• Cell endothelial barrier
• Cell membrane barrier
• Blood brain barrier
• Maternal fetal Barrier
• CSF blood barrier
• Blood testis barrier</td><td>b) Binding of drugs to -
• Tissue proteins
• Plasma proteins</td></tr>
</table>

1. **Tissue permeability of drugs:** The passage of drug across cell membrane to the extravascular tissue depends on the physiochemical nature of drug and various physiological barriers to diffusion of drugs. The influence of these is detailed below.

   (a) Physiochemical properties of drug: The physicochemical properties that influence drug distribution are molecular weight, lipophilicity and the degree of ionization. These are discussed below.

(i) ***Molecular weight*****:** Diffusion is a rapid process and the drugs with low molecular weight are able to readily cross the membrane. On the other hand the diffusion decreases on an increase in the molecular weight. The effect on molecular weight on diffusion of drugs is exemplified in Table 3.3.

If a drug of low molecular weight is water soluble, it can easily move through capillary junction into the extracellular fluid; however, it will not be able to cross the membrane to reach the intracellular fluid. On the other hand, if a drug has low molecular weight and is lipophilic, it can move to extracellular fluid and is able to cross membrane to reach intracellular fluid. The volume of extracellular fluid is around 20% of body weight i.e. around 14 L in a 70 kg individual. This extracellular fluid along with intracellular fluid together constitutes 60 % of the total body weight. Thus drug will distribute in to the 60% of total body weight i.e. 42 L in a 70 kg individual.

Table 3.3 Effect of molecular weight on the diffusion coefficient.

Molecule	Molecular weight (Daltons)	Diffusion coefficient across capillary (cm^2/sec x 100 g)
Urea	60	1.83
Glucose	180	0.64
Sucrose	342	0.35
Myoglobin	17,000	0.005
Heamoglobin	68,000	0.001
Serum albumin	69,000	<0.001

(ii) ***Lipophilicity*****:** The ability of drug molecule to cross the membrane depends on its solubility in the membrane, which is determined by drug partition coefficient between lipid membrane and aqueous phase (expressed as partition coefficient) and diffusion coefficient which is measure of mobility of molecules within lipid. The diffusion coefficient varies slightly among different drug molecules and therefore partition coefficient is the important variable. Direct relationship exists between the lipid solubility of the drugs and permeation through membrane.

(iii) ***Degree of ionization*****:** The charge on the drug molecule affects its ability to pass through the membrane. The ratio of ionized and unionized ions will be determined by its pKa value. Also the difference in the pH will influence the degree of ionization. As mentioned in the previous chapter the dissociation constant (pKa) can be determined by Henderson-Hasselbach equation and that can be used to predict the degree of ionization of weak acid and base at different pH. Generally, the ionized form of weak acid and weak base drugs are water soluble and will not able to cross the membrane and distribute tissue passively On other side the unionized. Form is considered to be lipid soluble and is able to cross the membrane.

(b) Anatomical barriers

(i) ***Cell endothelial barrier*:** The junctions present between capillary endothelial cells are not continuous and therefore allows free passage of molecules between cells. All drugs whether ionized or unionized having molecular weight less than 600 Daltons can easily diffuse through capillary endothelium into the extracellular fluid. The larger molecules of size 80,000-100,000 Dalton pass very slowly through it. Lipid soluble drugs however can pass through vascular endothelium rapidly as compared to water soluble drugs that penetrate more slowly. In kidney and liver there are larger gaps in between the junctions that make them more permeable, this allows rapid distribution of drugs outside the capillary. In contrast, in organs like CNS and placenta there are tight junctions present between the endothelial cells and endothelium is enclosed in impermeable membrane made of periendothelial cells. This prevents the passage of harmful substance from blood into these organs. In other organs like liver or spleen the drug distribution to tissue depends on the capillary permeability.

(ii) ***Cell membrane barrier*:** Once a drug moves from capillary wall to extracellular fluid, its further entry to intracellular fluid depends on its passage through the cell membrane. Cell membrane is lipoidal barrier similar to that of GIT (discussed in previous chapter). Lipid soluble drug molecules are able to diffuse more easily when compared to water soluble molecules as shown in Fig. 3.2

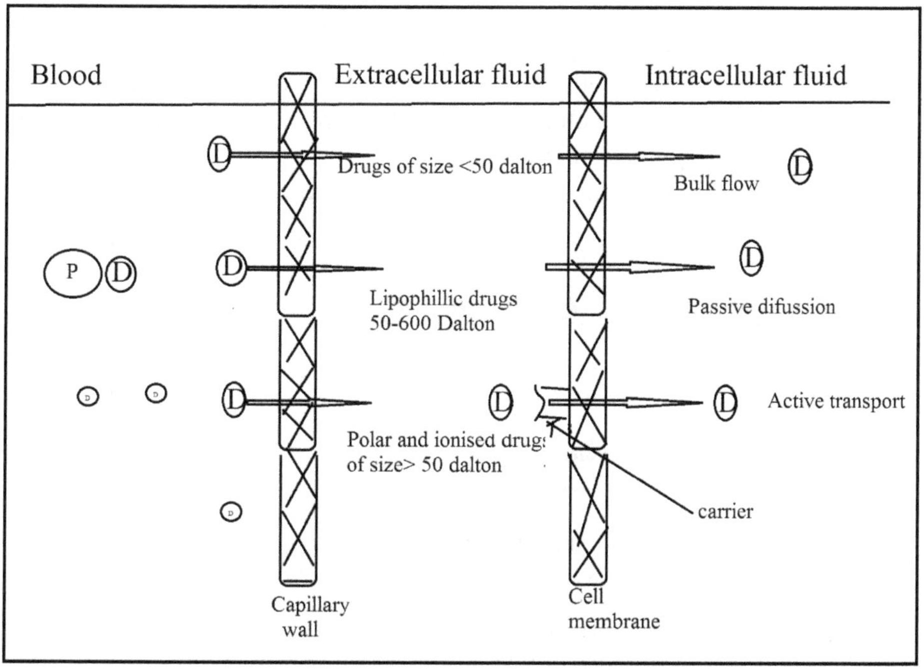

Fig. 3.2 Physiochemical properties affecting diffusion of drug across cell membrane barrier.

(iii) ***Blood-brain barrier (BBB):*** The BBB protects the brain from content of cerebrospinal fluid and blood. It consists of endothelial cells connected to each other by tight intracellular junctions that do not contain fenestrations, which is supported by the astrocytic sheath consisting of a layer of glial connective tissue cells (astrocytes) close to the basement membrane of the capillary endothelium (Fig 3.3). The brain remains inaccessible for many drugs including many anticancer drugs and antibiotics like aminoglycosides. Besides this, drug like dopamine, used in the treatment of Parkinson's disease is also not able to cross BBB and therefore levodopa is used which penetrates the BBB and converts to dopamine in brain tissue. Only drugs having high lipid water coefficient like certain anesthetics, barbiturate and benzodiazepine can pass through the tightly connected capillary endothelial cells. Highly ionized and water soluble drugs are unable to cross this barrier in significant amount. Inflammation may cause BBB to lose its integrity therefore allowing normally impermeable substance to pass through it.

The BBB is leaky in some parts of the central nervous system (CNS) including chemorceptor trigger zone (CTZ). For example domperidone (a dopamine receptor antagonist) which cannot cross BBB but can reach to CTZ and thus prevent nausea and vomiting caused by dopamine agonist e.g. apomorphine.

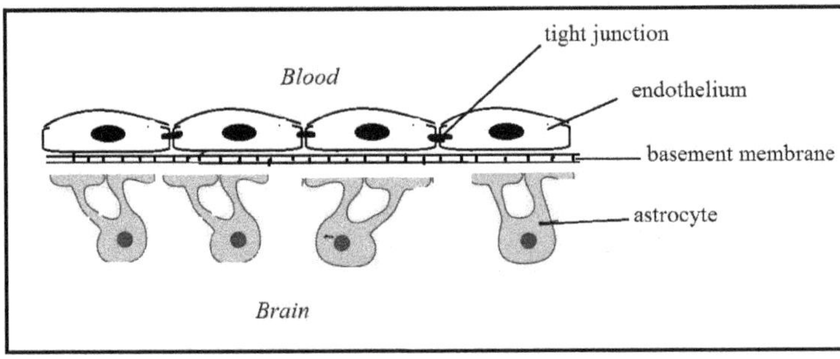

Fig. 3.3 Diagrammatic representation of blood brain barrier.

Targeting polar drugs to brain in certain conditions like tumor treatment is always challenging. Three different approaches have been rationalized for promoting drug transport across the BBB.

- Use of permeation enhancers such as dimethylsulfoxide in the formulation
- Osmotic disruption of the BBB by infusing the internal carotid artery with hyperosmolar solution. E.g. infusion of mannitol solution (3.5% w/v).
- Use of specialized drug carrier systems like dihyropyridine redox system. The lipophilic dihydropyridine is linked to the polar drug to generate a prodrug that can readily cross the BBB. The enzymes present in the brain breakdown the prodrug liberating the drug in the brain,

(iv) ***Maternal-fetal barrier:*** The composition of placenta includes a layer of trophoblastic cells which contains syncytiotrophoblast that encloses fetal capillaries. The placental syncytiotrophoblast and fetal capillary membranes fuse together to form a single membrane that acts as a lipid barrier and separates the mother's blood from the fetus blood. This barrier allows lipid soluble substances to cross easily as compared to water soluble one. The placenta is well perfused and is not effective barrier as that of brain. Moderately lipid-soluble drugs (example ethanol, barbiturates, narcotics analgesics and sulphonamides) can also easily pass through it by simple diffusion process. The passage of certain drugs across the placenta may damage the fetus. Teratogenicity refers to a condition of congenital malformation (birth defect) or the disturbance in the development of fetus due to administration of certain drugs. Such drugs are referred to as teratogens. For example thalidomide (prescribed in the 60's), was responsible for phocomelia. Roaccutane ® (retinoic acid, commonly used for treating acne), is highly teratogenic. Drugs are particularly hazardous to the fetus during two stages of pregnancy: (i) in the first trimester when fetal organs develop and teratogenic effects are pronounced. E.g. methotrexate, phenytoin, isotretinoin, testosterone

(v) ***Cerebrospinal spinal fluid-blood barrier:*** This barrier prevents the passage of drugs from blood to cerebrospinal fluid (CSF). It consists of three parts that include: choroidal epithelial cells (that secrete CSF and are interconnected by tight junctions), basal membrane and endothelium of the pia mater capillaries that contains fenestrations (Fig. 3.4). It is more permeable than BBB and thus many plasma proteins enter to CSF through pinocytosis or active transport. The concentration of plasma protein is lower in CSF as compared to its concentration in blood plasma and therefore any impairment in this barrier may lead to increase in concentration of proteins in CSF. The permeability characteristics are similar to BBB.

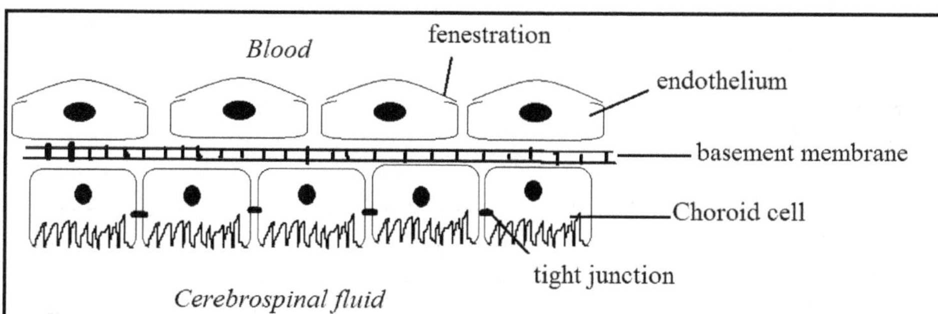

Fig. 3.4 Diagrammatic representation of the cerebrospinal spinal fluid-blood barrier.

(vi) **Blood-testis barrier:** This barrier is present in between the blood vessels and the somniferous tubules of testis. It is formed by tight junctions between the sertoli cells of somniferous tubules. The barrier prevents the entry of drugs into the somniferous tubules. However, steroids can pass through this barrier.

2. **Physiological factors affecting drug distribution**

(a) **Cardiac output, rate of blood flow to different organs and tissue size:** The distribution of drugs takes place via blood that flows in continuous manner from heart to all parts of the body. The primary stage for distribution of drugs depends on the cardiac output and blood flow to various regional organs. The rate of blood flow is high in highly perfused organs resulting in rapid drug distribution whereas drug distribution is slower for the organs that are not well perfused like adipose tissue and therefore the drug concentration is markedly less. Also, under normal condition there is limited blood flow to the muscles while during exercise the blood flow to muscles increases that result in increased distribution of drug towards muscles.

If the distribution to tissue is limited by slow diffusion across membrane then the process is termed as **permeability or diffusion limited.** Whereas for drugs that rapidly diffuse across membrane, if the blood flow becomes rate limiting step in drug distribution then the process is termed as **perfusion or flow limited.**

Table 3.4 Percent cardiac output and blood flow to tissue.

Tissue	Percent Body weight	Percent cardiac output	Blood flow (mL/100 g tissue/min)
Adrenals	0.02	1	550
Kidneys	0.4	24	450
Thyroid	0.04	2	400
Hepatic	2.0	5	20
Portal	----	20	75
Portal-drained viscera	2.0	20	75
Heart (basal)	0.4	4	70
Brain	2.0	15	55
Skin	7.0	5	5
Muscle (basal)	40.0	15	3
Connective tissue	7.0	1	1
Fat	15.0	2	1

Tissue size and tissue storage also play important role in distribution of drugs. The accumulation of the drug in tissue is referred to as tissue affinity. The various factors that determine the distribution constant (K_d) of a drug into the organ include blood flow to the organ (Q), volume of the organ (V) and partitioning of drug into the organ tissue (P) and is represented by Eq.3.4

$$K_d = \frac{Q}{VP} \quad .....(3.4)$$

The partitioning of drug into the organ tissue is referred to as the ratio of concentration of drug present in organ tissue to the concentration of the drug present in blood. Time taken by the drug to distribute is measured by distribution half life which is referred as time taken for 50% distribution ($t_{d1/2}$) and this can be calculated from distribution constant (K_d), assuming first order distribution (Eq. 3.5).

$$t_{d1/2} = \frac{0.693}{K_d} \quad .....(3.5)$$

When partitioning of drug to the tissue is same than the distribution half life depends on two factors, blood flow to the organ and volume or size of the organ. With increase in blood flow to the organ the distribution time decreases while in contrast to this with increase in organ volume or size, the distribution time increases as large organ volume will take longer time to fill with drug. Further some tissues have good ability to store or accumulate drug. As an example flutamide, an antiandrogenic drug concentration in prostate is twenty times more than that of plasma and therefore its full effect is achieved only after the complete distribution to the receptor site.

(b) **Binding of drugs to tissue and plasma protein:** The extent of drug distribution to the tissues depends on tissue binding and plasma protein binding of drug. Around 98 percent of all proteins are located extravascularly. These proteins and other tissue macromolecules may contain binding sites for drugs. Most of the drugs that bind to tissue may also bind to plasma protein. Thus binding competition may occur. Increase in plasma- protein bound fraction of drug in absence of tissue binding leads to a decrease in distribution whereas increase in tissue-bound fraction of drug, leads to increased distribution.

The body tissue comprises of 40% of the body weight that reflects importance of tissue binding in drug distribution. Drug accumulation may occur as a result of binding of drugs to tissue proteins or other macromolecules in a tissue. For example digoxin binds to proteins of the cardiac tissue that result in large volume of distribution.

Accumulation and storage of drug in adipose (fat) tissue is considered as a form of tissue binding. Drugs having high lipid/water coefficient (log P), tend to accumulate in adipose tissue. But due to the poor blood flow in adipose tissue the process of accumulation is slow and once the desired concentration is reached in tissue, its removal from adipose is also slow resulting in increased biological half life. For example, the chlorinated hydrocarbon, DDT (dichlorodiphenyl trichloroethane) is lipophilic and remains in fat tissue for years. A large number of drugs bind to extravascular tissue and follow the order: liver > kidney > lung > muscles.

The effect of binding of drugs to plasma protein will be discussed in detail in the next chapter (Chapter 4) on plasma protein binding of drugs.

Miscellaneous Factors Affecting Drug Distribution

(a) **Effect of age and fat deposition:** In general, with age muscle mass decreases and the total body water content declines to 10-15% until the age of 80. This leads to a decrease in distribution of hydrophilic drugs like aspirin, tubocurarine, edrophonium, famotidine and lithium .Use of diuretics further reduces the extracellular space that leads to increase in toxic effect of the drug. Generally speaking, the high fat content leads to large distribution of lipophilic drugs. The total body fat increases from 18 to 36% in men and from 33 to 45% in women. Although the fat content is higher in women than in men but change in distribution of lipophilic drugs is more marked in men than in women. Amiodarone, diazepam, teicoplanin, and verapamil are some of the drugs that represent increased distribution in old age. However, very old individuals loose weight with time and therefore the proportion of fat decreases leading to decrease in distribution of lipophilic drugs. Therefore, the doses of drug must not be overlooked for very old age patients. Low weight patients, on average, receive higher doses per unit body weight than heavier patients.

(b) **Pregnancy:** During pregnancy there is marked increase in plasma volume, with parallel increase in all body fluid compartments and total body water. Expanded extracellular volume and total body water will increase volume of distribution for hydrophilic drugs. However increased body weight and fat increases the volume of distribution for fat soluble drugs. Fall in serum albumin is observed in pregnancy; also the plasma protein binding sites are occupied with hormones that increase during pregnancy and thus more of the free drug is available for adverse effect and for placental transfer to fetus.

(c) **Disease state:** A number of mechanisms like altered concentration of plasma proteins, altered permeability of physiological barriers, diminished or altered perfusion to organs or tissues, change in tissue pH, disease states such as inflammation, liver disease, and diabetes can affect capillary barriers and therefore disable or enable entry of drugs and thus change the normal distribution pattern observed in the healthy state. In patients with hepatic impairment there is a decrease in plasma protein synthesis by the liver. This decrease may affect the volume of distribution of drugs that are extensively bound to these proteins. Diminished vascular perfusion of one or more parts of the body is encountered in conditions such as cardiac failure that may alter the drug distribution to certain organs.

Role of Transporters in Distribution

It has been recognized that transporter proteins provides assistance for the transport of most of the drugs. Every living cell comprises of these transporters in varying amounts that are distributed differentially throughout tissues and barrier membrane. These transporters play an important role in distributing drug molecules to their effector site including distribution to almost every organ and tissue in the body. Some of the transporters are described below.

(i) **ABC Transporters (ATP binding cassette):** It directly utilizes ATP as the energy source and therefore transfers molecules actively across the biological membrane. ABC transporters are present at barrier membrane and are therefore considered important for drug distribution. These are increasingly being implicated in regulation of the passage of endogenous and exogenous chemicals across cellular and tissue membranes, thereby playing a pivotal role in drug distribution

(ii) **SLC transporters:** SLC transporters do not directly access an energy source and they are able to function as uniporters (facilitated diffusion of substrates across membranes), symporters (transport of two compounds in the same direction at the same time), and antiporters (transport of two compounds in opposite directions at the same time). While the majority of the SLC transporters serve to facilitate transfer of highly specific endogenous substrates, a number of them can contribute to multi-drug resistance and limit accumulation by transporting drugs. Partition coefficients are useful in estimating the distribution of drugs within the body. Hydrophobic drugs with high n-octanol/water partition coefficients are mainly distributed to hydrophobic areas such as lipid bilayers of cells. Conversely, hydrophilic drugs (low n-octanol/ water partition coefficients) are found primarily in aqueous regions such as blood serum. If one of the solvents is a gas and the other a liquid, a gas/liquid partition coefficient can be determined. For example, the blood/gas partition coefficient of a general anesthetic measures how easily the anesthetic passes from gas to blood and out of cells. As an example, multiple statin drugs are substrates for organic anion transporting polypeptides (OATPs; SLC transporter) that are highly expressed in the basolateral membrane of hepatocytes and this contributes to their ability to accumulate into the liver.

Distribution Coefficient

The **distribution coefficient**, **log *D***, is the ratio of the sum of the concentrations of all forms of the compound (ionized + unionized) in each of the two phases, one essentially always aqueous; as such, it depends on the pH of the aqueous phase, and log *D* = log *P* for non-ionizable compounds at any pH. For measurements of distribution coefficients, the pH of the aqueous phase is buffered to a specific value such that the pH is not significantly perturbed by the introduction of the compound. The value of each **log *D*** is then determined as the logarithm of a ratio—of the sum of the experimentally measured concentrations of the drug's various forms in one solvent, to the sum of such concentrations of its forms in the other solvent; it can be expressed as

$$\text{Log D} = \frac{[\text{drug}]^{\text{ionized}}_{\text{octanol}} + [\text{drug}]^{\text{unionized}}_{\text{octanol}}}{[\text{drug}]^{\text{ionized}}_{\text{water}} + [\text{drug}]^{\text{unionized}}_{\text{water}}} \quad .....(3.6)$$

In the above equation, the superscripts "ionized" each indicate the sum of concentrations of all ionized species in their respective phases. In addition, since log D is pH-dependent, the pH at which the log *D* was measured must be specified. In drug discovery involving partition phenomena in biological systems such as the human body; the log D at the physiologic pH 7.4 is of great interest.

Questions

Multiple Choice Questions

1. The major mechanism of drug transport involved in the transport of drug out of the blood into tissues is:
   (a) Active transport (b) Passive diffusion
   (c) Carrier mediated transport (d) Pore transport
2. Volume of distribution equals to
   (a) Dose given/plasma concentration
   (b) Total amount of drug in the body/plasma concentration
   (c) Urine drug concentration/plasma concentration
   (d) Dose given/urine concentration
   (e) Urine drug concentration/plasma concentration
3. When considering drug delivery to the brain which of the following is false?
   (a) The cells in the blood vessels that supply the brain are tightly connected which restricts drug absorption
   (b) Only relatively small lipophilic molecules readily, passively diffuse in to the brain
   (c) Drugs with a low log P value show improved passive diffusion into the brain
   (d) Polar molecules can be taken up into the brain through active transport
4. The volume of distribution of the drug can be given as
   (a) 500 L^{-1} (b) 50 L
   (c) 50 ml (d) None of the above
5. The anatomical barrier that remain inaccessible to most of the drugs is
   (a) Cell membrane barrier (b) Epithelial barrier
   (c) Blood brain barrier (d) Maternal fetal barrier
6. Drugs having high lipid water coefficient will tend to accumulate in-
   (a) Skin (b) Plasma
   (c) Intracellular fluid (d) Adipose tissue

7. If the distribution to tissue is limited by slow diffusion across membrane process is termed as:
   (a) Permeability limited
   (b) Perfusion limited
   (c) Both a and b
   (d) None of the above
8. Drugs that have a volume of distribution 4 L or less are thought to be confined to
   (a) Plasma
   (b) Tissue
   (c) Plasma and red blood cells
   (d) None of the above
9. The volume of distribution of drug is
   (a) Total body volume
   (b) Indication of patient total blood volume
   (c) Indication of patient total fluid volume
   (d) Ratio of total amount of drug in the body to the plasma concentration of the drug
10. Transfer of drug from plasma to tissue depends on
   (a) Weight of the tissue
   (b) Size of the tissue
   (c) Blood perfusion rate of the tissue
   (d) None of the above

Long Questions

1. Define distribution and list the various factors affecting distribution of drug in the body.
2. Elaborate the anatomy and physiology of blood brain barrier. What are the characteristics required for a drug to penetrate BBB.
3. Define apparent volume of distribution. Calculate V_d of a drug administered at a dose of 300 mg and exhibiting 30 μg/ml instantaneous concentration in plasma.
4. What are the two major rate limiting steps in distribution of drugs?
5. Illustrate the role of transporters in drug distribution.
6. How is a polar drug targeted to the brain?
7. How does age affect distribution of the drug in the body?
8. The V_d of a drug is 3000 litres. Calculate the plasma concentration when the amount of the drug in the body is 2 mg.

CHAPTER

Protein Binding of Drugs 4

LEARNING OBJECTIVES

- Knowledge of plasma proteins and drug protein binding
- Understanding Tissue binding
- Learning the factors affecting protein binding
- Significance of protein binding

The plasma proteins serve many different functions, including transport of lipids, hormones, vitamins and minerals in activity and functioning of the immune system. Other blood proteins act as enzymes, complement components, protease inhibitors or kinin precursors. Contrary to the popular belief, haemoglobin is not a blood protein, as it is carried within red blood cells, rather than in the blood serum. Serum albumin accounts for 55% of blood proteins, is a major contributor to maintaining the oncotic pressure of plasma and assists, as a carrier, in the transport of lipids and steroid hormones. Globulins make up 38% of blood proteins and transport ions, hormones, and lipids assisting in immune function. Fibrinogen comprises 7% of blood proteins; conversion of fibrinogen to insoluble fibrin is essential for blood clotting. The remainder of the plasma proteins (1%) is regulatory proteins, such as enzymes, proenzymes, and hormones. All blood proteins are synthesized in liver except for the gamma globulins.

The drug in the body can interact with blood components and extravascular tissues. The interacting molecules are generally the macromolecules such as proteins, DNA or adipose tissue components. The proteins interact with the drugs considerably and the phenomenon is termed as protein binding of drugs. Thus the drug exists in the body as bound and unbound form and the efficiency of drug is affected by the degree to which it binds. The less bound a drug is, the more efficiently it can traverse cell membranes or diffuse. Common blood proteins that drugs bind to are human serum albumin, glycoprotein, lipoprotein, and globulins. Since albumin is basic in nature, acidic and neutral drugs will primarily bind to albumin. If albumin becomes saturated, then these drugs will bind to lipoprotein. On the other hand basic drugs will bind to the acidic alpha -1 acid glycoprotein. Protein binding is significant because various pathological conditions may affect the levels of albumin, lipoproteins and alpha-1 acid glycoprotein.

Depending on the affinity of a drug for plasma protein, a fraction of the drug may become bound to the plasma protein, with the remainder being unbound. If the process of protein binding is reversible, then a chemical equilibrium will establish between the bound and unbound drug, so that,

$$\text{Protein} + \text{drug} \rightleftharpoons \text{Protein} - \text{drug complex}$$

Protein binding affects pharmacokinetics (absorption, distribution and clearance) as well as pharmacodynamics (receptor/enzyme interaction) i.e. a protein bound drug is neither metabolized nor excreted nor is it pharmacologically active. A bound drug is also restricted since it remains confined to a particular tissue for which it has greater affinity. For example, the protein bound fraction of warfarin is 97%. This means that the unbound fraction is 3% that is actually active and may be excreted. Moreover, such a bound drug, because of its enormous size, cannot undergo membrane transport and thus its half-life is increased. The bound portion may act as a reservoir or depot from which the drug is slowly released as the unbound form. Since the unbound form is being metabolized and/or excreted from the body, the bound fraction will be released in order to maintain equilibrium. The drugs may be categorized based on the extent of binding (Fig. 4.1). Table 4.1 lists the drugs that are more than 90% protein bound.

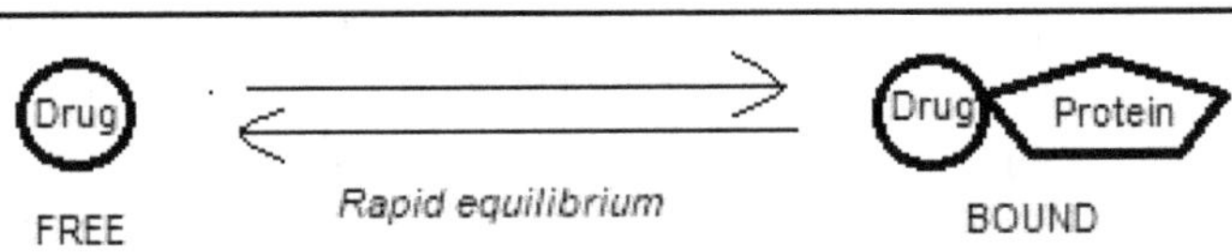

Percent bound	Magnitude of binding
0 - 50 %	Very Low
50 - 90%	Moderate
90 - 99 %	High
> 99 %	Very high

Fig. 4.1 Magnitude of drug protein binding.

Table 4.1 Examples of drugs that are more than 90% protein bound.

Therapeutic Category	Examples
Antibiotics	Ceftriaxone, doxycycline, ertapenem
Antipsychotics	Haloperidol, clozapine, chlorpromazine
Antiepilectic	Phenytoin, valproic acid
Antidiabetic	Glipizide
Chemotherapeutic agents	Paclitaxel, tamoxifen
Analgesics	Ibuprofen, buprenorphine, bupivacaine
Anxiolytics	Chlordiazepoxide, diazepam, lorazepam

Binding of drugs generally involves weak chemical bonds such as hydrogen bonds, hydrophobic bonds, ionic bonds or vander Waal's forces, and, therefore, is a reversible process. Irreversible drug binding is rare and arises as a result of covalent binding and is often a reason for the carcinogenicity or tissue toxicity of the drug. For example, covalent binding of paracetamol metabolites to liver results hepatotoxicity. Binding of drugs can be categorized into two classes:

1. Binding of drugs to blood components like plasma proteins, blood cells

2. Binding of drugs to extravascular tissue proteins, fats, bones, etc.

Of all types of binding, the plasma protein-drug binding is the most significant. Several factors have been shown to influence protein binding or displacement of therapeutic drugs from proteins. The *in vivo* variables include stress, inflammatory conditions, pregnancy, malignancies, liver disease, uremia, malnutrition, and competition of highly bound drugs with weaker binding drugs. Strongly protein-bound include classical anticonvulsants such as carbamazepine, phenytoin and valproic acid. *In vitro* factors that may impact the total-to free-drug ratio include the presence of drug displacement agents in blood collection tubes, heparin, and changes in pH with specimen age and/or exposure to air. For e.g. anticoagulants, particularly heparin, in blood collection tubes increases the concentration of free fatty acids that, in turn, affects binding of acidic drugs to albumin and basic drugs to alpha-1-acid glycoprotein, thus influencing measurement of the free drug.

As binding of drug to plasma proteins and more specifically to human serum albumin, is of significance, thus estimation of plasma protein binding is an important part of characterization of a new chemical entity during its development into a drug. Methods to determine plasma protein binding can be broadly divided into methods that either involve or obviate the need for prior separation of protein-bound and unbound drug.

(i) Methods requiring no separation of bound and unbound drug include surface plasmon resonance, capillary electrophoresis, NMR, fluorescence spectroscopy.

(ii) Equilibrium dialysis, ultracentrifugation, ultrafiltration, microdialysis, involve pre-separation of bound and free drug for the determination of free fraction of the drug. Some of the methods are amenable to automation and high throughput requirements of drug discovery, but equilibrium dialysis is still considered the 'gold standard' for estimation of drug protein binding.

In order to predict the extent of protein binding certain softwares are available. Those are:

(i) Quantum Plasma Protein Binding

(ii) S+ Plasma Protein binding

(iii) Albumin binding prediction

1. Binding of Drugs to Blood Components

(a) ***Plasma protein drug binding:*** After entering into the systemic circulation, the drug interacts with the blood components like plasma proteins; blood cells and hemoglobin (Table 4.2). The main interaction of drug in the blood compartment is with the plasma proteins which are present in abundant amounts and in large variety. The binding of drugs to plasma proteins is reversible. The extent or order of binding of drugs to various plasma proteins is: human serum albumin > α_1-acid glycoprotein > lipoproteins > globulins. Human serum albumin has attracted great interest in pharmaceutical industry since it can impact drug deliver, alter pharmacokinetic and pharmacodynamic properties of drug. Protein binding may be assayed by methods including equilibrium dialysis, ultrafiltration, ultracentrifugation, gel filtration, binding to albumin microspheres and circular dichroism.

Table 4.2 Brief description of blood proteins to which drugs bind.

Protein	Molecular Weight	Concentration (g %)	Drugs that bind
Human serum albumin (has 585 amino acids)	66, 500 Da	3.5 - 5.0	Large variety of drugs
α_1-acid glycoprotein	44000 Da	0.04-0.1	Basic drugs such as imipramine, lidocaine, quinidine, etc.
Lipoproteins	200000 to 3400000 Da	Variable	Propranol, verapamil, chlorpromazine, quinidine
α_1-Globulin	59000 Da	0.003-0.007	Thyroxine, steroids and cyanocobalamine
α_2-Globulin	1,34,0000 Da	015-0.06	Vitamin A, D, E and K and cupric ions
Heamoglobin	64500 Da	11-16	Phenytoin, pentobarbital, and phenothiazines

(i) ***Binding of drugs to human serum albumin:*** The human serum albumin (HSA) is the most abundant plasma protein (59 % of total plasma and 3.5 to 5.0 g %) with extensive drug binding capacity. HSA performs various physiological functions namely, regulates colloidal osmotic pressure, and transports numerous endogenous compounds such as fatty acids, hormones, bile acids, amino acids and toxic metabolites. The HSA can bind several compounds having varied structures. Both endogenous compounds such as fatty acids, bilirubin and tryptophan as well as drugs bind to HSA. A large variety of drugs ranging from weak acids, neutral compounds to weak bases, bind to HSA. It not only protects the bound drugs against oxidation and influences the *in vivo* distribution (Fig. 4.2), but also alters the pharmacokinetic and pharmacodynamic properties of drugs. Although there are eight binding sites with various affinities for the endogenous substances as well as drugs, HSA has two major binding sites known as warfarin-azapropazone (Site I) and diazepam binding site (Site II) (Table 4.3). Each of these sites binds several drugs of different chemical and pharmacological properties with relative high affinity. On the other hand the drug binding sites can be very specific and stereoselective. Despite its large size, HSA is not plasma limited but is distributed.

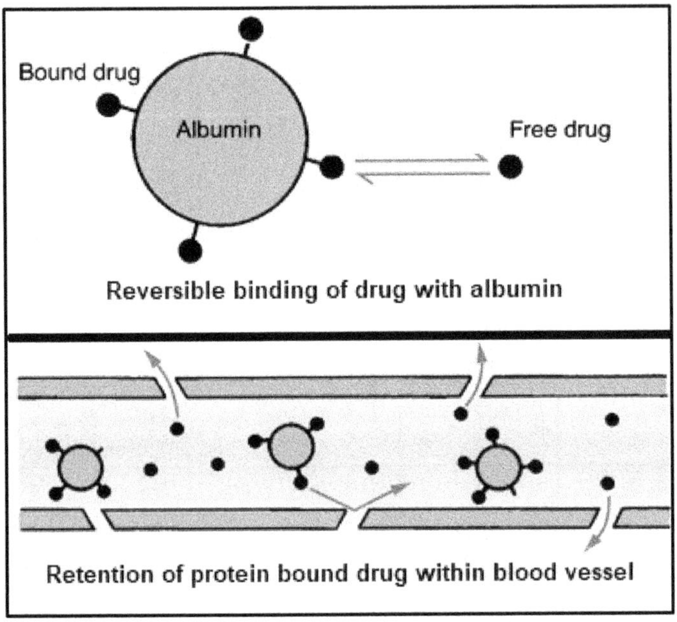

Fig. 4.2 Diagram showing effect of drug protein binding on *in vivo* distribution.

Table 4.3 Binding sites on human serum albumin.

Site number	Synonymn	Drugs that bind
Site I	Warfarin and azapropazone binding site	Large number of drugs binds to this site. e.g. several NSAIDs (naproxen, flubiprofen, suprofen, indomethacin), sulfonamides (sulfadimethoxine, sulfamethizole), phenytoin, sodium valproate and endogenous substance: bilirubin.
Site II	Diazepam binding site	benzodiazepines, medium chain fatty acids, ibuprofen, ketoprofen, tryptophan, cloxacillin, probenicid, etc.
Site III	Digitoxin binding site	Very few drugs bind to sites III and IV
Site IV	Tamoxifen binding site	

A drug can bind to more than one site in which case the main binding site is called as the primary site and the other as the secondary site. For example, site 1 is the primary site for dicoumarol and site II is the secondary site. Drugs that have affinity to bind to the same site will compete with each other for binding. The drugs that bind to one site do not competitively inhibit binding of drugs to other sites. However, they may either promote or retard binding of a drug to another site by energetic coupling mechanisms.

(ii) ***Binding of drugs to α_1-Acid Glycoprotein (α_1-AGP or AAG)***

AAG (also called as orosomucoid), synthesized in hepatocytes, is a member of the acute phase protein family, first described in 1950. It has a single polypeptide chain consisting of 183 amino acids with five glycan chains, accounting for ~45% of its total molecular weight (41-44). AAG is formed primarily in the liver and circulates from 0.5 to 1.0 mg/ml in the plasma of healthy humans. In most disease states including inflammation, infection, and cancer, AAG levels increase from 2 to 6-fold in humans. The levels of AAG may be particularly affected in HIV infection, however, in others it may remain unaffected but the binding capacity may diminish. AAG binding may also depend on gender, age, obesity, pregnancy, disease state, ethnicity and even daily changes It binds to a number of basic (positively charged) drugs like lidocaine, fluconazole, penbutol, atracurium, nortriptyline, propranolol, quinidine and dipyridamole. Binding of drugs to HSA and AAG involve hydrophobic bonds. Because AAG is a low capacity protein, it is possible to saturate its binding sites by drugs at normally encountered therapeutic concentration ranges.

(iii) ***Binding of drugs to Lipoproteins***

A lipoprotein is a biochemical assembly whose primary purpose is to transport hydrophobic lipid (fat) molecules in water, as in blood or extracellular fluid. They have a single layer phospholipid and cholesterol outer shell, with the hydrophilic portions oriented outward toward the surrounding water and lipophilic portions of each molecule oriented inwards toward the lipids molecules within the particles. Apolipoproteins are embedded in the membrane, both stabilizing the complex and giving it functional identity determining its fate. Thus the complex serves to emulsify the fats. Many enzymes, transporters, structural proteins, antigens, adhesins, and toxins are lipoproteins. The plasma concentration of lipoproteins is much less in comparison to HSA and AAG.

A drug that binds to lipoproteins does so by dissolving in the lipid core of the protein and thus its capacity to bind depends upon its lipid content. The plasma lipoprotein particles are classified as HDL, LDL, IDL, VLDL and ULDL (chylomicrons) lipoproteins, according to density / size (an inverse relationship), compared with the surrounding plasma water. These complex protein capsules enable fats to be carried in all extracellular water, including the blood stream. The five classes of lipoproteins are:

1. High density lipoproteins (HDL)
2. Low density lipoproteins (LDL) (predominant in humans)
3. Intermediate density lipoprotiens (IDL)
4. Very low density lipoproteins (VLDL)
5. Ultra low density lipoproteins (ULDL or chylomicrons)

The binding of drugs to lipoproteins is non-competitive. A number of acidic (diclofenac), neutral (cyclosporine A), and basic drugs (chlorpromazine) bind to lipoproteins. Basic, lipophilic drugs have relatively more affinity. Lipoprotein binding becomes significant in cases of drugs that predominantly bind to them, and secondly, when levels of HSA and AAG in plasma are decreased.

(iv) *Binding of drugs to Globulins*

Several plasma globulins have been identified and are labeled as α1, α2, β1, β2 and γ-globulins.

1. α1-globulin: Also called as transcortin or CBG (corticosteroid binding globulin), it binds to number of steroidal drugs such as cortisone and prednisone. It also binds to thyroxine and cyanocobalamin.
2. α2-globulin: Also called as ceruloplasmin, it binds vitamins A, D, E and K and cupric ions.
3. β1-globulin: also called as transferrin, it binds to ferrous ions.
4. β2-globulin: binds to carotenoids.
5. γ-globulin: binds specifically to antigens.

(b) Binding of Drugs to Blood Cells

The circulating blood volume consists of about 45 percent of blood cells. This fraction may, however, be increased to about 60 percent in newborns, and decreased to as low as 20 percent in anemia, for instance, due to uremia. The major cell body in the blood is the erythrocyte, also called the red blood cell (RBC). As the RBCs constitute 95% of the total blood cells, significant drug binding is possible. Leucocytes and thrombocytes are other cells of interest and comprise the additional 5 percent. The RBC comprises of three components each of which can bind to drugs:

Hemoglobin: It has a molecular weight of 64,500 and drugs like phenytoin, pentobarbital and phenothiazines bind to hemoglobin.

Carbonic anhydrase: Drugs that bind to it are acetazolamide and chlorthalidone.

Cell Membrane: Imipramine and chlorpromazine bind with the RBC membrane.

Different drugs have different affinities for the blood cells. The rate and extent of entry into RBC is more for lipophilic drugs whereas hydrophilic drugs do not enter RBC as exemplified by the antibiotic ampicillin. Two diuretic drugs, acetazolamide and chlorthalidone, have among the highest affinities to the blood cells that have been published so far.

The binding of drugs to erythrocytes will only be important for the total body distribution, if the binding to the cells is extremely strong and/or the distribution volume of the drug is low. We must also keep in mind that in the circulating blood, the erythrocytes are an isolated pharmacokinetic compartment. Equilibration to various organs does not take place against free concentrations in whole blood, but rather to free concentrations in plasma. Nevertheless, it is possible that the red cell may serve as an interesting model cell in the pharmacokinetic analysis of a drug

2. **Tissue Binding (Tissue Localization) of Drugs:** A drug can bind to one or more of the several tissue components. Tissue-drug binding is important in distribution from two viewpoints: firstly, it increases the apparent volume of distribution of drugs in contrast to plasma protein binding which decreases it; this is because the parameter is related to the ratio of amount of drug in the body to the plasma concentration of free drug and the latter is decreased under conditions of extensive tissue binding of drugs, and secondly, tissue-drug binding results in localization of a drug at a specific site in the body (with a subsequent increase in biological half-life). This is more so because a number of drugs bind irreversibly with the tissues (contrast to plasma protein-drug binding); for example, oxidation products of paracetamol, phenacetin, carbon tetrachloride and bromobenzene bind covalently to hepatic tissues. Tissue binding assay techniques can involve testing binding

to isolated organs, tissue slices, homogenates and isolated subcellular particles.

Factors influencing localization of drugs in tissues include lipophilicity and structural features of the drug, perfusion rate of the organ/tissue and pH differences. Extensive tissue-drug binding suggests that a tissue can act as the storage site for drugs. Drugs that bind to both tissue and plasma components present competition between drug binding sites. For majority of drugs that bind to extravascular tissues, the order of binding is: liver > kidney > lung > muscle. Several examples of extravascular tissue-drug binding are:

(i) **Liver:** Oxidation products of paracetamol, phenacetin, chloroform, carbon tetrachloride and bromobenzene bind covalently to hepatic tissues resulting in hepatotoxicity.

(ii) **Lungs:** The specific architectural arrangement of mammalian lung favors that so-called pneumophilic drugs are filtered out of the blood and are retained within the tissue as shown in particular for amphetamine, chlorphentermine, amiodarone, imipramine, chlorpromazine, propranolol, local anaesthetics, and some miscellaneous therapeutics.

(iii) **Kidneys:** Metallothionins, a family of protein present in kidneys, has a high content of cysteine residues that bind various heavy metals; these proteins are transcriptionally regulated by both heavy metals and glucocorticoids.

(iv) **Skin:** Drugs that can cause drug-induced pigmentation include antimalarials (chloroquine), chemotherapeutic agents, nonsteroidal anti-inflammatory drugs (NSAIDs), antipsychotics, amiodarone, minocycline accumulate in skin by interacting with melanin.

(v) **Eyes:** Drugs bind to melanin at varying extent that ranges from no binding to extensive binding. Binding may lead to drug accumulation to the pigmented tissues and prolonged drug retention in the melanin containing cells. Binding of chloroquine and phenothiazines to melanin in eyes causes retinopathy.

(vi) **Hairs:** With past drug use, the drug will be located in a small section of the hair at a distance from the root proportional to the number of months after the drug use. Chloroquine and phenothiazines get deposited in hair shafts.

(vii) **Bones:** Tetracycline binds to bones and teeth. Administration of this antibiotic to infants or children during odontogenesis results in permanent brown-yellow discoloration of teeth. Bisphosphonates, the gold-standard pharmacological treatment for osteoporosis, are unique in that they become physically bound to the bone matrix and therefore accumulate over time. There is no known method of removing the medication from the bones.

(viii) Fats: Lipophilic drugs such as thiopental and the pesticide DDT accumulate in adipose tissues by partitioning into it. However, high o/w partition coefficient is not the only criteria for adipose distribution of drugs since several highly lipophilic (more than thiopental) basic drugs like imipramine and chlorpromazine are not localized in fats. The poor perfusion of adipose could be the reason for such an ambiguity.

(ix) Nucleic Acids: Molecular components of cells such as DNA interact strongly with drugs like chloroquine and quinacrine resulting in distortion of its double helical structure. Distamycin and netropsin interact with AT-rich regions of DNA in the minor groove by forming hydrogen bonding and hydrophobic interactions. The terminal amidine group of the small molecule is basic, and serves to attract the drug molecule to the negatively charged DNA phosphodiester backbone.

Factors Affecting Protein-Drug Binding

Drug related factors	Protein/Tissue related factors	Drug interactions	Patient related factors
(a) Physicochemical characteristics of the drug (b) Concentration of drug in body (c) Affinity of a drug for a particular binding component	(a) Physicochemical characteristics of the protein or binding agent (b) Concentration of protein or binding component (c) Number of binding sites on the binding agent	(a) Competition between drugs for the binding site (displacement interactions) (b) Competition between drugs and normal body constituents (c) Allosteric changes in protein molecule	(a) Age (b) Intersubject variations (c) Disease states

A. Drug Related Factors

(a) **Physicochemical characteristics of the drug:** Protein binding is primarily related to the lipophilicity of the drug. Hence, an increase in the lipophilicity of drug increases its extent of protein binding, For example, cloxacillin a highly lipophilic drug exhibits 95% protein binding. Thus on intramuscular injection, low absorption is observed as only ≤ 5% free drug is available. Highly lipophilic drugs such as thiopental tend to accumulate in the adipose tissues. The anionic (acidic) drugs have strong binding affinity for HSA whereas the cationic (basic) drugs tend to bind to AAG. The unionized, neutral drugs bind predominantly to the lipoproteins.

(b) **Concentration of drug in the body:** The extent of drug-protein binding is affected by changes in the concentration of both drug as well as protein. As the concentration of HSA in the blood is very high, any drug that has tendency to bind to HSA does not have much influence on drug-protein binding as the therapeutic concentration of any drug is not sufficient enough to saturate it. However, the therapeutic concentration of lidocaine can tend to saturate AAG as the concentration of AAG is quite less in comparison to that of HSA in blood.

(c) **Drug-protein/tissue affinity:** Each drug has affinity to bind to a specific plasma protein or tissue depending on its physicochemical characteristics. As mentioned, lidocaine has higher affinity for AAG than for HSA. Likewise, digoxin tends to bind to the proteins of cardiac muscles rather than those of plasma or skeletal muscles.

B. Protein/Tissue Related Factors

(a) **Physicochemical properties of protein binding component:** The adipose tissue and lipoproteins tend to bind lipophilic drugs by solubilizing them in their lipid core. HSA is best known for its drug binding capacity, providing a depot for a wide variety of drugs that may be available in quantities well beyond their solubility in plasma. The presence of active anionic and cationic groups on the albumin molecules is determined by the physiological pH that in turn affects binding of drugs to HSA.

(b) **Concentration of protein binding component:** HSA is present in the highest concentration in blood amongst all the plasma proteins. Hence, drug-protein binding predominantly occurs with HSA. The concentration of several proteins and tissue binding components available for binding gets altered in disease states that affect the extent of binding.

(c) **Number of binding sites on the protein:** HSA has abundant binding sites on it in comparison to other plasma proteins and displays high binding capacity. Carbamazepine has affinity to bind to site II of HSA. Many drugs are capable of binding to HSA at more than one site. For example ketoprofen, dicoumarol, fluocloxacillin, tamoxifen, flurbiprofen and ketoprofen bind to both the primary and secondary sites on HSA. Indomethacin binds to three different sites on HSA. Drug binding to HSA is an important determinant for their biological efficacy. The plasma protein AAG has limited binding capacity owing to its low concentration in blood and low molecular size. Although AAG has only one binding site for lidocaine; two binding sites are reported in presence of HSA due to direct interaction between HSA and AAG.

C. Drug Interactions

(a) **Competition between drugs for the binding sites:** Competition between drugs results when two or more drugs tend to bind to the same site on protein. Assume two drugs: A and B that tend to bind to the same protein site. If drug A is bound to such a site, then administration of drug B (same/higher affinity) will result in displacement of drug A from its binding site. Such a drug-drug interaction for the common binding site is called as displacement interaction. The drug A is termed as the displaced drug and drug B as the displacer. For e.g. carbamazepine has direct competition with L-tryptophan for binding with site II of HSA. Similarly, phenylbutazone and warfarin have same degree of affinity for HSA. If a patient on warfarin therapy is administered phenylbutazone (higher affinity) it will result in displacement of warfarin from its binding site. Thus high circulating levels of free warfarin may cause adverse hemorrhagic reactions. Phenylbutazone is also known to displace sulfonamides from their HSA binding sites causing high circulating levels of free sulphonamides. Such displacement interactions can result in unexpected rise in free drug concentration of the displaced drug in blood which may either enhance clinical response or may result in toxicity. Even a drug metabolite can cause displacement interaction.

Clinically significant interactions will result when:

The displaced drug	The displacer drug
Is more than 95% bound	Has a high degree of affinity as the drug to be displaced
Has a small volume of distribution (less than 0.15 L/Kg)	Competes for the same binding sites.
Shows a rapid onset of therapeutic or adverse effects	The drug/protein concentration ratio is high (above 0.10)
Has a narrow therapeutic index	Shows a rapid and large increase in plasma drug concentration.

The extent of displacement is dependent on both the concentration of the displacer drug, and its affinity for the binding sites in comparison to that of the drug to be displaced from protein. Consider a drug that is 95% protein bound. For such drug a displacement of mere 5% will result in a 100% rise in its free drug concentration. If the displaced drug has a small V_d, it will remain confined to the central (blood) compartment and display toxic responses. On the other hand, if such a drug has a large V_d, it will tend to redistribute into a large volume of body fluids and thus clinical effects may be negligible. The increase in free drug concentration following displacement also makes the drug more available for elimination by liver and kidneys. If the drug is readily metabolizable, its displacement results insignificant reduction in elimination half-life. Displacement interaction becomes insignificant with potent, low dose drugs. Table 4.3 lists few displacer and displaced drugs.

Table 4.4 Cases on change in plasma protein binding on coadministration.

Displaced drug	Displacer
Carbamazepine	Valproate
Diazepam	Valproate
Ketoprofen	Probenecid
Methotrexate	Probenecid
Cefatriaxone	Probenecid
Tolbutamide	Sulfaphenazole
Phenytoin	Phenylbutazone

(b) **Competition between drugs and normal body constituents:** As mentioned earlier, the free fatty acids normally present in body interact with a number of drugs that bind primarily to HSA. The free fatty acid levels are increased in physiological (fasting), pathological (diabetes, myocardial infarction and alcohol abstinence) and pharmacologically induced conditions (after caffeine and heparin administration). Under physiological conditions, HSA normally binds up to two moles of unesterified fatty acids although in certain disease states it may accommodate up to six moles. The fatty acids, which also bind to albumin, influence binding of several benzodiazepines and propranolol (decreased binding); and warfarin (increased binding). Binding of the endogenous substance bilirubin to HSA may be impaired by certain drugs and is of clinical concern in neonates whose bilirubin metabolizing capacity is not well developed. The acidic drugs such as sodium salicylate and sulfonamides displace bilirubin from its HSA binding site. The free bilirubin is not subjected to conjugation reactions in the liver of the preterm infants or neonates and thus crosses the BBB to cause kernicterus.

Allosteric changes in protein molecule

Allosteric changes refer to alteration(s) of the protein structure by the drug or its metabolite thereby modifying the binding capacity of protein. Such agents are called as allosteric effectors. E.g. aspirin acetylates the lysine component of HSA thereby modifying its capacity to bind with NSAIDs like phenylbutazone (increased affinity) and flufenamic acid (decreased affinity). Allosteric interactions have been reported to affect stereoselective binding equilibria between HSA and ibuprofen, warfarin and lorazepam.

D. Patient Related Factors

(a) **Age:** Modification in protein-drug binding as influenced by age of the patient is due to differences in the protein content in various age groups.

(i) **Neonates:** Low albumin content in the newborn results in an increase in the unbound concentration of drug that binds to HSA. For example drugs like phenytoin and diazepam.

(ii) **Young infants:** Infants inflicted from congestive cardiac failure are given a digitalizing dose that 4 to 6 times the adult dose on the basis of body weight. This is quite in contrast to the concept that infants should be given low doses considering their underdeveloped drug eliminating system. The reason for use of a higher digoxin dose is attributed to two factors (i) greater binding of the drug to plasma proteins in infants, and (ii) abnormally large renal clearance of digoxin in infants.

(iii) **Elderly:** The albumin content is lowered in old age and hence the free concentration of drug(s) that bind to it is increased requiring dose reduction. On the other hand the AAG levels increase in old age and thus lower free concentration is observed for drugs that bind to it. This requires higher dose of such drugs. The situation is complicated for the drugs that bind to both HSA and AAG, e.g. lidocaine and propranolol.

(b) **Intersubject variations:** Intersubject variability in drug protein binding has been studied for few drugs and the results depicted small difference and not exceeding two fold. These insignificant differences can be attributed to genetic and environmental factors.

Disease states

Several pathological conditions result in alteration of the blood protein content. Since HSA is the major drug binding protein, hypoalbuminemia can severely affect drug-protein binding. Hypoalbuminemia is caused by several conditions like trauma, inflammatory states, burns, renal and hepatic disorders, aging, pregnancy, cancer and surgery etc. Invariably every chronic illness is characterized by reduced HSA content. A lowered binding of frusemide is associated with hypoalbuminaemia and hyperbilirubinaemia. Hyperlipo-proteinemia, is observed in hypothyroidism, alcoholism and obstructive liver diseases etc., affects binding of lipophilic drugs. Some of the diseases that alter drug-protein binding are depicted in Table 4.5.

Table 4.5 Influence of disease states on drug-protein binding.

Disease	Influence on plasma protein	Influence on drug-protein binding
1. Renal failure (uremia)	Decreased albumin content	Decreased binding of acidic drugs; neutral and basic drugs unaffected.
2. Nephrotic syndrome	Decreased albumin concentration	Decreased binding of acidic drugs; neutral and basic drugs unaffected.
3. Hepatic failure	Decreased albumin synthesis	Decreased binding of acidic drugs; binding of basic drugs is normal or reduced depending on AAG levels.
4. Inflammatory states (trauma, surgery, burns, infections, etc.)	Increased AAG levels	Increased binding of basic drugs; neutral and acidic drugs unaffected.

In conclusion, all factors, specifically displacement interactions and the factors related to patient(s) exhibit significant affect on drug-protein or drug-tissue binding that in turn influence:

1. **Pharmacokinetics of drug:** An increase in drug- protein binding will result in a decrease in unbound drug concentration. This favors confinement of drug in blood. On the other hand a decrease in drug-protein binding will increase the unbound drug concentration favouring tissue redistribution and clearance of drugs from the body due to enhanced biotransformation and excretion.
2. **Pharmacodynamics of drugs:** An increased concentration of unbound drug results in increased intensity of action (therapeutic/toxic) and vice versa.

Significance of Protein/Tissue Binding of Drugs

For a drug showing little protein binding, the plasma acts simply as a watery solution in which the drug is dissolved. Where protein binding does occur the behaviour of the drug may be influenced in several ways. This has been explained in the following text.

Absorption

The absorption equilibrium is achieved when the concentration of free drug between the site of administration and the systemic circulation becomes equal. Once equilibrium is achieved it is likely that absorption may stop. However, binding of the absorbed drug to the plasma proteins decreases the free (unbound) drug concentration and disturbs the equilibrium. As a result sink condition and the concentration gradient is reestablished which now act as the driving force for further absorption of the drug. This is particularly useful in case of ionized drugs which are transported with difficulty. Extensive plasma protein binding will increase the amount of drug that has to be absorbed before effective therapeutic levels of unbound drug are reached. For example, acidic dugs (such as acetyl salicylic acid – aspirin) are often substantially bound to albumin.

Distribution

Binding of drugs to plasma protein restricts their entry to certain tissues for which they have specific affinity. This prevents accumulation of drug in such tissues and thus, subsequent cumulative toxicity. Plasma protein-drug binding thus favors uniform distribution of drugs throughout the body by its buffer function (maintains equilibrium between the free and the bound drug). A protein bound drug does not cross the BBB, the placental barrier and the glomerulus.

The former two are hence protected against undue exposure to drugs. Water insoluble drugs, neutral endogenous macromolecules such as heparin and several steroids, and oil soluble vitamins are distributed to the tissues by binding primarily to the lipoproteins which act as a carrier for such hydrophobic compounds. A drug that is extensively bound to plasma proteins remains confined to the blood thus limiting its volume of distribution. On the other hand, a drug that shows extravascular tissue binding, has large volume of distribution. In both cases, the bound drug serves as a depot for that drug. For example, erythrocytes are a storage site for the lipophilic compound tetrahydrocannabinol.

The negative impact of protein binding can be exemplified through antibiotics. Protein binding of antibiotics may affect the efficacy of antimicrobial therapy in two ways. First, only the non-protein-bound fraction of a drug in plasma can penetrate into and equilibrate with the extravascular space. Penetration into the extravascular space is highly important for antimicrobial therapy, as the majority of bacterial and fungal infections occur in the interstitial fluid of tissues or in other body fluids than blood.

Elimination

Only the free or unbound drug is capable of being eliminated. This is because the drug-protein complex cannot enter into the metabolizing organ (liver). Elimination of a highly bound drug may be delayed. Since the concentration of free drug is low, drug elimination by metabolism and excretion may be delayed. This effect is responsible for prolonging the effect of the drug digoxin. Furthermore, the large molecular size of the drug-protein complex also prevents it from getting filtered through the glomerulus. Thus, drugs which are more than 95% bound are eliminated slowly i.e. they have long elimination half-lives. For example, tetracycline, which is only 65% bound, has an elimination half-life of 8.5 hours in comparison to 15.1 hours of doxycycline which is 93% bound to plasma proteins. However, penicillins have short elimination half-lives despite being extensively bound to plasma proteins. This is because rapid equilibration occurs between the free and the bound drug and the free drug is equally rapidly excreted by active secretion in renal tubules.

Displacement interactions

Drugs may compete for binding with plasma proteins leading to interactions. This is significant for highly bound drugs such as the anticoagulant warfarin since even a small change in binding will greatly affect the amount of free drug. Such an effect is produced by the concurrent administration of aspirin, which displaces warfarin and increases the amount of free anticoagulant. As stated earlier, displacement interactions are significant in case of drugs which are more than 95% bound. This is explained from the example given in Table 4.6. A displacement of just 1% of a 99% bound drug results in doubling of the free drug concentration i.e. a 100% rise. For a drug that is bound to a lesser extent e.g. 90%, displacement of 1% results in only a 10% rise in free drug concentration which may be insignificant clinically.

Table 4.6 Influence of percent binding and displacement on change in free concentration of drugs.

	Drug A	Drug B
% drug before displacement		
Bound	99	90
Free	1	10
% drug after displacement		
Bound	98	89
Free	2	11
% increase in free drug concentration	100	10

Kernicterus in infants is a typical example of a disorder caused by displacement of bilirubin from albumin binding sites by the NSAIDs. Since displacement interactions may precipitate toxicity of displaced drug, a reduction in its dose is required. This may become necessary for a drug having a small V_d such as warfarin since displacement can result in a large increase in free drug concentration in plasma. With a drug of large V_d such as digoxin, even a substantial increase in the degree of displacement of drug in plasma may not effect a large increase in free drug concentration and dose adjustment may not be required.

Therapy

Treatment of brain disease is difficult as majority of drugs cannot pass through the blood brain barrier. HSA delivery systems have been extensively used for treating brain disease since HSA can pass through BBB. HSA can directly form a "nano- drug" thus increasing drug bioavailability. These have been exploited to improve the targeting of anticancer drugs and decrease their side effects.

The binding of drugs to lipoproteins can be used for site-specific delivery of hydrophilic moieties. This is particularly useful in cancer therapies since certain tumor cells have greater affinity for LDL than normal tissues. Lipoproteins carry high-drug payload and are used as delivery vehicles for transportation of chemotherapeutic agents. These bear unique targeting capabilities because of their easy transportation to cancer and tumor sites. LDL loaded with r11-DOX is used to treat cancer cells. LDL follows receptor pathway is used to deliver radionucleotides for the treatment of neoplasms and tumors. Another example is site-specific drug delivery in cancer treatment is that of estramustine. Besides natural HDL molecules, reconstituted high density lipoprotein (rHDL) is also prepared to deliver therapeutic agents. Reconstructed high density lipoproteins made with phospholipids and apolipoproteins and used as a vehicle for systemic delivery of drugs, therapies and as imaging agents. These are highly useful for targeted and efficacious systemic delivery of siRNAs.

Questions

Multiple Choice Questions

1. β_2- globulins bind to
   (a) Carotenoids (b) Thyroxine
   (c) Antigens (d) cupric ions
2. Both HSA and heamoglobin have a molecular weight of
   (a) 44,000 (b) 59,000 (c) 65,000 (d) 64,5000
3. Site III in HSA is also called as
   (a) Tamoxifen binding site (b) Warfarin binding site
   (c) Digoxin binding site (d) Diazepam binding site
4. Irreversible drug binding arises as a result of
   (a) Covalent bonding (b) Hydrophobic bonds
   (c) Ionic bonding (d) Hydrogen bonding
5. The red blood cell is how many times larger in diameter than HSA
   (a) 400 (b) 450 (c) 500 (d) 550

6. Drugs bind to extravascular tissues; least binding is observed with which of the following:
   (a) Lungs (b) Kidney
   (c) Muscle (d) Liver
7. Clinically significant drug interactions occur when V_d of displaced drug is
   (a) 2 L/Kg (b) < 0.5 L /Kg
   (c) 1 L/Kg (d) < 0.15 L/Kg
8. Renal failure (Uremia) results in
   (a) Decreased binding of acidic drugs
   (b) Decreased binding of basic drugs
   (c) Increased binding of acidic drugs
   (d) Increased binding of basic drugs
9. The neonates have low albumin content consequently the unbound fraction of phenytoin will
   (a) Increase (b) Remain unchanged
   (c) Decrease (d) None of the above
10. A drug that shows extravascular tissue binding has
    (a) A large V_d (b) Same as free drug
    (c) A small V_d (d) None of the above

Short Questions

1. A protein bound drug is both pharmacokinetically as well as pharmacodynamically inert. Why?
2. When is drug-binding considered irreversible? What could be the consequence of such an interaction?
3. Classify the body components to which drugs normally bind.
4. Why does binding of a drug to plasma proteins occur to a large extent in comparison to binding to other tissue components?

5. Why is HSA considered a versatile protein for drug binding? Name the various drug binding sites on HSA.
6. From distribution viewpoint, what is the significance of tissue-drug binding?

Long Questions

1. What is the influence of drug related factors on plasma protein level and drug-binding?
2. Explain the significance of protein/tissue binding.
3. Explain the drug binding interaction with (i) Human serum albumin and (ii) lipoproteins.
4. With suitable examples, discuss tissue binding of drugs.
5. Elaborate the patient related factors that influence protein binding.

Biotransformation of Drugs

CHAPTER

5

LEARNING OBJECTIVES

- Understanding the concept of biotransformation
- Chemical pathways of biotransformation
- Factors affecting of biotransformation

The duration and intensity of drug action depends upon the rate of drug removal from the body/site of action that can be correlated to the rate of elimination and tissue redistribution of drug. Elimination is the major process for removal of a drug from the body and termination of its action. It occurs by two processes viz. biotransformation and excretion. ***Biotransformation of drugs is defined as the conversion of the drug (chemical compound) to another chemical (metabolites).*** The chemical changes are usually affected enzymatically in the body. Drugs are xenobiotics which enter the body and are absorbed by virtue of their lipophilicity. A drug needs to be sufficiently lipid soluble for absorption but because of this it is able to bypass excretion. This is because only water-soluble agents undergo renal excretion whereas lipid soluble substances are passively reabsorbed from the renal tubules into the blood after glomerular filtration. Thus, if such a phenomenon continues, drugs would accumulate in the body and precipitate toxic reactions. However, to prevent such a consequence, the body is armed with the metabolic system which transforms the water insoluble, lipophilic, non-polar drugs into polar and water-soluble products that can be easily excreted by the kidneys. For e.g., hippuric acid, the metabolite of benzoic acid, is two times more water-soluble and gets readily excreted. Thus drug biotransformation can be seen as a detoxification process. However, occasionally biotransformation may lead to products of decreased water solubility. For instance, the N-acetyl derivatives of sulfonamides are less water-soluble than the parent drug and thus have a tendency to cause crystalluria.

Biotransformation normally results in pharmacologic inactivation of drugs, i.e. formation of metabolites with little or no pharmacological activity, e.g. conversion of phenytoin to p-hydroxyphenytoin. Biotransformation may occasionally yield metabolites with equal activity, and the process rarely leads to toxicologic activation of drugs. Inactive drugs (prodrugs) also depend upon biotransformation for activation, the process being called as pharmacologic activation; e.g. conversion of enalapril to enalaprilat. A change in the pharmacologic activity of the drug on metabolism can also been observed (see Table 5.1).

Table 5.1 Metabolites and relative activity of drugs.

Drugs	Metabolites
Pharmacologic Inactivation	
Active	*Inactive*
Phenobarbital	Hydroxyphenobarbital
Phenytoin	p-hydroxy phenytoin
Salicylic acid	Salicyluric acid
No Change in Pharmacologic activity	
Active	*Active*
Amitriptyline	Nortriptyline
Imipramine	Desiprarnine
Phenylbutazone	Oxyphenbutazone
Digitoxin	Digoxin
Toxicologic Activation	
Active	*Reactive intermediates*
Isoniazid	Tissue acylating intermediate
Paracetamol	Imidoquinone of N-hydroxylated metabolite (causes hepatic necrosis)
Pharmacologic Activation	
Inactive (Prodrug)	*Active*
Aspirin	Salicylic acid
Pivampicillin	Ampicillin
Enalapril	Enalaprilat
Change in Pharmacologic Activity	
Iproniazid (antidepressant)	Isoniazid (antitubercular)
Diazepam (tranquilizer)	Oxazepam (anticonvulsant)

In comparison to xenobiotics, the natural endogenous substances such as neurotransmitters (epinephrine, norepinephrine, dopamine, GABA, etc.), steroids (testosterone, progesterone, cortisol, etc) and insulin which are also used as therapeutic agents, are inactivated rapidly due to well developed system of human body for metabolizing such agents. These substances are therefore called as **soft drugs**. Such soft drugs do not precipitate unexpected toxicity when used in concentrations close to their normal levels.

Drug Metabolizing Organs

Liver is the primary site for metabolism of almost all drugs (and other xenobiotics) because it has a large variety of enzymes in abundance. Metabolism by organs other than liver (called as extrahepatic metabolism) is of minor importance since lower level of drug metabolizing enzymes is present in such tissues. The decreasing order of drug metabolizing ability of various organs is: liver > lungs > kidneys > intestine > placenta > adrenals > skin. Brain, testes, muscles, spleen also metabolize drugs to a small extent.

Drug Metabolizing Enzymes

The enzymes that biotransform xenobiotics are versatile and non-specific in nature. The biotransformation enzymes can be broadly divided into two categories: **microsomal and non-microsomal**. The microsomal enzymes catalyze oxidative, reductive, hydrolytic and glucuronidation biotransformations.

Some important characteristics of microsomal enzyme system are:

1. The intact nature of lipoidal membrane bound microsomal enzymes is essential for its selectivity towards lipid-soluble substrates.
2. A number of lipid-soluble xenobiotics can interact non-specifically with the microsomal enzymes while the natural water soluble endogenous substances do not interact.
3. The lipid soluble substrate is biotransformed into a water-soluble metabolite by the microsomal enzymes which can be readily excreted.

The non-microsomal enzymes include those that are present in soluble form in the cytoplasm and those attached to the mitochondria but not to endoplasmic reticulum. These are also non-specific enzymes that catalyze few oxidative reactions, a number of reductive and hydrolytic reactions and conjugation reactions other than glucuronidation. In contrast to the microsomal enzymes, the non-microsomal enzymes, especially the soluble ones, act on relatively water-soluble xenobiotics (as well as endogenous compounds).

Chemical Pathways of Drug Biotransformation

The drug metabolism pathways can be primarily categorized into phase I and phase II reactions. Little is also known about phase III reactions.

Phase I Reactions

These reactions generally precede phase II reactions and include oxidative, reductive hydrolytic and reactions. In these reactions, a polar functional group (e.g. -OH, -COOH, -NH_2 and –SH) is either introduced or unmasked if already present on the lipid soluble substrate. Thus, phase I reactions are also called as **functionalization** reactions. These transformations are also called as **asynthetic reactions.** The resulting product of phase I reaction is susceptible to phase II reactions. Table 5.2 summarizes various phase I reactions under the subheadings of oxidative, reductive and hydrolytic reactions.

Table 5.2 A summary of Phase I biotransformation reactions.

Oxidative reactions	Reductive Reactions	Hydrolytic reactions
1. Oxidation of aromatic carbon atoms 2. Oxidation of olefins (C–C bonds)	1. Reduction of carbonyl functions (aldehydes/ ketones) 2. Reduction of alcohols and C=C bonds	1. Hydrolysis of esters and ethers 2. Hydrolysis of amides
3. Oxidation of benzylic, allylic carbon atoms and carbon atoms alpha to carbonyl and imines	3. Reduction of N-compounds (nitro, azo and N-oxide)	3. Hydrolytic cleavage of non-aromatic heterocycles
4. Oxidation of aliphatic carbon atoms 5. Oxidation of alicyclic carbon atoms	4. Miscellaneous reductive reactions	4. Hydrolytic dehalogenation 5. Miscellaneous hydrolytic reactions

Contd...

Oxidative reactions	Reductive Reactions	Hydrolytic reactions
6. Oxidation of carbon-heteroatom systems: a. *Carbon-Nitrogen systems* i. N-Dealkylation ii. Oxidative deamination iii. N-Oxide formation iv. N-Hydroxylation *b. Carbon-Sulfur systems*: i. S-Dealkylation ii. Desulfuration iii. S-oxidation *c. Carbon-Oxygen systems* i O-dealkylation) 7. Oxidation of alcohol, carbonyl and acid functions 8. Miscellaneous oxidative reactions		
The oxidative deamination and oxidation of alcohol, carbonyl and acid functions are catalyzed by microsomal and non-microsomal enzymes. Rest all are catalyzed by microsomal enzymes only.	*All are catalyzed by both microsomal and non-microsomal enzymes except reduction of alcohols and C+ C bonds that is catalyzed by microsomal enzymes only.*	*1, 2, 3 are catalyzed by both microsomal and non- microsomal enzymes*

The most important enzyme system of phase I metabolism is cytochrome P-450 (CYP450), a microsomal superfamily of isoenzymes that catalyzes the oxidation of many drugs. The electrons are supplied by NADPH–CYP450 reductase, a flavoprotein that transfers electrons from NADPH (the reduced form of nicotinamide adenine dinucleotide phosphate) to CYP450. CYP450 enzymes can be induced or inhibited by many drugs and substances resulting in drug interactions in which one drug enhances the toxicity or reduces the therapeutic effect of another drug.

Oxidative Reactions

Oxidative reactions are the most important and most common metabolic reactions. Almost all drugs that undergo phase I biotransformation undergo oxidation at some stage or the other. A simple reason for oxidation being a predominant reaction is that energy in animals is primarily derived by oxidative combustion of organic molecules containing carbon and hydrogen atoms. Oxidative reactions increase hydrophilicity of xenobiotics by introducing polar functional groups such as -OH. Such a polar metabolite can thus rapidly undergo phase II reaction or is excretable by the kidneys. Oxidation of xenobiotics is non-specifically catalyzed by a number of enzymes located in the microsomes. Such enzymes require both molecular oxygen (O_2) and the reducing agent NADPH to effect reaction. They are therefore referred to as the mixed function oxidases. The overall stoichiometry of this reaction involving the substrate RH which yields the product ROH, is given by the following equation:

$$RH + O_2 + NADPH + H^+ \longrightarrow ROH + H_2O + NADP^+$$

where NADPH is reduced nicotinamide adenine dinucleotide phosphate.

The various steps in the oxidation of xenobiotics are as follows:

1. Binding of the substrate (RH) to the oxidized form of the cytochrome P-450 (Fe^{+++}) to form a complex.
2. A one electron transfer from NADPH to the complex by cytochrome P-450 reductase to form reduced (Fe++) P-450 substrate complex; this step is considered as the rate-limiting step in the overall oxidation of xenobiotics.
3. The reduced enzyme-substrate complex combines with a molecule of oxygen to form a ternary complex.
4. The ternary complex combines with a second electron supplied by NADH in presence of enzyme cytochrome b_5 reductase to form a ternary activated oxygen P-450 substrate complex.
5. One atom for oxygen from the activated oxygen complex is transferred to the substrate to yield the oxidized product and the other atom forms water. The free oxidized form of cytochrome P-450 is now ready to attach to yet another molecule of substrate.

Reductive reactions

Bioreductions are also capable of generating polar functional groups such as hydroxyl and amino which can undergo further biotransformation or conjugation. Large number of reductive reactions is just opposite of oxidation. For example:

Alcohol dehydrogenation ⟷ Carbonyl reduction

N-Oxidation ⟷ Amine oxide reduction

This means bioreduction comprises one-half of the reversible reactions. Such reactions may be catalyzed by the same enzyme (true reversible reaction) or by different enzymes (apparent reversible reaction). Since reversible reactions usually lead to conversion of inactive metabolites into active drug, they may result in delay of drug removal from the body and hence prolongation of action.

Hydrolytic Reactions

These reactions differ from oxidative and reductive reactions in three respects:

1. The reaction does not involve change in the state of oxidation of respects.
2. The reaction results in large chemical change in the substrate brought about by loss of relatively large fragment of the molecule.
3. The hydrolytic enzymes that metabolize xenobiotics are the ones that also - act on endogenous substrates; moreover, their activity is not confined to liver as they are found in many other organs like kidney, intestine, etc.

A number of functional groups are hydrolyzed namely. esters, ethers, amides, hydrazides, etc.

Phase II Reactions

These reactions generally involve covalent attachment of small polar endogenous molecules such as glucuronic acid, sulfate, glycine, etc. to either unchanged drugs or phase I products having suitable functional groups and form highly water-soluble conjugates which are readily excretable by the kidneys (or bile), Thus, these reactions are called as **conjugation** reactions. Since the outcome of such processes are generally products with increased molecular size (and altered physicochemical properties), they are also called as synthetic reactions. Quite often, a phase I reaction may not yield a metabolite that is sufficiently hydrophilic or pharmacologically inert but conjugation reactions generally result in products with total loss of pharmacologic activity and high polarity. Hence, phase II reactions are better known as true detoxification reactions. Since these reactions generally involve transfer of moieties to the substrate to be conjugated, the enzymes responsible are called as transferases. A summary of Phase II reactions is presented in Table 5.3.

Table 5.3 Summarized Phase II biotransformation reactions.

1. Conjugation with glucuronic acid	(M)
2. Conjugation with sulfate moieties	(N)
3. Conjugation with alpha amino acids	(N)
4. Conjugation with glutathione and mercapturic acid formation	(N)
5. Acetylation reactions	(N)
6. Methylation reactions	(N)
7. Miscellaneous conjugation reactions	(N)

*M indicates reaction catalyzed by microsomal enzymes and N indicates reaction catalyzed by non- microsomal enzymes.

Phase II reactions involve transfer of a suitable moiety such as glucronic acid, sulfate, glycine, etc. in presence of enzyme transferase to drugs or metabolites of phase I reactions having suitable functional groups to form highly polar, readily excretable and pharmacologically inert conjugates. Tissue reactive and carcinogenic metabolites are rendered harmless by conjugation with glutathione. The two phase II reactions namely acetylation and methylation that do not generate polar products, also terminate the pharmacologic activity of xenobiotics. Thus, phase II reactions are the true drug detoxification pathways.

The moieties transferred to the substrates in a phase II reaction possess three characteristics:

1. Are simple endogenous molecules.
2. Are of large molecular size.
3. Are strongly polar or ionic in nature in order to render the substrate water-soluble.

A significant aspect of conjugation reaction is that they are capacity-limited due to the availability of endogenous conjugating molecules. Thus, when doses of drugs are higher than normal levels of conjugating molecules, saturation of metabolism occurs and the unconjugated drug/metabolite precipitates toxicity. The order of capacities of important conjugation reactions is: *glucuronidation > amino acid conjugation > sulfation and glutathione conjugation*. The increase in the molecular weight of the drug(s) following conjugation with glucuronic acid, sulfate and glutathione is 176, 80 and 300 daltons respectively. The molecular weight of the conjugate is important in dictating its route of excretion. High molecular weight conjugates are excreted predominantly in bile while the low molecular weight ones are excreted in urine. The biotransformation reactions generally proceed sequentially and the combination of several phase I and phase II reactions yield a range of metabolites as depicted in Figure 5.1.

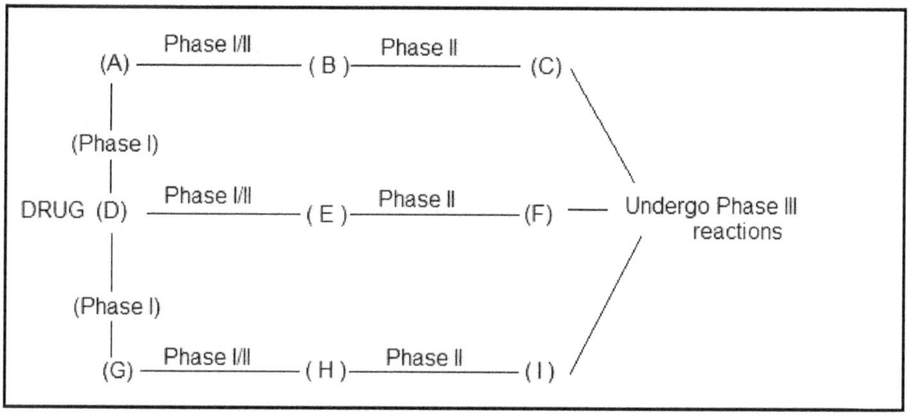

Fig. 5.1 Drug (D) undergoing various biotransformations to yield a range of metabolites (B, E, H). Phase II reactions lead to products (C, F, I) followed by Phase III reactions to yield products ready to be excreted.

Glucuronidation, the most common phase II reaction, is the only one that occurs in the liver microsomal enzyme system. Glucuronides are secreted in bile and eliminated in urine. Thus, conjugation makes most drugs more soluble and easily excreted by the kidneys. Amino acid conjugation with glutamine or glycine produces conjugates that are readily excreted in urine but not extensively secreted in bile. Aging does not affect glucuronidation. However, in neonates, conversion to glucuronide is slow, potentially resulting in serious effects (e.g., as with chloramphenicol). Conjugation may also occur through acetylation or sulfoconjugation. Sulfate esters are polar and readily excreted in urine. Aging does not affect these processes.

Phase III reactions

The biotransformation of drug metabolites, particularly the glutathione conjugates which are excreted via bile in the gut, by the intestinal microflora, is considered by few researchers as phase III reactions. After phase II reactions, the xenobiotic conjugates may be further metabolized. For example conversion of glutathione conjugates to acetylcysteine (mercapturic acid) conjugates. The reaction involves enzymatic removal of γ-glutamate and glycine residues in the glutathione molecule followed by acetylation of the cysteine residue in the conjugate. Phase III reactions thus act to remove phase II products to the extracellular medium, where they may be further metabolized or excreted.

Factors Affecting Biotransformation of Drugs

The therapeutic efficacy, toxicity and biological half-life of a drug depend upon its metabolic rate. A number of factors may influence the rate of drug metabolism they are:

1. Physicochemical properties of the drug
2. Chemical factors:
   (i) Induction of drug metabolizing enzymes
   (ii) Inhibition of drug metabolizing enzymes
   (iii) Environmental chemicals
3. Biological factors:
   (i) Species differences
   (ii) Strain differences
   (iii) Sex differences
   (iv) Age
   (v) Diet
   (vi) Altered physiologic factors: Pregnancy, hormonal imbalance, disease state.
   (vii) Temporal factors: Circardian rhythm

1. **Physicochemical properties of the drug:** Molecular size and shape, pK_a, acidity/basicity, lipophilicity and steric and electronic characteristics of a drug influence its interaction with the active sites of enzymes and the biotransformation processes to which it is subjected.

2. **Chemical factors**

   (i) ***Induction of drug metabolizing enzymes:*** The phenomenon of increased drug metabolizing ability of the enzymes (especially of microsomal monooxygenase system) by several drugs and chemicals is called as enzyme induction and the agents which bring about such an effect are known as inducers. Most inducers are in general lipophilic compounds with long elimination half-lives. The inducers can be classified into two categories as follows:

   1. ***Phenobarbital type inducers*** include several drugs and pesticides which increase the metabolism rate of a large number of drugs.
   2. ***Polycyclic hydrocarbon type inducers*** include 3-methyl cholanthrene and cigarette smoke which stimulate the metabolic rate of few drugs.

Some drugs such as carbamazepine, meprobamate, cyclophosphamide, rifampicin, etc. stimulate their own metabolism; the phenomenon is called as auto-induction or self-induction.

The mechanisms involved in enzyme induction may be increased enzyme synthesis, decreased rate of enzyme degradation, enzyme stabilization or enzyme activation. Enzyme induction results in decreased pharmacologic activity of most drugs, increased activity where the metabolites are active and altered physiologic status due to enhanced metabolism of endogenous compounds such as sex hormones. Some examples of inducers and the drugs affected by them are given in Table 5.4.

Table 5.4 Drug metabolizing enzyme inducers and drugs commonly affected by them.

Inducers	Drugs with enhanced metabolism
Barbiturates	Coumarins, cortisol, phenytoin, testosterone, oral contraceptives
Alcohol	Phentobarbital, phenytoin
Phenytoin	Cortisol, coumarins, oral contraceptives, tolbutamide
Rifampicin	Oral contraceptives, tolbutamide, rifampicin
Cigarette smoke	Nicotine, amino azo dyes

(ii) ***Inhibition of drug metabolizing enzymes:*** The process of enzyme inhibition that causes a decrease in metabolizing activity may be either direct or indirect.

Direct inhibition may result from interaction at the enzymic site wherein the net outcome is a change in enzyme activity. Direct enzyme inhibition may be divided into competitive or non-competitive type.

(a) ***Competitive inhibition*** results when structurally similar compounds compete for the same site on an enzyme. Such an inhibition due to substrate competition is reversible and can be overcome by high concentration of one of the substrates, e.g. methacholine inhibits metabolism of acetylcholine by competing with it for cholinesterase.

(b) ***Non-competitive inhibition*** arises when a structurally unrelated agent interacts with the enzyme and prevents the metabolism of drugs. Since the interaction is not structure- specific, metals like lead, mercury and arsenic and organophosphorus insecticides inhibit the enzymes non-competitively. Isoniazid inhibits the metabolism of phenytoin by the same mechanism.

Direct inhibition also results when the metabolic product competes with the substrate for the same enzyme (called as product inhibition). Certain specific inhibitors such as xanthine oxidase inhibitors (e.g. allopurinol) and MAO inhibitors (e.g. phenelzine) also inhibit the enzyme activity directly.

Indirect inhibition is accomplished by one of the two mechanisms:

(a) ***Repression*:** It is defined as the decrease in enzyme content which may be either due to a reduction in the enzyme synthesis rate (as affected by ethionine, puromycin and actinomycin D) or because of increase in the rate of enzyme degradation (as affected by carbon tetrachloride, carbon disulfide, disulfiram, etc.)

(b) ***Altered physiology*** due to nutritional deficiency or hormonal imbalance.

Direct enzyme inhibition is usually rapid (a single dose of inhibitor may be sufficient) and therefore more important than indirect enzyme induction. Enzyme inhibition generally results in prolonged pharmacologic action of a drug. Some examples of inhibitors and drugs affected by them are given in Table 5.5.

Table 5.5 Enzyme inhibitors and drugs affected by them.

Inhibitors	Drugs with decreased metabolism
MAO inhibitors	Barbiturates, Tyramine
Coumarins	Phenytoin
Allopurinol	6-Mercaptopurine
PAS	Phenytoin, Hexobarbital

(ii) ***Environmental chemicals:*** Several environmental agents influence the drug metabolizing ability of enzymes. Halogenated pesticides such as DDT and polycyclic aromatic hydrocarbons contained in cigarette smoke have enzyme induction effect. Organophosphate insecticides and heavy metals such as mercury, tin, nickel, cobalt and arsenic inhibit drug metabolizing ability of enzymes. Other environmental factors that may influence drug metabolism are temperature, altitude, pressure, atmosphere, etc.

3. **Biological Factors**

(i) ***Species differences:*** The effect of differences in species has been observed in both phase I and phase II reactions. In phase I reactions, both qualitative and quantitative variations in the enzyme and their activity have been observed. For e.g.: amphetamine and ephedrine are primarily metabolized by oxidative deamination in humans and rabbit whereas in rats, the aromatic oxidation is the major route of biotransformation of these drugs. In case of phase II reactions, the variations are mainly qualitative and characterized either by the presence of, or complete lack of certain conjugating enzymes. For example, in pigs, phenol is excreted mainly as glucuronide whereas its sulfate conjugate dominates in cats. Certain birds utilize ornithine for conjugating aromatic acids instead of glycine.

(ii) ***Strain differences (Pharmacogenetics):*** Enzymes influencing metabolic reactions are under the genetic control and hence the differences in enzymic activity between strains of the same animal species are likely. The intersubject variability in drug response is called as pharmacogenetic variation. The intersubject variations in drug biotransformation may either be monogenically or polygenically controlled. A *polygenic control* has been observed in studies in twins. In identical twins (monozygotic), very little or no difference in the metabolism of phenylbutazone, dicoumarol and antipyrine was observed but large variations were apparent in fraternal twins (dizygotic; twins developed from two different eggs) for the same drugs.

Furthermore, the differences observed in the metabolism of a drug among different races are called as *ethnic variations*. Such a variation may be *monomorphic* or *polymorphic*. An example of monomorphism is: the entire human race acetylates PABA and PAS to only a small extent. Example of polymorphism is the acetylation of isoniazid (INH) in humans. The human population comprises of slow acetylators (inactivator phenotypes that metabolize INH slowly) and rapid acetylators (activator phenotypes that metabolize INH rapidly). Other drugs known to exhibit pharmacogenetic differences in metabolism are debrisoquine, succinyl choline, phenytoin, dapsone and sulfadimidine.

(iii) ***Sex differences:*** Sex related differences in the rate of metabolism can be attributed to regulation of such processes by sex hormones since variations among male and female are generally observed following puberty. Such sex differences are widely studied in rats; the male rats have greater drug metabolizing capacity. In humans, women metabolize benzodiazepines slowly than men and several studies show that women on contraceptive pills metabolize a number of drugs at a slow rate.

(iv) ***Age:*** Differences in the drug metabolic rate in different age groups are mainly due to variations in the enzyme content, enzyme activity and hemodynamics. In neonates (up to 2 months), the microsomal enzyme system is not fully developed and many drugs are biotransformed slowly; for example, caffeine has a half-life of 4 days in neonates in comparison to 4 h in adults. A major portion of this drug is excreted unchanged in urine by the neonates. Conjugation with sulfate is well developed (paracetamol is excreted mainly as sulfate) but glucuronidation occurs to a very small extent. As a result, hyperbilirubinemia precipitates kernicterus and chloramphenicol leads to cyanosis or Gray baby syndrome in new born. Similarly, sulfonamides cause renal toxicity and paracetamol causes hepatotoxicity. Infants (between 2 months and one year) show almost a similar profile as neonates in metabolizing drugs with improvement in the capacity as age advances and enzyme activity increases. Children (between one year and 12 years) and older infants metabolize several drugs much more rapidly than adults as the rate of metabolism reaches a maximum somewhere between 6 months and 12 years of age. As a result, they require large mg/kg doses in comparison to adults; for example, the theophylline half-life in children is two-third of that in adults. In very elderly persons, the liver size is reduced, the microsomal enzyme activity is decreased and hepatic blood flow also declines as a result of reduced cardiac output all of which contribute to decreased metabolism of drugs. Drug conjugation however, remains unaffected.

(v) ***Diet:*** The enzyme content and activity is altered by a number of dietary components. In general, low protein diet decreases and high protein diet increases the drug metabolizing ability. This is because the enzyme synthesis is promoted by protein diet which also raises the level of amino acids for conjugation with drugs. The protein-carbohydrate ratio in the diet is also important; a high ratio increases the microsomal mixed function oxidase activity. Fat free diet depresses cytochrome P-450 levels since phospholipids, which are important components of microsomes, become deficient. Dietary deficiency of vitamins (e.g. vitamin A, B2, B3, C and E) and minerals such as Fe, Ca, Mg, Cu and Zn retards the metabolic activity of enzymes. Starvation results in decreased amount of glucuronides formed than under normal conditions. Malnutrition in women results in enhanced metabolism of sex hormones.

(vi) ***Altered physiologic factors***

***Pregnancy*:** Studies in animals have shown that the maternal drug metabolizing ability (of both phase I and phase II reactions) is reduced during the later stages of pregnancy. This was attributed to high levels of steroid hormones in circulation during pregnancy. In women, the metabolism of promazine and pethidine is reduced during pregnancy or when receiving oral contraceptives. Higher rate of hepatic metabolism of anticonvulsants during pregnancy is thought to be due to induction of drug metabolizing enzymes by the circulating progesterone.

***Hormonal imbalance*:** The influence of sex hormones on drug metabolism has already been discussed. The effect of other hormones is equally complex. Higher levels of one hormone may inhibit the activity of few enzymes while inducing that of others. Adrenolectomy, thyroidectomy and alloxan induced diabetes in animals showed impairment in the enzyme activity with a subsequent fall in the rate of metabolism. A similar effect was observed with pituitary growth hormone. Stress related changes in ACTH levels also influence drug biotransformation.

***Disease states*:** As liver is the primary site for metabolism of most drugs, all pathologic conditions associated with it result in enhanced half-lives of almost all drugs. Thus, a reduction in hepatic drug metabolizing ability is apparent in conditions such as hepatic carcinoma, hepatitis, cirrhosis, obstructive jaundice, etc. Biotransformations such as glycine conjugation of salicylates, oxidation of vitamin D and hydrolysis of procaine which occur in kidney, are impaired in renal diseases. Congestive cardiac failure and myocardial infarction which result in a decrease in the blood flow to the liver, impair metabolism of drugs having high hepatic extraction ratio e.g. propranolol and lidocaine. In diabetes, glucuronidation is reduced due to decreased availability of UDPGA.

(vii) *Temporal factors*

***Circadian rhythm*:** The variations in the enzyme activity with light cycle are called as circadian rhythm in drug metabolism. The enzyme activity is maximum during early morning (6 to 9 a.m.) and minimum in late afternoon (2 to 5 p.m.) which corresponds with the high and low serum levels of corticosterone . Clinical variation in therapeutic effect of a drug at different times of the day is therefore apparent. The study of variations in drug response as influenced by time is called as chronopharmacology. Time dependent change in drug kinetics is known chronokinetics. The main aim of chronokinetic studies is to control the time of administration, which among others, can be responsible for variations of drug kinetics but also may explain chronopharmacological effects observed with certain drugs.

There are some instances in which a chronopharmacokinetics is important like:

* When possible daily variations in pharmacokinetics may be responsible for time dependent variations in drug effects (e.g. certain antimicrobial agents are more effective at a specific time of day)

* When drugs have a narrow therapeutic range.

* When symptoms of a disease are clearly circadian phase-dependent (e.g. nocturnal asthma, myocardial infarction, angina pectoris, ulcer disease)

* When drug plasma concentrations are well correlated to the therapeutic effect in case the latter is circadian phase-dependent

* When the drug has some serious adverse effects that can be avoided or minimized because they are related to time of administration (e.g. aminoglycoside nephrotoxicity)

DEFINITIONS:

Xenobiotics: All chemical substances that are not nutrients for the body and enter the body through, ingestion, inhalation or absorption are called as xenobiotics (Greek: xenos = foreign) or exogenous compounds.

Microsomes: The microsomes are basically artifacts which resulted when attempts were first made to isolate endoplasmic reticulum of the liver homogenate. These vesicular fragments or microsomes are derived from rough endoplasmic reticulum due to the presence of RNA rich ribosomes on the membrane surface whose function is protein synthesis) which shed their ribosomes to become smooth surfaced.

Questions

Multiple Choice Questions

1. In context to biotransformation which of the following is not true.
   (a) Normally leads to pharmacologic inactivation of drugs.
   (b) Occasionally yields metabolites with equal activity.
   (c) Rarely leads to toxicological activation
   (d) It is a reversible process.
2. Upon biotransformation, the metabolite of which of the following drug shows no change in pharmacological activity.
   (a) Amphetamine (b) Isoniazid
   (c) Phenylbutazone (d) Salicylic acid

3. Which of the following organ is not a drug metabolizing organ?
   (a) Lungs (b) Pancreas
   (c) Intestine (d) Skin
4. The non-microsomal enzymes are present in
   (a) Soluble form in cytoplasm
   (b) Soluble form in endoplasmic reticulum
   (c) Insoluble form in cytoplasm
   (d) Insoluble form in endoplasmic reticulum
5. Which of the following is not a Phase I reaction?
   (a) Oxidative (b) Reductive
   (c) Sulfation (d) Hydrolytic
6. Which of the following Phase II biotransformation is catalyzed by microsomal enzymes?
   (a) Acetylation
   (b) Glucoronidation
   (c) Methylation
   (d) Conjugation with glutathione
7. Which of the following physicochemical property of drug does not affect biotransformation?
   (a) Molecular size (b) pKa
   (c) Solubility (d) Lipophilicity
8. Which of the following drugs is not an inducer of drug metabolizing system?
   (a) Barbiturates (b) Phenytoin
   (c) Rifampicin (d) Tolbutamide
9. In humans, amphetamine and ephedrine are metabolized by
   (a) Oxidative deamination (b) Sulfate conjugation
   (c) Aromatic oxidation (d) Methylation
10. Select among the following the physiological factor whose alteration does not affect biotransformation of drugs.
   (a) Hormonal imbalance (b) Diabetes
   (c) Pregnancy (d) Bacterial infection

Short Questions

1. Name and define the pharmacokinetic processes involved in the termination of drug action.
2. Define the fate of a lipophilic drug that is not metabolized upon absorption.
3. Why are drugs referred to as xenobiotics?
4. What would be the consequence if biotransformation of a drug leads to generation of a less soluble metabolite?
5. What are soft drugs? Why do they have short half-lives?
6. Why is liver considered the major site for metabolism of drugs?
7. What are the characteristics microsomal enzymes?
8. Which metabolic reactions are considered phase III reactions?
9. Why oxidative reactions are predominant in comparison to other phase II reactions?
10. What is the interesting phenomenon observed with acetylation reactions in human race?

Long Questions

1. Classify the chemical pathways of drug metabolism. Why are phase I reactions called as functionalization reactions and Phase II reactions as true detoxification reactions? Explain.
2. Outline the steps involved in the oxidation of xenobiotics. What is the rate-limiting step in such a process?
3. In what respects the hydrolytic reactions differ from oxidative and reductive reactions?
4. What are the possible mechanisms of enzyme induction and enzyme inhibition by xenobiotics? What are their consequences? Why enzyme inhibition is considered more dangerous than enzyme induction?
5. Explain the biological factors that affect biotransformation of drugs.

CHAPTER 6

Excretion of Drugs

LEARNING OBJECTIVES

- Understanding drug elimination pathways
- Renal excretion of drugs
- Factors affecting renal excretion
- Non-renal excretion of drugs
- Dosing adjustments in renal and hepatic failure

Drug elimination is a process of irreversible removal of drug(s) from the body by all the possible routes of excretion. The drugs may be eliminated after being chemically altered (metabolized), or they may be eliminated intact. Drug elimination constitutes into two major processes: Biotransformation and excretion. *Biotransformation* or *drug metabolism* is the process by which the drug is chemically converted in the body to a metabolite. Biotransformation is usually an enzymatic process. However, a few drugs may also be changed chemically by a non-enzymatic process (e.g. ester hydrolysis). The enzymes involved in the biotransformation of drugs are located mainly in the liver. Other tissues such as kidney, lung, small intestine, and skin also contain biotransformation enzymes.

Drug excretion is essentially the removal of intact drug. Most drugs, particularly water-soluble, non-volatile drugs and their metabolites are eliminated largely by the kidneys in urine. Renal excretion plays an important role in eliminating unchanged drugs or their metabolites into urine. In some cases, drugs may also be excreted from the body through the lungs, milk, sweat, tears, skin, hair, genital secretions or saliva (Figure 6.1). Thcse are considered secondary processes for drug excretion.

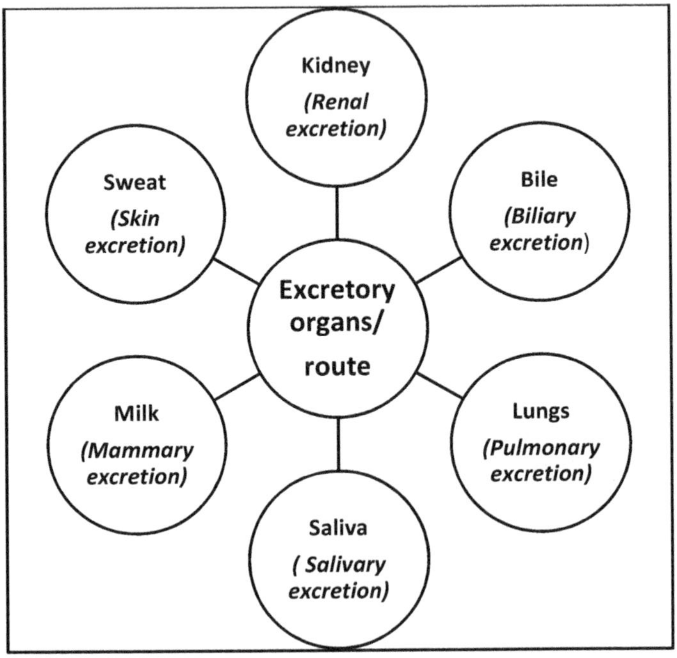

Fig. 6.1 Principal routes of excretion.

Renal Excretion

Renal excretion is the most important route of excretion of drugs and their metabolites (ketamine and fentanyl); it involves three mechanisms: glomerular filtration, tubular secretion, and passive reabsorption. Fig 6.2 presents an overview of renal excretion mechanisms.

- *Glomerular filtration* of unbound drug: Highly bound drugs such as the NSAIDs are not excreted by glomerular filtration.
- *Tubular secretion* of anionic (e.g., NSAIDs, glucuronic acid conjugates) and cationic (e.g., cimetidine) drugs occur.
- *Passive reabsorption* of lipophilic drugs: The pH of urine can have profound effects on the extent of tubular reabsorption.

Glomerular filtration and active tubular secretion tend to increase the concentration of drugs in lumen and hence facilitate excretion whereas tubular reabsorption decreases it and hinders the drug movement out of the body. Thus,

Total renal excretion = excretion by filtration + excretion by secretion – retention by reabsorption

If an active drug is metabolized primarily to inactive compounds, renal function will not greatly affect elimination of the parent compound. However, if the drug or an active metabolite is excreted unchanged via the kidneys, changes in renal function (i.e. chronic renal failure) will influence its elimination. Therefore, dose adjustment of the drug should be recommended.

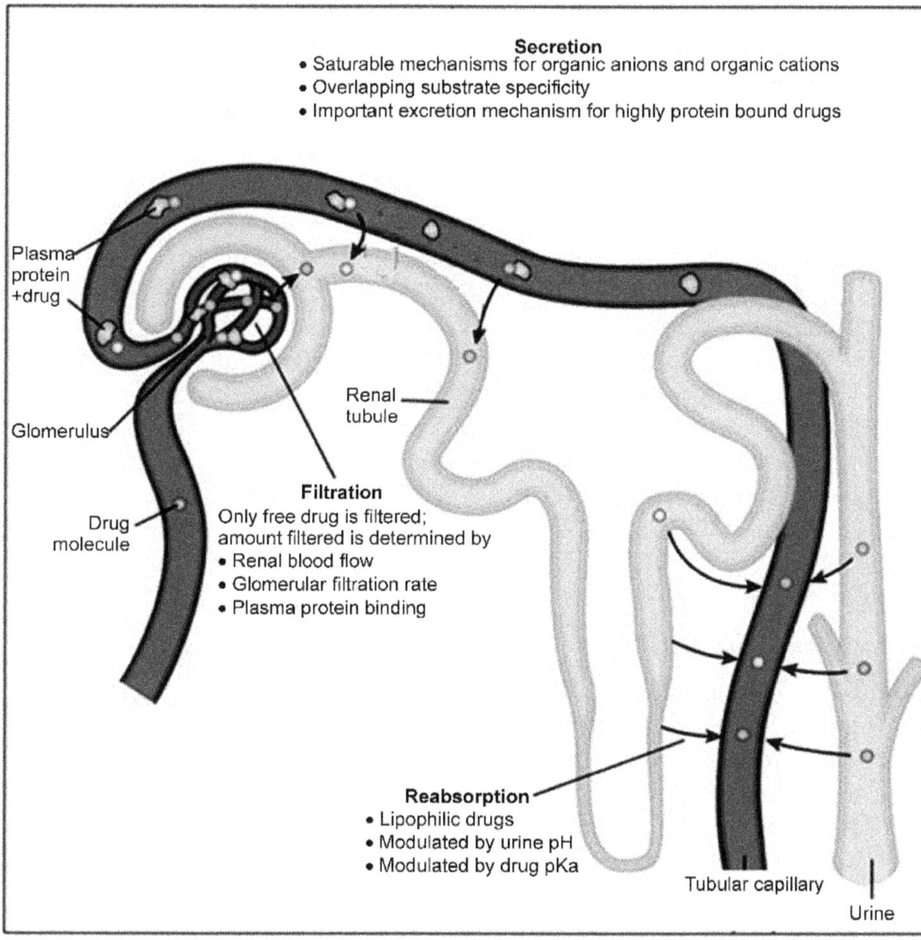

Fig. 6.2 Mechanisms of renal excretion of drugs.

Glomerular filtration

Glomerular filtration is the first step in the formation of urine and is a physiological function of kidney nephrons. The ultrafiltrate, which appears in the lumen of the proximal convoluted tubule, is composed of water and solutes that can pass through the filtering membrane of the capillaries. Under physiological conditions, the large molecular weight proteins and blood cells do not pass through the capillary wall and hence do not appear in the luminal fluid. Therefore, glomerular filtration is relatively non-selective. The benefits of the filtration process are that it disposes of excess fluid, solutes, and metabolism byproducts and that it serves to detoxify the system by disposing of substances identified as foreign. In general, the glomerular filtration rate (GFR) is relatively stable and is the most important index of intrinsic renal function. Water content and ingredients are maintained by varying the amount of water and solute(s) reabsorbed by the different parts of the nephron beyond the glomerulus. Filtration does not require the expenditure of metabolic energy; rather it is caused by a balance of hydrostatic and oncotic forces.

Glomerular filtration results in production of about 180 L of glomerular fluid each day. Glomerulus filters 20 % of the plasma entering the kidney (filtration fraction = 20 %). Normal renal plasma flow is 625 ml/min; 20% of which yields a normal GFR of 125 ml/min in males, slightly less in females. About 99% of the glomerular filtrate is reabsorbed in the tubules, so normal urine production is 1 ml/min. A high GFR makes it possible for the kidney to process (filter and reabsorb) body fluids many times a day. GFR is reduced in newborns, the elderly, patients with kidney and heart disease. Reduced GFR means the drug dose be reduced, increase the dose interval, or both. The process of filtration plays a crucial role in the pharmacological actions of diuretics. The diuretics must undergo glomerular filtration to exert their action on reabsorption process.

Factors that influence the filtration of solutes and large molecules

(i) ***Size***: Small electrolytes (e.g., sodium) and small organic molecules (e.g., glucose) are freely filtered by the glomerular capillary membrane, and they are assigned a filterability factor of 1.0. The filterability factor significantly decreases as the molecular weight increases to a level equal to, or more than the molecular weight of albumin. That is why under normal conditions, albumin does not appear in urine. Water soluble drugs with molecular weight less than 300 D are excreted through kidney. Drugs of molecular weight in the range of 300 to 500 Daltons are excreted both through urine and bile.

(ii) ***Electric charge***: Although the size of the molecule determines, to a large extent, the filterability of the molecule, electric charge makes a difference as well. For example, the diameter of albumin molecule (6 nm) is somewhat smaller than the pores of the glomerular membrane (8 nm). Nonetheless, albumin is not filtered into the lumen mainly because of the negative charge shared by albumin and the basement membrane, resulting in electrostatic repulsion. This is clearly demonstrated by the significantly greater filterability of positively charged dextran molecule, compared with negatively, charged dextran for any given molecular radius. The relative filterability of neutral dextran falls between the two values but is closer to the positively charged dextran. In general, for a given molecular weight, negatively charged molecules are less readily filtered than are positively charged or even neutral molecules. If a pathological loss of the negative charges occurs, such as with chronic diabetes or streptococcal infection, some of the larger molecular weight proteins, like albumin, are filtered and appear in the urine.

(iii) ***Glomerular capillary hydrostatic pressure*****:** Under normal conditions, this pressure amounts to approximately 60 mm Hg. There is a direct relationship between this pressure and GFR, with an increase in the glomerular capillary hydrostatic pressure, GFR increases, and vice versa. The main determinants of glomerular capillary hydrostatic pressure are arterial pressure, and afferent arteriolar resistance and efferent arteriolar pressure that affect GFR in a manner detailed below.

A direct relationship between arterial pressure and glomerular capillary hydrostatic pressure, and hence GFR
An inverse relationship between afferent arteriolar resistance and glomerular capillary hydrostatic pressure, hence GFR
A biphasic effect on glomerular capillary hydrostatic pressure and, hence on GFR. With moderate increase in efferent arteriolar resistance the GFR increases slightly, whereas with a substantial increase in resistance, GFR decreases.

Under physiological conditions, GFR can be defined, and calculated, as the clearance of inulin. This calculation is based on the assumption that inulin is freely filtered by the glomerulus and is not reabsorbed or secreted by the renal tubule. Creatinine is also cleared from the body predominantly by glomerular filtration, so plasma creatinine levels reflect glomerular filtration.

Glomerular filtration agents used to measure glomerular filtration rate are:

- Technetium 99 diethylenetriamine pentaacetic acid (99mTc-DTPA)
- Technetium 99 mercaptoacetyl triglycine (99mTc-MAG3)
- Iodine 131 o-iodohippurate (131I-OIH)

Active Tubular Secretion

Tubular secretion takes place in the proximal tubule of the nephron. Many organic compounds are actively secreted, but there are separate carrier systems for anions and cations. Anions appear to be transported actively over the basolateral membrane and by a less efficient non-active carrier-mediated process (facilitated diffusion) over the brush border membrane. As a result of these mechanisms, anions tend to accumulate in proximal tubular cells. For cations, however, the active transport step operates over the brush border membrane, whereas the uptake of the cation in the cell occurs via facilitated diffusion over the basolateral membrane.

Active reabsorption is most prominent for many nutrients and endogenous substrates (amino acids, glucose, vitamins), but various exogenous compounds also have a certain affinity for the reabsorptive carrier systems. Uricosuric drugs, for instance, interfere with carrier-mediated reabsorption of urate.

Tubular function reduces the 180 L/day of filtered fluid to about 1 L/day of excreted fluid, altering its composition through active and passive transport. Substances may be either resorbed or secreted from tubules and may move bidirectionally, taking advantage of both active and passive transport. The direction of transit for resorbed substances is from tubule to interstitium to blood, whereas the direction for secreted substances is from blood to interstitium to tubule. Secretion is the major route of elimination for drugs and toxins, especially when they are plasma protein bound. Tubular secretion agents to estimate effective renal plasma flow are 99mTc-MAG3, 131I-OIH.

Many drugs do not enter the kidney tubule by glomerular filtration but do so by tubule secretion. This is an active process since drugs are carried against a favourable chemical gradient from the capillary network into the tubule. The process of tubule secretion can have a big impact on the rate at which the drug is eliminated from the body. Renal secretion is unaffected by pH and protein binding but is dependent on renal blood flow.

For example, penicillin readily enters the nephron by tubule secretion and is rapidly excreted from the body in the urine. In a situation where the therapeutic effect needs to be prolonged, agents can be administered that block tubule secretion to slow the excretion of the drug. The first clinical application of this concept was undertaken with penicillin after World War II. During the war, this antibiotic was widely used and physicians faced difficulties in maintaining therapeutic blood levels of the drug because of its fast renal elimination. In 1951, probenecid was introduced as a competitive inhibitor of penicillin renal secretion that allowed physicians to diminish the antibiotic renal elimination and thus to maintain adequate drug levels for a longer time. In 1988, the racing cyclist Pedro Delgado was proved of using probenecid in order to inhibit the renal secretion and thus the urinary detection of steroids. This short historical outline describes well that drugs are actively secreted into renal tubules, via transporters.

Tubule secretion involves two carrier systems – basic carriers which transport basic drugs (amiloride, dopamine, histamine), and acidic carriers for acidic drugs (frusemide, penicillin, indomethacin). There are many renal tubular drug transporters. They belong to different families among which the main ones are the organic anion transporters (OATs) and the organic cation transporters (OCTs) families, Organic Anion-Transporting Polypeptide Family (OATPs) and the Multidrug Resistance-Associated Protein Transporters (MRPs). Clinically, these transporters are not only necessary for the renal tubular secretion and reabsorption of various drugs, but are also responsible in part for the drug's pharmacologic response (e.g., furosemide), drug-drug interactions of therapeutic or toxic importance, and drug nephrotoxicity.

Two structurally similar drugs carrying similar ionic charge and utilizing the same carrier- mediated process for excretion may compete with each other. Consequently, a drug with higher rate of excretion will inhibit the excretion of other drug in competition. Thus, the half-life of both the drugs is increased as the total number of sites for active secretion is constant. Such competition may result in therapeutic benefits. For e.g. probenicid inhibits active tubular secretion of the drugs p-aminosalicylic acid, penicillin, 17- ketosteroids and hence increases their plasma concentration by two fold. Such competitions may also result in clinical disadvantage. For example inhibition of nitrofurantoin secretion by probenecid decreases the therapeutic efficacy of the former.

The occurrence of saturable excretion routes causes dose-dependent, non-linear pharmacokinetics. In clinical pharmacokinetics, tubular secretion can adequately be described with the use of a Michaelis-Menten equation. This implies that a compound undergoing tubular secretion exhibits a concentration-dependent renal clearance. At low plasma concentrations the clearance will be maximal, and for several drugs may be as high as the effective renal plasma flow. Increasing concentrations cause decreasing renal clearance, until eventually the secretion mechanism becomes fully saturated. Then the excretion of the drug in urine will depend primarily on its net rate of filtration. It is important to realize that the non-linear kinetics will be evident from the plasma kinetics only when the saturable pathway contributes to at least some 20% of the total body clearance. Non-linear kinetics inevitably leads to disproportionate accumulation. Therefore, for any drug that is actively secreted, careful consideration should be given to the possibilities of drug-drug interaction and of unwanted drug accumulation with increasing doses.

Tubular Reabsorption

Reabsorption is referred to as passive diffusion since the process does not require energy. Tubular reabsorption takes place all along renal tubule. So, drugs and their metabolites enter the kidney tubule but some may be reabsorbed back into the blood stream. This flow of drug back into the blood occurs because water is reabsorbed from the kidney tubules by diffusion. In fact, majority of water that initially enters the nephron is reabsorbed back into the blood as a means of conserving body fluid. As this movement occurs, some drugs are transported along with it, which increases half-life of the drug(s). Tubular reabsorption can either be (i) an active process or (ii) passive process.

Active tubular reabsorption is also observed for high threshold endogenous substances or those nutrients that the body needs to conserve. For example: vitamins, glucose, uric acid, electrolytes and amino acids. There are few examples of drugs also which undergo this process.

Passive reabsorption may occur throughout the nephron. The driving force is largely supplied by reabsorption of water which concentrates the urine with respect to plasma. Since normal urine flow is about 1-2 ml/min, drug may be concentrated in the urine at least 100 fold compared to the concentration of unbound drug in plasma. Passive tubular reabsorption is seen with exogenous substances like drugs. Concentration gradient is the prime driving force for it. The primary determinant of passive reabsorption is lipophilicity of the drug. Lipophilic substances are extensively reabsorbed whereas polar substances are not. As a majority of drugs are weak electrolytes their diffusion across the lipoidal tubular membrane depends on the degree of ionization of drugs which in turn is dependent on two factors namely: pH of the urine and pKa of the drug. Reabsorption is also influenced by urine flow rate.

(i) **pH of Urine:** Urine comprises water, salts, and waste products from the kidneys. The balance of these compounds affects the pH. The average value for urine pH is 6.0, but it can range from 4.5 to 8.0. Urine under 5.0 is considered acidic, and urine higher than 8.0 is alkaline. The factors affecting urinary pH are diet, drug intake and pathophysiology of patients. Food has an important role on the urinary pH. Acidic foods like grains, fish, sodas, high-protein foods and sugary foods lower the urinary pH and alkaline foods including nuts, vegetables, most fruits result in higher pH. Urine pH influences the rate of excretion of drugs and in some clinical situations is manipulated to control the excretion of certain drugs from the body. Most drugs are either weak acids or weak bases. In alkaline urine, acidic drugs are more readily ionized. In acidic urine, alkaline drugs are more readily ionized. Ionized substances are more soluble in water so dissolve in the body fluids more readily for excretion. This is important in a situation such as blood poisoning that requires rapid excretion of drug from the body. For example, in aspirin poisoning, the urine is made more alkaline with sodium bicarbonate that increases the ionization of salicylic acid (its metabolite) thereby increasing its excretion from the body. Drugs that alkalinize the urine (e.g. sodium bicarbonate, potassium or sodium citrate, thiazide diuretics, carbonic-anhydrase inhibitors) increase the rate of salicylate renal excretion. Acidification of the urine is used to accelerate the excretion of amphetamine in patients with overdosage. *Drugs that acidify the urine* (ascorbic acid, aluminum chloride) increase the renal elimination and those which alkalize urine decrease renal elimination (Fig. 6.3). The excretion of the unchanged form of a drug through the urine may depend on the urinary pH only if the pKa of the drug differs from the pH by about two units. Since the pH of the urine ranges approximately from 4.8 to 7.5, the urinary excretion of a large number of drugs may be urinary pH-dependent.

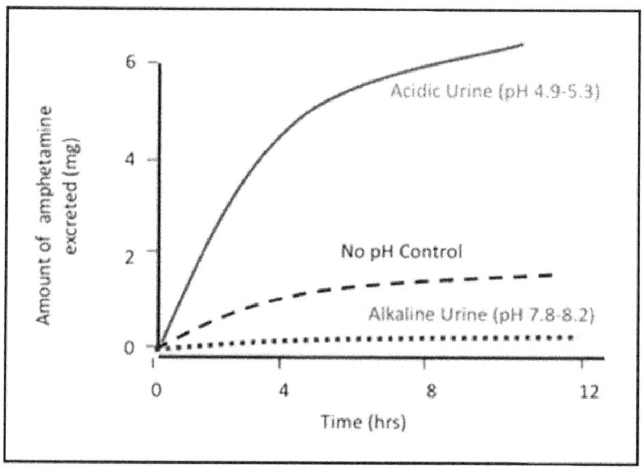

Fig. 6.3 Effect of urinary pH on the renal excretion of amphetamine.

The relative amount of unionized and ionized drug in the urine at a particular pH and the percent drug ionized at the given pH can be given by Henderson-Hasselbach equation.

For weak acids

$$pH = pKa + \log\frac{[ionized]}{[unionized]} \quad .....(6.1)$$

$$\%\ Drug\ ionized = \frac{10^{pH - pKa}}{1 + 10^{pH - pKa}} \times 100 \quad .....(6.2)$$

For weak bases

$$pH = pKa + \log\frac{[unionized]}{[ionized]} \quad .....(6.3)$$

$$\%\ Drug\ ionized = \frac{10^{pKa - pH}}{1 + 10^{pKa - pH}} \times 100 \quad .....(6.4)$$

The concentration ratio R of a drug in urine to that in plasma (U: P) can be given by the following equations.

For weak acids

$$R = \frac{U}{P} = \frac{1 + 10^{pH\ urine - pKa}}{1 + 10^{pHplasma - pKa}} \quad .....(6.5)$$

For weak bases

$$R = \frac{U}{P} = \frac{1 + 10^{pKa - pH\ urine}}{1 + 10^{pKa - pHplasma}} \quad .....(6.6)$$

(i) **pKa of drug:** As demonstrated by Henderson Hasselbach equation, pKa of a drug governs its ionization at a given pH. A polar and ionized drug will be poorly reabsorbed passively and excreted rapidly. Tubular reabsorption is also affected by lipid solubility of the drug. Thus an ionized lipophilic drug will be reabsorbed while a unionized polar drug will be excreted. The combined effect of urinary pH and pKa of drug is summarized in Table 6.1.

Table 6.1 Effect of urinary pH and pKa of drug on its renal excretion.

Nature of drug	Example	Impact on excretion
Acidic / basic drugs *Polar in their unionized form*	Penicillin Gentamicin	Not reabsorbed passively irrespective of the extent of ionization Excretion is independent of urine pH and its flow rate

Contd...

Nature of drug	Example	Impact on excretion
		Rate of excretion = Rate of filtration + rate of active secretion
Very weakly acidic, non-polar drugs (pKa > 8.0) ; Very weakly basic, non-polar drugs (pKa < 6.0) *Mostly unionized throughout the entire range of urinary pH*	Phenytoin Propoxyphene	Extensively reabsorbed passively in the entire range of urinary pH Rate of excretion is always low and independent of urinary pH
Strongly acidic drugs (pKa ≤ 2.0) Strongly basic drugs (pKa ≥ 12.0) *Completely ionized throughout the entire range of urinary pH*	Cromoglycic acid Guanethidine	Rate of excretion is always high and independent of urinary pH
Acidic drugs (pKa = 3.0 to 8.0) Basic drugs (pKa = 6.0-8.0)	Several NSAIDs Morphine analogs	Extent of reabsorption depends on pH

The toxicity due to overdose of drugs whose excretion is sensitive to pH change can be treated by acidification or alkanization of the urine with ammonium chloride or sodium bicarbonate respectively. Thus excretion of basic drugs can be promoted by acidification of urine and that of acidic drugs by alkanization of urine. For e.g. enhanced excretion of sulfonamides by alkanization of urine minimizes its precipitation and hence limits crystalluria. Change in urinary pH can also improve therapeutic efficacy of a drug. For e.g. Conversion of urinary antiseptic hexamine to its active form (formaldehyde), takes place in acidic urine.

In addition to pH modification, urinary excretion of drugs can also be enhanced by forced diuresis. Forced diuresis is the increase in urine flow by large intake of fluid or administration of mannitol or other diuretics. This can be used to treat toxicity of drugs that are excreted primarily by renal route, if the drug is extensively reabsorbed passively from the renal tubules and reabsorption is sensitive to urine pH.

(ii) Urine flow rate: Polar drugs whose excretion is independent of urine pH and are not reabsorbed, are unaffected by urine flow rate (e.g. gentamicin, penicillin); only their concentrations in urine will be affected. An increase in flow rate in case of such drugs results in a dilute urine. For the drugs whose reabsorption is pH dependent (weak bases and weak acids), reabsorption is inversely proportional to the urinary flow rate. Such drugs can be divided into two categories depending on the extent of reabsorption relative to water.

1. Drugs that are reabsorbed to an extent equal to or greater than water. In such case a linear relationship is observed between renal clearance and urinary excretion.
2. Drugs that are reabsorbed to an extent lower than water. In such case a curvilinear relationship is observed between renal clearance and urinary excretion.

Clearance

Clearance may be defined as the hypothetical volume of body fluids containing drug which is cleared off the drug in a specific time. It is expressed in ml/min and is a constant for given plasma drug concentration.

$$\text{Clearance} = \frac{\textit{Elimination rate}}{\textit{Plasma drug concentration}} \quad .....(6.7)$$

The renal clearance of a drug (Cl_R) is a measure of the functional ability of the kidney to remove it from the body independent of other pharmacokinetic processes. It is defined as the hypothetical volume of plasma or blood from which the drug is completely removed per unit time by the kidneys. Obviously this is a virtual volume, not a real volume. No single millilitre of plasma has its entire drug removed in one transit through the kidney; rather a fraction is removed from each of the many millilitres of plasma perfusing the organ.

$$\text{Renal clearance } (Cl_R) = \frac{\text{Rate of drug excretion at time t}}{\text{concentration of drug in plasma at time t}} \quad .....(6.8)$$

Although the term 'clearance' usually refers to irreversible removal, in the context of the renal route it often represents the net excretion process as some drug may be transferred back from the kidney to the plasma. Thus, physiologically speaking,

$$\text{Renal clearance } (Cl_R) = \frac{\text{Rate of filtration + Rate of secretion} - \text{Rate of reabsorption}}{\text{concentration of drug in plasma}} \quad .....(6.9)$$

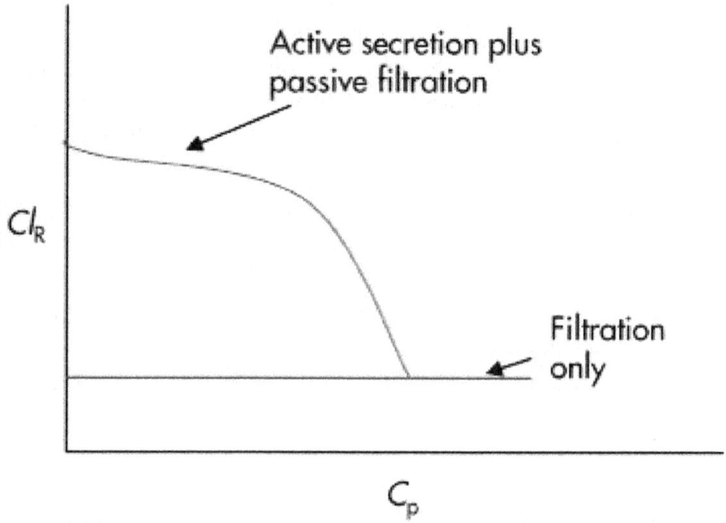

Fig. 6.4 Plot between plasma drug concentration and renal clearance.

The contribution of each process for a drug cannot be determined by direct measurement. The rate of filtration (GFR) can be determined by comparing clearance value for a drug with that of a marker like creatinine/ inulin cleared by glomerular filtration. The ratio of these two values is called renal clearance ratio/ excretion ratio (Eq. 6.10).

$$\text{Renal clearance ratio} = \frac{Cl_R \text{ of drug}}{Cl_R \text{ of creatinine}} \quad .....(6.10)$$

Significance of renal clearance

(a) The measurement of renal clearance is of primary value in determining the mechanism(s) of drug excretion since it can be used to characterize the process of drug removal in the kidney, whether it is constant or changing, capacity-limited or otherwise.

(b) If renal excretion contributes significantly to the overall elimination of a drug, that is, renal clearance is about 50% or more of total clearance, changes in renal clearance may have profound effect on the duration of pharmacological or toxic effects.

(c) It is especially important to know about the renal clearance of drugs that are predominantly excreted in an unchanged form in the urine when dosing patients with lowered kidney function, namely the very young, the elderly and those with renal disease.

(d) Renal clearance may help in the management of overdose.

(e) Measurement of renal clearance may also contribute to an understanding of the mechanisms of specific drug interactions.

(f) In drug development it might be preferable to select those compounds with relatively high renal contributions to total clearance since inter-individual variability in metabolic clearance is greater and less predictable than variability in renal clearance.

(g) When performing cross-over bioavailability studies on drugs with relatively high renal clearances corrections for intrasubject variability in renal clearance may improve estimates of drug absorption.

(h) Its measurement can form the basis of a method of determining the absolute extent of drug absorption without use of an i.v. reference dose.

Factors Affecting Renal Excretion

1. **Physicochemical properties of drug:** The size of molecule to be filtered has considerable impact on the renal excretion. Only unbound or free drug (small molecular size) appears in glomerular filtrate. Drugs that are bound to plasma proteins behave as macromolecules and are not filtered across glomerulus. Consequently, protein bound drugs have longer half lives than unbound drugs.

2. **Biological factors**: Factors like species, strain difference, age, sex etc. alter the excretion of the drug from the body. Renal excretion of drugs is about 10% lower in female than in males. The renal clearance of drugs per unit of body surface area is generally lower in neonates and infants and in the elderly compared to that in normal young adults. However, the exact effect of age on clearance may vary considerably depending upon the particular drug since the different processes involved in renal excretion mature and deteriorate at different rates. Also, in the newborn, the effects of a low GFR and immature secretory systems may be offset to some extent by relatively low plasma drug binding compared to that in adults and by a low reabsorptive capacity owing to a relative inability to concentrate urine and, possibly, to the presence of protein in the glomerular filtrate. A relatively low urinary pH in neonates could further help to reduce the reabsorption of basic drugs. As the fraction of water reabsorbed is constant, these considerations suggest that changes in urine flow should have less effect on renal drug clearance in newborn babies compared to adults. The rate of urinary excretion of pethidine is specifically sensitive to urine flow in the neonates.

3. **Drug interaction:** Any drug-drug interaction that has potential to alter renal blood flow, urinary pH, active secretion of drugs, forced diuresis and binding characteristics would cause changes in renal clearance of drug. Alkalinization of urine on administration of citrates and bicarbonates promotes renal excretion of acidic drugs. Displacement interactions can result in high renal clearance of the displaced drug and may result in nephrotoxicity. For e.g. potentiation of gentamicin induced nephrotoxicity by furosemide.
4. **Disease state renal dysfunction:** Renal dysfunction impairs the excretion of drugs primarily excreted by kidney. Renal failure may result due to diabetes, hypertension and pyelonephritis. Renal failure (uremia) is characterized by impaired glomerular filtration rate and accumulation of fluids and protein metabolites in the body that leads to impairment of renal excretion of the drugs. As a result the half- life of drug(s) gets increased and if the dose is not adjusted it may result in drug accumulation and clinical toxicity.

Non-Renal Routes of Drug Excretion

Various non-renal excretion routes include biliary excretion, salivary excretion, pulmonary excretion, mammary excretion, gastrointestinal excretion, skin/dermal excretion and genital excretion.

(i) **Biliary excretion:** Bile is steadily secreted by the hepatic cells of liver at a rate of 0.5 to 1 ml /min. Around 90% of bile is reabsorbed from intestine and transported back to the liver for resecretion. Compounds excreted by biliary route include sodium, potassium, bilirubin, glucose, glucuronides, inulin, sucrose etc. As a matter of fact, greater the polarity better the excretion. Like the listed compounds, drug metabolites also get excreted by this route. As the drug metabolites are more polar than parent drug these get predominantly excreted via bile. The factors affecting biliary excretion are detailed below.

***Nature of biotransformation process*:** The drugs undergoing certain phase-II reactions namely glucuronidation and conjugation with glutathione form drug metabolites with increased tendency for biliary excretion. The examples of such drugs are indomethacin, chloromphenicol and morphine. Glutathione conjugates have high molecular weight and hence are not excreted in urine. The primary requirement for a drug to be excreted in bile is to have polar groups like –COOH, -SO_3H. Clomiphene citrate is essentially removed from the body by biliary excretion.

The enterohepatic circulation: In some cases, drugs that are excreted as glucuronides or as glutathione conjugates are hydrolyzed to the parent drugs by intestinal or bacterial enzymes, and are reabsorbed. The reabsorbed drugs are again carried to back to the liver for resecretion via bile into the intestine. This process of drug cycling between the intestine and the liver is termed as enterohepatic circulation. The process holds significance in conservation of vitamins and hormones. The process also results in extending the half-lives of drugs like carbenoxolone. Some drugs that undergo enterohepatic circulation are rifampicin, cardiac glycosides and chlorpromazine.

Other factors: The ability of liver to excrete drug in bile is expressed as biliary clearance and is expressed by the following equation.

$$\text{Biliary clearance} = \frac{\textit{Biliary excretion rate}}{\textit{Plasma drug concentration}} \qquad .....(6.11)$$

The efficacy of excretion of drug by biliary system can be assessed by an agent that is completely excreted in bile. For example, sulfobromophthalein is excreted in half an hour in intestine when hepatic function is normal. Any delay in its excretion suggests hepatic and biliary malfunction.

(ii) **Pulmonary excretion:** The lungs are the major organ of excretion for gaseous volatile and gaseous substances after absorption in lungs by simple diffusion. Most of the gaseous anesthetics are eliminated by expired air. Only the intact gaseous drugs are excreted and not their metabolites. Factors affecting pulmonary excretion are rate of respiration, pulmonary blood flow and solubility of the drug. Ethanol which is highly soluble in blood and tissues is excreted slowly by lungs.

(iii) **Salivary excretion:** Salivary excretion is a form of salivary recycling as the drug which is swallowed is reabsorbed. Drug excretion into saliva is dependent on pH partition and protein binding. The unionized fat soluble drugs are excreted passively from saliva. This may result in bitter after taste in the mouth of a patient. Drugs excreted in saliva are phenytoin, caffeine and theophylline. In most cases salivary concentration represents the free drug concentration. However drugs like spiramycin are higher in saliva than in plasma.

(iv) **Mammary excretion:** Excretion of drug in milk is important as the drug can gain entry in breast feeding infants. The transfer of drugs into the breast milk is influenced by protein binding, lipid solubility and ionization capacity of the drug. Highly plasma bound drug like diazepam is less secreted in milk as it gets bound to the proteins present in milk. As the pH of milk varies from 6.4 to 7.6, primarily the free unionized and fat soluble drugs diffuse passively into the milk. However, the amount of drug excreted in milk is less than 1% and the fraction consumed by an infant is too less to elicit toxic effects. Nicotine is secreted in the milk of mothers who smoke. Some potent drugs like morphine and barbiturates may induce adverse effects. The adverse effects associated with excretion of drugs in milk are jaundice due to interaction of bilirubin with sulfonamides and discoloration of teeth with tetracycline.

(v) **Skin excretion:** Drugs are excreted through skin via sweat. The process of dermal excretion of drugs is governed by pH partition hypothesis. Drugs like salicylic acid, benzoic acid, alcohol and heavy metals like lead, mercury and arsenic are excreted via sweat. In certain cases drugs excreted through skin may cause dermatitis and urticaria.

(vi) **Gastrointestinal excretion:** While this is not a major route of elimination, a large number of drugs can be excreted into the gastrointestinal tract and eliminated via feaces. Excretion of drugs through gastrointestinal tract via feaces usually occurs after parenteral administration of drugs. Water soluble and ionized froms of weakly acidic and basic drugs are excreted in gastrointestinal tract. Examples are nicotine and quinine. Drugs excreted in GIT are reabsorbed into systemic circulation and undergo recycling. Intestinal excretion is relatively a slow process and is an important elimination route only for those drugs that undergo slow biotransformation, or slow urinary and biliary excretion.

Renal Dysfunction

Chronic kidney disease is a common, progressive illness that is becoming a global public health problem. In patients with kidney dysfunction, the renal excretion of parent drug and/or its metabolites will be impaired, leading to their excessive accumulation in the body. In addition, the plasma protein binding of drugs may be significantly reduced, which in turn could influence the pharmacokinetic processes of distribution and elimination. The activity of several drug-metabolizing enzymes and drug transporters has been shown to be impaired in chronic renal failure. In patients with end-stage renal disease, dialysis techniques such as hemodialysis and continuous ambulatory peritoneal dialysis may remove drugs from the body, necessitating dosage adjustment.

Inappropriate dosing in patients with renal dysfunction can cause toxicity or ineffective therapy. Therefore, the normal dosage regimen of a drug may have to be adjusted in a patient with renal dysfunction. Dosage adjustment is based on the remaining kidney function, most often estimated on the basis of the patient's glomerular filtration rate (GFR) estimated by the Cockroft-Gault formula. Net renal excretion of a drug is a conjunction of three processes: glomerular filtration, tubular secretion and tubular reabsorption. Therefore, dosage adjustment based on GFR may not always be appropriate and a re-evaluation of markers of renal function may be required.

According to EMEA and FDA guidelines, a pharmacokinetic study should be carried out during the development phase of a new drug that is likely to be used in patients with renal dysfunction and whose pharmacokinetics are likely to be significantly altered in these patients. This study should be carried out in carefully selected subjects with varying degrees of renal dysfunction. In addition to this two-stage pharmacokinetic approach, a population PK/PD study in patients participating in phase II/phase III clinical trials can also be used to assess the impact of renal dysfunction on the drug's pharmacokinetics and pharmacodynamics.

Drug Dosing in Renal Diseases

Chronic kidney disease (CKD) and renal dysfunction can alter medications' renal elimination and lead to subtherapeutic or supratherapeutic drug concentrations, which may decrease efficacy or increase toxicity. Chronic kidney disease can affect glomerular blood flow and filtration, tubular secretion and reabsorption, and renal bioactivation and metabolism. Drug absorption, bioavailability, protein binding, distribution volume and non-renal clearance (metabolism) also can be altered in these patients. Because of age-related decline in renal function and the use of multiple medications to treat co-morbid conditions older patients are particularly at a higher risk of developing advanced disease and related adverse events.

Chronic kidney disease is defined as the presence of kidney damage or a reduction in the GFR for 3 or more months. Based on GFR, chronic kidney disease is classified as-

Description	Kidney damage with
Stage 1	Normal or increased GFR ≥ 90 mL/min/1.73 m^2
Stage 2	Mild decrease in GFR (60 - 89 mL/min/1.73 m^2)
Stage 3	Moderate decrease in GFR (30 - 59 mL/min/1.73 m^2)
Stage 4	Severe decrease in GFR (15 - 29 mL/min/ 1.73 m^2)
Stage 5	GFR less than 15 mL/min/1.73 m (KIDNEY FAILURE)

Renal damage can alter clearance of active drug metabolites, causing accumulation. Altered renal function can also affect dosing intervals of renally eliminated medications. The following drugs require renal dosage adjustments:

- Allopurinol (Zyloprim)
- Lithium (Lithobid)
- Acyclovir (Valtrex)
- Arnantadine (Symmetrel)
- Fexofenadine (Allegra)
- Cephalexin (Keflex)
- Amoxycillin (Amoxy)
- Cefuroxime (Certin)
- Ciprolloxacin (Cipro)

Gabapentin (Neurontin)
Metoclopramide (Reglan)
Ranitidine (Zantac)
Rivaroxaban (Xarelto)
Fesoterodine (Toviaz)
Clarithromycin (Biaxin)
Levofloxacin (Levaquin)
Nitrorurantoin (Macrobid)
Piperacillint razobactam (Zosyn)

Drug dosing errors are common in patients with renal impairment.

- To avoid these errors, dosages of drugs cleared renally should be adjusted based on creatinine clearance or glomerular filtration rate (GFR).
- These calculations are valid only when renal function is stable and the serum creatinine level is constant.
- The K/DOQI clinical practice guideline advocates using the traditional Cockcroft Gault (CG) equation or the Modification of Diet in Renal Disease (MDRD) study equation for routine estimation of GFR.
- However, in patients with a GFR lower than 60 mL per minute per 1.73 m^2, the MDRD equation has been shown to be superior to the Cockcroft-Gault equation. Because the production and excretion of creatinine declines with age, normal serum creatinine values may not represent normal renal function in older patients.
- The MDRD equation has been shown to be the best method for detecting a GFR lower than 90 mL per minute per 1.73 m^2 in older patients. The (MDRD) Study equation and the Chronic Kidney Disease Epidemiology Collaboration (CKD-EPI) equation are the most widely used equations for estimating GFR in patients age 18 and over. For estimating GFR from serum creatinine in patients under age 18 (including infants, toddlers, children, and teens), the Bedside Schwartz equation should be used.

Dosing Adjustments

Loading dose(s) usually does not need to be adjusted in patients with CKD. For maintenance dosing adjustments, recommended methods are dose reductions, less frequent dosing interval, or both. Dose reduction involves reducing each dose while maintaining the normal dosing interval. This approach maintains more constant drug concentrations, but it is associated with a higher risk of toxicities if the dosing interval is inadequate to allow for drug elimination. Normal doses are maintained with the extended interval method, but the dosing interval is lengthened to allow time for drug elimination before redosing. Lengthening the dosing interval has been associated with a lower risk of toxicities but a higher risk of subtherapeutic drug concentrations, especially toward the end of the dosing interval. The dose of any drug is adjusted according to the estimated creatinine clearance generally using the Cockroft-Gault equation for patients ≥ 18 years old and the Schwartz equation for patients < 18 years old.

Dosage adjustment in patients with hepatic dysfunction

Both the FDA and the European Medicines Agency (EMEA) have published guidance for industry on the evaluation of the pharmacokinetics of medicinal products in patients with impaired hepatic function. These guidelines recommend that a pharmacokinetic study be carried out during development of a medicinal product that is likely to be used in patients with impaired hepatic function and when hepatic impairment is likely to significantly alter the pharmacokinetics of the drug substance or its active metabolite(s). The primary objective of such a study is to identify patients at risk and to assess whether a dosage adjustment is required for patients with impaired hepatic function. When no recommendations for dosage adjustment in patients with hepatic dysfunction are available, the following general considerations will be helpful. It is assumed that the drug is mostly eliminated by hepatic mechanisms (metabolism, biliary excretion).

1. **Drugs with a relatively high hepatic extraction ratio:** The oral bioavailability of these drugs can be drastically increased in patients with chronic liver disease, and the dosage should be reduced accordingly. Following systemic administration (i.v., i.m., s.c., etc.), the plasma clearance may be reduced if hepatic blood flow is decreased.
2. **Drugs with a low hepatic extraction and high plasma protein binding (> 90%):** The oral and intravenous clearance of these drugs is determined by the intrinsic capacity of the hepatic elimination mechanisms and the unbound drug fraction in blood or plasma. The intrinsic clearance will be reduced to a degree determined by the functional status of the liver and the specific metabolic pathway(s) involved in the elimination of the drug.

Because the unbound fraction of drug in blood or plasma may be significantly increased in patients with chronic liver disease, pharmacokinetic evaluation should be based on unbound blood/plasma concentrations, and dosage adjustment may be necessary even though total blood/plasma concentrations are within the normal range.

3. **Drugs with a low hepatic extraction ratio and low plasma protein binding (< 90%):** Fluctuations in the unbound drug fraction in blood or plasma are rather small and \will not significantly affects blood/plasma clearance of the drug. Dosage adjustment may be necessary and should be aimed at maintaining normal total (i.e., bound plus unbound) plasma concentrations.
4. The elimination of drugs that are partly excreted in unchanged form by the kidneys will be impaired in patients with the hepato-renal syndrome. It should be taken into account that creatinine clearance significantly overestimates glomerular filtration rate in these patients.
5. The volume of distribution of hydrophilic drugs may be increased in patients with chronic liver disease who have edema or ascites. As a consequence, the loading dose may have to be increased in these patients if a rapid and complete effect of the drug is required. Since many hydrophilic drugs are eliminated primarily in unchanged form by the kidneys, renal function should be taken into consideration.
6. Extreme caution is recommended when using drugs with a narrow therapeutic index in patients with liver disease and when administering any drug to patients with severe liver dysfunction.

Questions

Multiple Choice Questions

1. Clearance is a function of:
   (a) The blood flow to clearing organs and the efficiency of the organ in extracting the drug.
   (b) Volume of distribution
   (c) Half life of the drug
   (d) Both b and c

2. Dosage adjustment of renally eliminated drugs at what creatinine clearance value?
   (a) 90 ml/min (b) 30 ml/min
   (c) 60 ml/min (d) 15 ml/min
3. Which of the following factors can affect the renal clearance of a drug?
   (a) Oral bioavailability (b) pKa
   (c) Route of administration (d) Administered dose
4. The drug with molecular weight in the range of 300-500 daltons is excreted through
   (a) Urine (b) Both urine and bile
   (c) Bile (d) None of the above
5. The creatinine clearance value of 20 to 50 ml/min indicates:
   (a) Mild renal dysfunction (b) Normal renal function
   (c) Severe renal impairment (d) Moderate renal failure
6. As majority of drugs are weak electrolytes, their diffusion across the lipoidal tubular membrane depends on degree on ionization which in turn is dependent on:
   (a) pH of Urine only
   (b) Both pH of urine and pKa of drug
   (c) pKa of the drug only
   (d) None of the above
7. Inhibition of active tubular secretion of organic acids such as penicillins, by probencid increases the plasma concentration by:
   (a) Two fold (b) Five fold
   (c) Four fold (d) No change
8. Glomerular filtration does not facilitate filtration of:
   (a) Ionized drugs (b) Ionized metabolites
   (c) Unionized drugs (d) Protein bound drugs
9. Active reabsorption is affected by:
   (a) Changes in pH (b) Protein binding of drug
   (c) Renal blood flow (d) pKa of drug
10. State true or false: Contrary to tubular secretion, reabsorption results in an increase in the half life of a drug.

Short Questions

1. What's the difference between clearance and the rate of drug elimination?
2. Why is clearance a useful pharmacokinetic parameter?
3. Unlike glomerular filtration, active secretion of a drug is unaffected by protein binding. Explain.
4. How does pulmonary excretion affect drug elimination?
5. How can dose be adjusted in patients with renal failure?

Long Questions

1. In context to the factors affecting renal excretion, discuss the following:
   (i) Physicochemical properties of drug,
   (ii) Distribution and binding characteristics of drug.
2. How does urine pH and pKa of drug influence tubular reabsorption of drugs?
3. With the help of neat diagram, illustrate the processes involved in urinary excretion of drugs. Write about excretion via glomerular filtration.
4. Write a descriptive note on biliary excretion.
5. Excretion of drug in milk is highly significant. Explain why?

Bioavailability and Bioequivalence

CHAPTER

7

LEARNING OBJECTIVES

- Understanding the concept of bioavailability
- Absolute and Relative bioavailability
- Bioequivalence and its legal requirements
- Methods of assessing bioavailability
- In vitro in vivo correlation

Bioavailability

Dosage forms or formulations are designed and developed to deliver the medicament to its site of action in a safe, efficient and stable way so that the rate and amount of drug is sufficient to elicit the desired pharmacological response. For most of the drugs the pharmacological response is directly related to the amount of drug present in the blood (plasma). Since the concentration of drug at the site of action is not convenient to be measured and there is direct relation between the amount of drug at site of action and in plasma. The concentration of drug in plasma/blood is directly related to the concentration at site of action.

As indicated in Chapter 21 CFR (Codes of *Federal Regulations*) Part 320.1, *bioavailability* of a drug is defined as the rate and extent to which the active drug ingredient or active moiety from the drug product is absorbed and becomes available at the site of drug action. The extent and rate of drug absorption are usually measured by the area under the blood or plasma concentration-time curve (AUC) and the maximum concentration (C_{max}), respectively. A blood concentration-time curve (achieved by serial measurements over time) reflects not just the release of the active ingredient from the drug and its absorption from the GI tract, but also other factors including presystemic metabolism, distribution, and elimination. The rate or rapidity of absorption plays a very important role in deciding the regimen and dose of the drug. A rapid rate of action is desired in case of drugs used for treatment of acute conditions such as asthma attack, pain, angina while a slower rate of absorption is desired when the aim of therapy is to prolong the duration of action and to avoid the adverse effects.

Bioavailability problems are observed mainly after oral administration due to either of the following reasons.

1. The drug may not be completely available after oral administration due to low permeability and slow absorption even when given in solution. Examples: cromolyn sodium, neomycin, riboflavin etc. The reason may be decreased residence time of the drug at the site of absorption. In order to increase bioavailability reduce GIT motility by use of drugs, or administer the dosage form of the drug with food, or else develop lipid soluble prodrugs.
2. The drug has poor water solubility thereby resulting in incomplete dissolution during the period of time available for absorption. E.g. phenytoin, griseofulvin etc. To increase bioavailability either change the dosage form, affect size reduction of the drug particles, or make water soluble prodrugs.
3. The drug may show incomplete bioavailability because of chemical degradation of the drug in stomach (penicillin G), pre-absorptive metabolism by enzymes in proximal intestine (aspirin) or by bacteria in distal intestine (digoxin), presystemic metabolism in gut wall (isoprotorenol) or liver (propranolol) during absorption. If a drug undergoes presystemic metabolism it may be completely absorbed but incompletely available as a part of dose is metabolized to other products as the drug passes from gut lumen to systemic circulation.

Purpose of Bioavailability Studies

- It is important to conduct bioavailability study in the primary stages of development of dosage forms to obtain evidence regarding the clinical utility of the drug product.
- The studies are also important in selection of excipients and methods used in the formulation of dosage forms.
- In the development of generic versions of the already patented product to compare the quality.
- Development of new dosage forms/formulations of already existing drug.
- As a quality control parameter of drug products.

Estimation of Bioavailability

Bioavailability is assessed using three main pharmacokinetic variables namely (i) Area under the blood drug concentration versus time curve (AUC), (ii) maximum blood concentration (C_{max}), and (iii) the time to reach maximum concentration (t_{max}). While the AUC relates to the extent of drug absorption, the latter two are the determinants of rate of absorption. Using AUC one can estimate absolute and relative bioavailability.

Absolute (systemic) Bioavailability

The fraction/percent of an administered dose that actually reaches the systemic circulation can be determined from blood level or urinary excretion data after oral administration with respect to similar data after intravenous administration. Thus absolute bioavailability (denoted as F) is very useful in characterizing the drug's inherent properties related to absorption. It is calculated by comparing the $(AUC)_{total}$ under the plasma concentration time curve(s) obtained after single dose of the drug by extravascular (oral) route with the equivalent single dose of the drug via the intravenous route to the same subject.

$$\text{Absolute bioavailability (F)} = \frac{[AUC_{total}]_{ev} \text{ X } Dose_{iv}}{[AUC_{total}]_{iv} \text{ X } Dose_{ev}} \quad .....(7.1)$$

Usually bioavailability studies are terminated before drug concentration in the blood returns to negligible levels and AUC beyond the last concentration data point C* at t* is estimated as:

$$(AUC)_{t^*-\alpha} = C^*/\,K_E \quad .....(7.2)$$

$$(AUC)_{total} = (AUC)_{0-t^*} + (AUC)_{t^*-\alpha} \quad .....(7.3)$$

Similarly, the urinary excretion data can also be utilized for calculation of absolute bioavailability by determining the cumulative amount(s) of the unchanged drug or its metabolite excreted in urine. The method may not be useful for drugs where the fraction excreted unchanged in too small for quantitative measurement using standard analytical techniques. On the other hand, for some drugs urinary excretion data is the method of choice (e.g. thiazide diuretics). Thus F is calculated as

$$\text{Absolute bioavailability (F)} = \frac{[X_u^{\infty}]_{ev} \text{ X } Dose_{iv}}{[X_u^{\infty}]_{iv} \text{ X } Dose_{ev}} \quad .....(7.4)$$

where, X_u^{∞} is the total amount of the unchanged drug or its major metabolite excreted in the urine in infinite time. In contrast to the blood levels that change with the dose, urinary fraction remains same irrespective of the dose.

Absolute bioavailability (F) can be determined for few drugs as not all drugs are approved for IV use. Alternatively, intramuscular route may be used for absolute bioavailability determination of soluble drugs. Nevertheless, very few drugs are approved for intramuscular use. Hence the term relative bioavailability (F_r) is frequently used.

Relative Bioavailability

It is defined as the ratio of bioavailability of an oral drug product (test) with that of an oral product (standard) of the same drug. It is denoted by the symbol Fr. The standard may be either aqueous oral solution of the drug or non aqueous oral solution or aqueous oral suspension or any other solid dosage form. The test may be single dose of drug as test product or oral solution. The blood levels or urinary excretion data is collected and AUC_{total} or X_u^{∞} is determined respectively. The relative bioavailability is determined as

$$\text{Relative bioavailability } (F_r) = \frac{[AUC_{total}]_{test} \text{ X } Dose_{std}}{[AUC_{total}]_{std} \text{ X } Dose_{test}} \qquad .....(7.5)$$

From urinary excretion data,

$$\text{Relative bioavailability } (F_r) = \frac{\left[X_u^{\infty}\right]_{test} \text{ X } Dose_{std}}{\left[X_u^{\infty}\right]_{std} \text{ X } Dose\ test} \qquad .....(7.6)$$

The value of F_r is generally ≤ 1, sometimes it may exceed the value of 1 when the drug administered is poorly soluble in gastric pH and precipitates as coarse crystals in stomach on swallowing aqueous solution or it undergoes acid hydrolysis to which the dosage form provides protection not afforded by solution. A value of $F_r = 1$ does not necessarily imply complete bioavailability. It rather means that the availability of drug from the test is equal to that from standard.

The limitations of F_r determination are:

1. The bioavailability studies are carried out by giving a single dose of the drug to ambulatory, healthy subjects after an overnight fast which may provide misleading information.
2. The drug availability may practically depend on food, activity (sleeping versus awake), disease and concomitant drugs ingested. All these have differential effects on the drug availability.

Therefore steady state studies are required for evaluation of F_r i.e. constant dose of drug given at constant dosing intervals. Based on the fact that AUC during single dosing interval will be equal to AUC after single dose. Thus F_r

from multiple dose steady state condition from plasma concentration data may be calculated as:

$$\text{Relative bioavailability } (F_r) = \frac{[AUC_{SS}]test \text{ X } Dose_{std}}{[AUC_{SS}]std \text{ X } Dose_{test}} \quad .....(7.7)$$

From urinary excretion data,

$$\text{Relative bioavailability } (F_r) = \frac{[X_{u,ss}]_{test} \text{ X } Dose_{std}}{[X_{u,ss}]std \text{ X } Dose\ test} \quad .....(7.8)$$

where, $X_{u,ss}$ is the amount excreted unchanged in urine during a single dosing interval.

The steady state studies for F_r determination takes into account the general conditions of drug use. If with single dose of drug, a drug is more bioavailable it is not clear whether it is due to faster absorption or it is more bioavailable. The steady state studies provide clear indication of bioequivalence.

Practice Problem

In a clinical trial, the patients were administered a drug either as a single oral tablet containing 200 mg of the drug, 5 mL of a pure aqueous solution containing 200 mg of the drug, or a single IV bolus injection containing 50 mg of the drug. Plasma samples were obtained periodically up to 48 hours after the dose and assayed for drug concentration. The average AUC values (0–48 hours) are given in the table below. From the data, calculate (a) the relative bioavailability of the drug from the tablet compared to the oral solution and (b) the absolute bioavailability of the drug from the tablet.

Drug Product	Dose (mg)	AUC (g hr/mL)	Standard Deviation
Oral tablet	200	89.5	19.7
Oral solution	200	86.1	18.1
IV bolus injection	50	37.8	5.7

Methods of Assessment of Bioavailability

There are several direct and indirect methods of assessing bioavailability in humans. The selection of a method depends upon the (i) purpose of the study,

(ii) nature of drug product, and (iii) the analytic method of drug measurement. The methods available for bioavailability assessment are classified as below:

1. Pharmacokinetic methods
    - (a) Plasma level- time data
    - (b) Urinary excretion data
2. Pharmacodynamic methods
    - (a) Acute pharmacological response methods
    - (b) Clinical response method

1. Pharmacokinetic methods

(a) Plasma level-time data: The most widely and accepted method for the assessment of bioavailability of drug products is plasma concentration time profile graph/data unless plasma samples cannot be assayed or collected due to any particular reasons. By appropriate blood sampling, an accurate description of the plasma drug concentration–time profile of the therapeutically active drug substance(s) can be obtained using a validated drug assay. The parameters t_{max} and C_{max} are the measures of the rate of absorption whereas AUC reflects the extent of absorption of drug.

t_{max} : The *time of peak plasma concentration*, t_{max}, corresponds to the time required to reach maximum drug concentration after drug administration. At t_{max}, peak drug absorption occurs and the rate of drug absorption exactly equals the rate of drug elimination. Drug absorption still continues after t_{max} is reached, but at a slower rate. When comparing drug products, t_{max} can be used as an approximate indication of drug absorption rate. This parameter cannot be utilized for comparing the bioavailabilities of modified release products and is mainly used for immediate release products.

C_{max} : The *peak plasma drug concentration*, C_{max}, represents the maximum plasma drug concentration obtained after oral administration of drug. The concentration of drug at the target site is hard to measure and a direct relationship exists between the pharmacodynamic drug effect and the plasma drug concentration, in most of the cases. C_{max} provides indications that the drug is sufficiently systemically absorbed to provide a therapeutic response. In addition, C_{max} value also has significance in deciding the chances of occurrence of adverse drug reaction related to a particular drug.

***AUC_{total}* or $[AUC]_0^\infty$:** The *area under the plasma level–time curve* (AUC) is a measurement of the extent of drug that reaches the systemic circulation. The AUC is the area under the drug plasma level–time curve from $t = 0$ to $t = \infty$, and is equal to the amount of unchanged drug reaching the general circulation divided by the clearance.

$$[AUC]_0^\infty = [AUC]_0^t + [AUC]_t^\infty \quad .....(7.9)$$

$$[AUC]_0^\infty = \int_t^\infty C\,dt \quad .....(7.10)$$

$$[AUC]_0^\infty = \frac{FDo}{\text{clearance}} = \frac{FDo}{KE\ V_d} \quad .....(7.11)$$

where, F = fraction of dose absorbed, D_0 = dose, K_E = elimination rate constant, and V_d = volume of distribution.

The AUC can be determined by following methods:

1. **Counting method:** Plot the plasma concentration versus time data on a numeric (Cartesian) graph paper and count the number of squares enclosed by the curve. Determine the area of curve by adding the area of squares.
2. **Cut and weigh method**: In this method plasma concentration versus time data is plotted on a Cartesian/ texture paper that can be cut out and weighed on electronic balance. The weight is proportional to the area under the curve.

   The above two methods give rough estimate of AUC, while for exact AUC determination following two methods are used.
3. **Trapezoidal method**: The most common method of estimating the AUC is with the help of trapezoidal rule. In this method the plasma concentration time profile curve is divided into series of suitable trapezoids having adjacent plasma concentration values as parallel sides and time difference as height of trapezoid. Finally the total area is calculated by adding area of individual trapezoids as depicted in equation 7.12.

$$[AUC]_0^t = \frac{Co+C1}{2}(t_1 - t_0) + \frac{C1+C2}{2}(t_2 - t_1) + \frac{Cn-1+Cn}{2}(t_n - t_{n-1}) \quad .....(7.12)$$

$$[AUC]_0^\infty = [AUC]_0^t + [AUC]_t^\infty \quad .....(7.13)$$

   where $[AUC]_t^\infty$ is area under the curve from time of the last measurable plasma concentration (C_p) till infinity (∞), and is determined as C_p / K_E.

4. **Integration method:** The rate of change of plasma concentration is determined by

   dC/dt = Rate of absorption – Rate of elimination

$$= Ka\ Xa - K_E\ X \qquad .....(7.14)$$

where, Ka and KE are absorption and overall elimination rate constants. While Xa and X represent the amount of drug in the gastrointestinal tract and body respectively. On integrating this term between limits we have final equation as

$$AUC = X\left[\frac{1}{K^E} - \frac{1}{Ka}\right] \qquad .....(7.15)$$

(b) Urinary excretion data: Urinary drug excretion data is an indirect method for estimating bioavailability. The method is based on the fact that rate of excretion of drug is directly proportional to the concentration of the drug in blood. The method holds promise when the drug is excreted in significant quantities as unchanged drug in the urine and the samples are calculated for at least seven half lives.

Average rate of drug excretion *(dX_u/dt)*: It is a well known fact that most of the drugs are eliminated out from the body following first order kinetics. The rate of drug excretion is dependent on the first-order elimination rate constant K_E and the concentration of drug in the plasma *C*. Since, the elimination process is directly proportional to the concentration of drug in plasma the maximum rate of excretion will be at a point when the concentration is at its peak that is C_{max}. Thus, a graph comparing the rate of drug excretion with respect to time should be similar in shape as the plasma level-time curve for that drug and $(dX_u/dt)_{max}$ would be analogous to C_{max} (Fig. 7.1).

Cumulative amount of drug excreted in the urine (X_u^∞): The X_u^∞ is directly related to the total amount of drug absorbed. Experimentally, urine samples are collected periodically after administration of a drug product. Each urine specimen is analyzed for free drug using a specific assay. A graph is constructed that relates the cumulative drug excreted to the collection-time interval. When the drug is almost completely eliminated, the plasma concentration approaches zero and the maximum amount of drug excreted in the urine, X_u^∞, is obtained and is found to be maximum. It is analogous to the area under the curve (AUC). The samples must be collected for a longer period of time so that the concentration could achieve the zero value and we would get a closure estimate of X_u^∞.

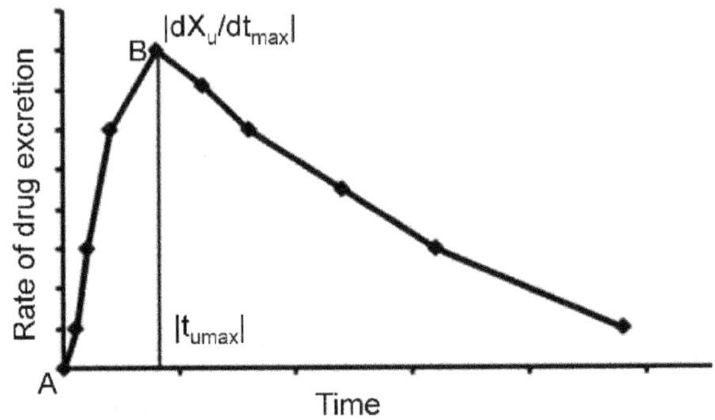

Fig. 7.1 A plot between urinary excretion rate and time.

Total time for the drug to be excreted $t_{u\ max}$: The slope of the curve segment *A–B* is related to the rate of drug absorption. It is analogous to t_{max} and is a useful parameter in bioequivalence studies that compare several drug products, as will be described later in this chapter.

1. **Pharmacodynamic methods:** The pharmacokinetic methods are based on the assumption that the drug concentration in blood or the drug excretion in the urine is related to the observed therapeutic effect. But due to issues of inaccuracy, non-reproducibility and certain other problems, pharmacokinetic methods sometimes does not hold good. In such cases pharmacodynamic methods are used.

   (a) **Acute pharmacological response method:** For locally acting, non-systemically absorbed drug products, such as topical corticosteroids, plasma drug concentrations may not reflect the bioavailability of the drug at the site of action. An acute pharmacodynamic effect, such as an effect on forced expiratory volume, FEV_1 (inhaled bronchodilators) or skin blanching (topical corticosteroids) can be used as an index of drug bioavailability. This method is utilized to construct a plot between acute pharmacological response verses time. Two important criteria should be fulfilled for applying this method:

      (a) An established dose related response curve should be present.

      (b) The response should be easily measurable. (Blood pressure, pupil diameter, ECG graph).

Measurements of the pharmacodynamic effect should be made with sufficient frequency and accuracy to permit a reasonable estimate for a time period at least three times the half-life of the drug.

(b) **Clinical response method:** This method is the most accurate method of comparison as it signifies the formulation differences and its affect on therapeutic responses. This difference also can be due to different pharmacodynamic and kinetic behavior of drug in different individuals. In this method the clinical response of the drug for which it is intended to be utilized is measured. E.g. For antiinflammatory drugs the reduction in inflammation is measured, for anti-diabetic drug reduction in blood glucose level is measured.

In vitro studies and bioavailability

The best way of assessing the therapeutic efficacy of drugs with a slow dissolution rate is *in vivo* determination of bioavailability. But in case of generic medicines and batch to batch production of same dosage forms it will be highly costly, tedious and time consuming and can bring hazards to the patients. Currently available drugs in market and most new research compounds have dissolution rate limited absorption. Hence, *in vitro* dissolution rate is the best available tool which can quantitatively assure about the biological availability of drug from its formulation. Ideally, the *in vitro* drug dissolution rate should correlate with *in vivo* drug bioavailability (see text on *in vivo in vitro* correlation (IVIVC).

In vitro dissolution testing models

The *in vitro* drug dissolution testing would be successful only if it predicts the *in vivo* behavior of drug accurately and precisely. The efforts are laid down basically for following purposes:

1. The dissolution apparatus characteristics from size, design, and shape to nature of agitation, speed should be clearly defined and SOP should be clear.
2. The medium composition, viscosity, temperature and volume should be well defined and the procedure should be followed as under guidelines.
3. Process parameters should be controlled.

These factors are considered important and are mainly aimed at mimicking the biological conditions outside. Table 7.1 summarizes the official dissolution apparatuses listed in USP.

Table 7.1 Types of USP compendial dissolution apparatus and their applications.

Apparatus	Name	Formulations tested
Apparatus 1	Basket type	Conventional and controlled release tablets
Apparatus 2	Paddle type	Tablets, orally disintegrating tablets, capsules and controlled release
Apparatus 3	Reciprocating cylinder	Controlled release formulations
Apparatus 4	Flow through cell	Formulations containing poorly soluble drug, powders and granules, microparticles
Apparatus 5	Paddle over disc	Transdermal formulations
Apparatus 6	Cylinder	Transdermal formulations
Apparatus 7	Reciprocating disc	Controlled release non-disintegrating formulations

In Vitro in Vivo Correlation (IVIVC)

A simple *in vitro* dissolution test on the drug product will not be sufficient enough to determine the therapeutic efficiency. So it is quiet essential to have a correlation between the *in vitro* dissolution behavior of a drug and its bioavailability. *In vitro in vivo* correlation is defined as the predictive mathematical model that describes the relationship between an *in vitro* property (such as rate of dissolution) of a dosage form and an *in vivo* response (such as plasma drug concentration). The main objective of this important relationship (IVIVC) is to enable the *in vitro* dissolution test to serve as surrogate for an *in vivo* bioavailability studies in human beings as conducting *in vivo* studies for every new product. Another important aspect is to develop a tool to evaluate a new dosage form with desired *in vivo* performance.

***In vitro in vivo* correlation levels**

Three IVIVC levels have been defined and categorized in descending order of usefulness:

Level A: The highest category of correlation is level A correlation. It represents point to point relationship between *in vitro* dissolution and *in vivo* rate of absorption i.e. the two curves are superimposible and mathematical equation for both the curves should be same. The *in vitro* dissolution studies serves as a surrogate for *in vivo* performance and change in manufacturing procedure or small change in additives/excipients can be justified without additional human studies.

Level B: It utilizes the principles of statistical moment theory. The mean *in vitro* dissolution time (MDT) is compared with mean residence time (MRT). Level B correlation uses entire *in vitro* and *in vivo* data, yet it is not a point to point correlation since there are various *in vitro* curves which may have same MRT values. It cannot have the ability to justify SUPAC and bioawaiver.

Level C: It is single point correlation relating one dissolution time point ($t_{50\%}$ or $t_{90\%}$) to one mean pharmacokinetic parameter (t_{max} or C_{max}). This is utilized in early stages of formulation development. Level C correlations can be useful when pilot formulations are being selected. Biowaiver is generally not possible.

Bioequivalence

Equivalence: Equivalence refers to the comparison of drug products with respect to certain characteristics or functions. It may be in terms of bioavailability, therapeutic response, or a set of established standards of one drug product to another. There are several types of equivalence:

Pharmaceutical equivalent: Drug products that contain the same active ingredient(s), i.e., the same salt or ester, in the same dosage form, use the same route of administration, and are identical in strength or concentration are called as pharmaceutical equivalents. Pharmaceutically equivalent drug products meet the same compendia or other applicable standards (i.e., strength, quality, purity, and identity), but they may differ in characteristics such as shape, scoring configuration, release mechanisms, packaging, excipients (including colors, flavors, preservatives), expiration time, and, within certain limits, labeling. When applicable, pharmaceutical equivalents must meet the same content uniformity, disintegration times, and/or dissolution rates.

Bioequivalent drug products: The term is defined under 21 CFR 320.1 as "the pharmaceutical equivalent or pharmaceutical alternative products that display comparable rate and extent of absorption of the test drug do not show a significant difference from the rate and extent of absorption of the reference drug when administered at the samc molar dose of the therapeutic ingredient under similar experimental conditions in either a single dose or multiple doses"

Therapeutic equivalent: Drug products are considered to be therapeutic equivalent only if they are pharmaceutical equivalents and if they can be expected to have the same clinical effect and safety profile when administered to patients under the conditions specified in the labeling. Therapeutic equivalent drug products must be (i) safe and effective, (ii) pharmaceutically equivalent, (iii) bioequivalent, (iv) adequately labeled, and (v) manufactured in compliance with GMP.

What is difference between bioavailability and bioequivalence?
Bioavailability is the percent of a drug's dose that reaches the systemic circulation. (Intravenously administered drugs have 100% bioavailability.) Bioequivalence is a measure of comparability between two dosage forms of the same drug and is used to determine whether the two drug products can be used interchangeably.

Bioequivalence Studies

Bioequivalence is used to evaluate the expected *in vivo* biological equivalence of two proprietary preparations of a drug. Bioavailability (BA) and bioequivalence (BE) studies are of considerable importance for regulatory bodies to ensure that the therapeutic response of two pharmaceutically equivalent drugs is comparable. Although bioequivalence is most commonly discussed in relation to generic medicines, it is important to note that bioequivalence studies are also performed for innovator medicines in situations such as:

1. Between early and late clinical trial formulations or between the formulations used in clinical trials and the product to be marketed for new medicines.
2. When changes in formulation have occurred after an innovator product has been approved, for example a change in one or more excipients.

Significance of bioequivalence (BE) studies

1. BE studies are surrogate marker for clinical effectiveness and safety data as it would not normally be practical to repeat clinical studies for generic products. It is accepted that if plasma concentrations of the active ingredient of generic and innovator drug formulations are the same, then their concentration at the site of action and therefore their safety and effectiveness will be the same. In addition to being bioequivalent, a generic medicine must conform to high quality standards in terms of the method of manufacture and the purity of the final pharmaceutical form. The measurement and

assessment of bioequivalence is carried out by internationally agreed standards.

2. BE studies are used to define early and late clinical trials.
3. BE studies allow the generic versions of branded products to reach the patients in a much easier way and in cost effective manner.

Acceptance Criteria for Bioequivalence

Bioequivalence is determined based on the relative bioavailability of the innovator medicine versus the generic medicine. It is measured by comparing the ratio of the pharmacokinetic variables for the innovator versus the generic medicine where equality is 1. The acceptance criteria are such that to be classified as bioequivalent, plasma concentrations of the generic medicine will not differ significantly compared with the innovator medicine. Studies have demonstrated that actual differences between observed mean plasma concentrations of generic and innovator medicines were no greater than 5%. In order to determine that two medicines are bioequivalent there must be no more than a 20% difference between the AUC and C_{max}. This is based on international consensus that differences less than this are not clinically significant. In order to establish this, the AUC and C_{max} for the generic medicine are compared to that for the innovator medicine (Fig. 7.2).

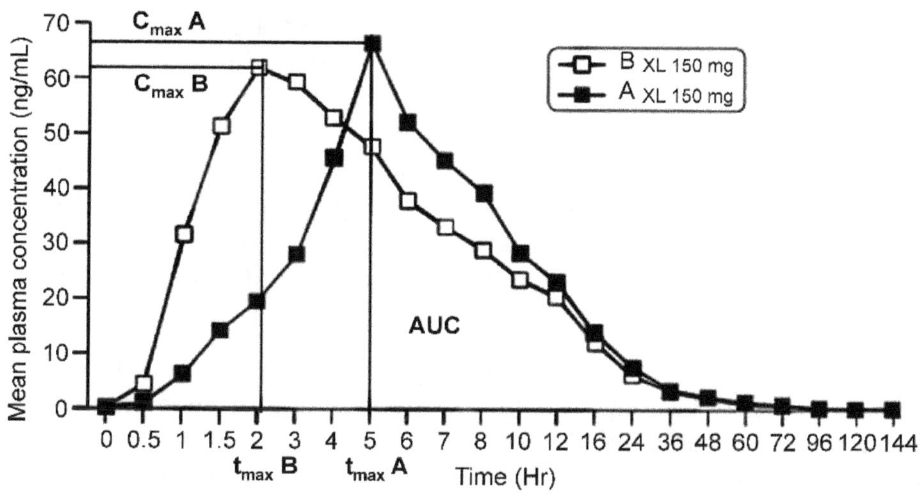

Fig. 7.2 Drug concentration versus time curve for two drug products.

Bioequivalence is based on a comparison of ratios where the ratio of generic to innovator for each pharmacokinetic variable does not differ by more than 8:10. This is how the range for the confidence intervals is defined: 8/10 = 0.80 gives the lower limit and 10/8 = 1.25 gives the upper limit. The 90% confidence intervals for the ratios of both C_{max} and AUC should be contained within the limits 0.80–1.25 (Fig. 7.3).

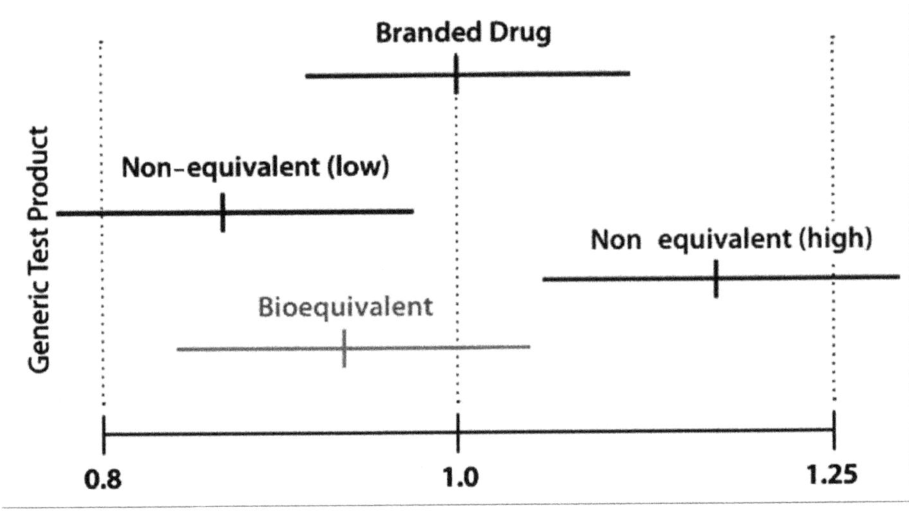

Fig. 7.3 Criteria for acceptance: 90% confidence interval of the ratios of AUC, C_{max}, t_{max} fall between 0.80 and 1.25 of the branded (innovator) drug.

Bioequivalence studies are cross-over studies in which each subject acts as their own control. This model, (*in vivo* healthy volunteers) is regarded as adequate to detect formulation differences. The results obtained allow extrapolation to populations in which the reference product is approved (e.g. the elderly, children, patients with renal or liver impairment).

Bioequivalence studies usually involve single doses of a medicine. It is theoretically possible that excipients used in the generic formulation (preservatives, pH adjusters, thickening agents etc) could affect the absorption and metabolism at steady state without producing these differences from a single dose. However this is extremely unlikely and would normally be apparent from differences observed in the bioequivalence study. Any difference that may exist is negligible compared to the variability of the conditions in the gastrointestinal tract and its effect on absorption.

Table 7.2 Bioequivalence study protocol.

1. Title Principal investigator Project number and date	5. Clinical Procedures • Dosage and drug administration • Biological sampling schedule
2. Study objective	6. Ethical considerations
3. Study design (a) Experimental design (b) Drug products (c) test product and recognized standard (d) Dosage Regimen (e) Frequency and duration of sampling (f) Randomization of drug administration (g) Analytical methods (h) Single *versus* multiple dose study	7. Methods of assessment • Plasma data • Urine data • Acute pharmacological data • Clinical response
4. Study population (a) Subjects (b) Subject selection • Medical history • Physical examination • Laboratory tests	8. Data analysis • Statistical treatment of data analysis • Format of data • Analytical validation procedure.

Test Procedures

Several *in vivo* and *in vitro* methods are appropriate to document BA and BE. In descending order of preference, the US regulations include pharmacokinetic, pharmacodynamic, clinical, and *in vitro* studies. Willingness to rely on test procedures other than clinical studies is based on the assumption that pharmacokinetic and pharmacodynamic approaches and/or *in vitro* approaches adequately reflect clinical safety and efficacy outcomes.

(i) Pharmacokinetic studies: The statutory definition of BA and BE, expressed in rate and extent of absorption of the active moiety or ingredient to the site of action, emphasizes the use of pharmacokinetic parameters to indicate release of the drug substance from the drug product with absorption into the systemic circulation. This approach is based on the fact that measurement of the active moiety or ingredient at the site(s) of action is generally not possible and that some predetermined relationship exists between the drug concentrations at the site of action relative to that in the systemic circulation.

A typical BE study is conducted as a crossover study, in which clearance and physiologic variables (e.g., gastric emptying, motility, and pH) are assumed to have less variability within an individual compared with variability between individuals. Where needed, a pilot study may be useful to validate analytic methodology, to assess intra- and intersubject variability in systemic exposure measures, and to optimize sample collection times. Although multiple dose studies are useful in establishing BA and BE; single dose studies to document BE may be preferred because they are generally more sensitive in assessing *in vivo* release of the drug substance from the drug product. Extent of absorption is readily measured by AUC either to the last sampled time point (AUC_{0-t}) or following extrapolation to time infinity ($AUC_{0-\alpha}$). Measurement of the true rate of absorption is difficult, given that rate varies continuously over time. A recent FDA guidance, therefore, has recommended that measures of systemic exposure be used to reflect clinically important differences between test and reference products in BA and BE studies. These measures include (i) total exposure (AUC_{0-t} or $AUC_{0-\alpha}$) for single-dose studies and AUC_{0-t} for steady-state studies), (ii) peak exposure (C_{max}), and (iii) early exposure (partial AUC to peak time of the reference product for an immediate release drug product).

Pharmacologic Effect (Pharmacodynamic studies): Locally acting drug products include oral inhalation drug products, such as metered dose inhalers and dry powder inhalers, and topically applied dermatologic drug products such as creams and ointments. These drug products deliver an active moiety or active ingredient to local sites of action where they exert their primary clinical effects. Pharmacokinetic studies measure systemic exposure but are generally inappropriate to document local delivery. In such cases, BA may be measured, and BE may be established, based on a pharmacodynamic (PD) study, providing an appropriate PD endpoint is available, which can be studied with sufficient accuracy, sensitivity, and reproducibility. Bronchodilator drug products, such as albuterol metered dose inhalers, produce relaxation of airway smooth muscle. For these drug products, a PD endpoint, based either on increase in forced expiratory volume in 1 sec (FEV 1) or on measurement of PD20 or PC20 (the dose or concentration, respectively, of a challenge agent), is clinically relevant and may be used for BA and BE studies. An essential component of a BA or BE study based on a PD response is documentation of a dose-response relationship.

In vitro bioequivalence studies

In vitro studies, i.e. dissolution studies can be used in lieu of in vivo bioequivalence under certain circumstances called as biowaivers (exemptions).

1. The drugs product differs only in strength of the active substances it contains, provided all the following conditions hold, namely: (i) pharmacokinetics is linear, (ii) the qualitative composition is the same, (iii) the ratio between active substance and the excipients is the same, or the ratio between the excipients is the same, (iv) both products are produced by the same manufacturer at the same production site, (v) a bioavailability or bioequivalence study has been performed with the original product, and (vi) under the same test conditions, the *in vitro* dissolution rate is the same.
2. The drugs product has been slightly reformulated or the manufacturing method has been slightly modified by the original manufacturer in ways that can convincingly be argued to be irrelevant for the bioavailability.
3. The drugs product meets all of the following requirements: (i) The product is in the form of solution or solubilized form (elixir, syrup tincture, etc), (ii) The product contains active ingredient in the same concentration as the approved drug product, and (iii) The product contains no excipients known to significantly affect absorption of the active ingredient.
4. An acceptable IVIVC and the *in vitro* dissolution rate of the new product is equivalent with that of the already approved medicinal product. Moreover, (i) the product is intended for topical administration (cream, ointment, gel, etc) for local effect, (ii) the product is for oral administration but not intended to be absorbed (antacid or radioopaque medium), and (iii) the product is administered by inhalation as a gas or vapour.

Bioequivalence study designs

There are various types of study designs some of most commonly used ones are discussed here.

1. **Parallel design:** The aim of experimental designs is to minimize the experimental variabilities and to get more accurate and precise results. In a parallel design, the two formulations are administered to two groups of volunteers. The formulations are administered randomly to the volunteers to avoid any bias. The most negative point of this design is that inter-subject variation is not corrected which is far much greater than variation between formulations. It is most preferred when (i) the inter-subject variability is

relatively small as compared to intra subject variability; or (ii) the drug is potentially very toxic or potent or has very long elimination half life.

2. **Cross over design:** Usually cross over designs are used to minimize the effect of inter-subject variability by using each subject as his/her own control. Generally two types of designs are used in bioavailability or bioequivalence studies. The two types of designs are,
   (a) Latin square cross-over design
   (b) Balanced incomplete block design
   (a) Latin square cross over design: It is a standard approach for conducting a comparative BA study. In this design each subject receives each formulation and each formulation is administered just once in each study period. The design is shown in Table 7.3 and the advantages and disadvantages are summarized in Table 7.4.

Table 7.3 Latin square design.

Two way crossover				
Group no.	Subjects in group	Treatment for period no.		
		I	II	
1	1,2,3,4,5,6	A	B	
2	7,8,9,10,11,12	B	A	
Three way crossover				
Group no.	Subjects in group	Treatment for period no.		
		I	II	III
1	1,2,3,4,5,6	A	C	B
2	7,8,9,10,11,12	B	A	C
3	11,12,13,14,15,16,17,18	C	B	A

Table 7.4 Advantages and disadvantages of Latin Square design.

Advantages	**Disadvantages**
1. It minimizes the effect of intersubject variability. 2. It minimizes the carry over effect of one drug which is administered in first study on the dosage forms which is to be administered on subsequent administration. 3. It minimizes the time effect. 4. It requires very less number of subjects to get meaningful results.	1. It requires longer time to complete the study since a washout period is needed between two study periods. 2. Increased number of study periods leads to high subject dropouts. 3. Very tedious if the number of formulations is large.

(b) Balanced incomplete block design: A balanced incomplete block design (BIBD) eliminates many of the difficulties encountered within the Latin square design. The main features of this design are (i) Each subject receives not more than two formulations, and (ii) each formulation is administered the same number of times to same number of volunteers Table 7.5.

Table 7.5 BIBD for four formulations (A, B, C, D).

Subject	Treatment for period no.	
	I	II
1	A	B
2	B	A
3	A	C
4	C	A
5	A	D
6	D	A
7	B	C
8	C	B
9	B	D
10	D	B
11	C	D
12	D	C

Terms used in the Bioequivalence studies:

- **Brand name (The trade name of the drug):** This name is privately owned by the manufacturer or distributor and is used to distinguish the specific drug product from competitor's products (e.g., Tylenol, McNeil Laboratories).
- **Chemical name:** The name used by organic chemists to indicate the chemical structure of the drug (e.g., N-acetyl-p- aminophenol).
- **Abbreviated New Drug Application (ANDA).** Drug manufacturers must file an ANDA for approval to market a generic drug product. The generic manufacturer is not required to perform clinical efficacy studies or non-clinical toxicology studies for the ANDA.
- **Drug product:** The finished dosage form (e.g., tablet, capsule, or solution) that contains the active drug ingredient, generally, but not necessarily, in association with inactive ingredients.

- **Generic name:** The established, non-proprietary, or common name of the active drug in a drug product (e.g., acetaminophen).
- **Generic substitution:** The process of dispensing a different brand or an unbranded drug product in place of the prescribed drug product. The substituted drug product contains the same active ingredient or therapeutic moiety as the same salt or ester in the same dosage form but is made by a different manufacturer.
- **Therapeutic equivalence:** This term indicates that two or more drugs that contain the same therapeutically active ingredient elicit identical pharmacological effects and can control the disease to the same extent.
- **Pharmaceutical equivalence:** This term implies that two or more drugs products are identical in strength quality, purity, content uniformly and disintegration and dissolution characteristics. They may, differ in containing different excipients.
- **Reference Product:** A reference product is a pharmaceutical product with which the new product is intended to be interchangeable in clinical practice. The reference product would normally be the innovator product for which efficacy, safety and quality have been established. When the innovator product is not available the product which is the market leader may be used as a reference product, provided that it has been authorized for marketing and its efficacy, safety and quality have been established and documented.
- **Generic products:** Products whose active pharmaceutical ingredients, dosage form strengths and regimen are the same as those of new products. Generic and new products should be the same in the application area of dosage and their physiochemical characteristics should be similar to those of new products.
- **Bioequivalence range:** Acceptable range of bioequivalence is generally 0.8% - 1.25% for the test or reference ratio of average values, when the parameters are logarithmically transformed. The acceptable range is generally + 0.2 for the relative difference *in vivo* parameters between reference and test products, when the raw data arc used.

Additional information on BA/ BE requirements in India can be retrieved from https://cdsco.gov.in/opencms/opencms/en/bioequi_bioavail/, maintained by Central Drugs Standard Control Organization, Directorate General of Health Services, Ministry of Health & Family Welfare, Government of India. The site provides link for

1	List of Approved BA/BE Centers
2	Documents to be submitted for Bioequivalence Study for export applications
3	Guidance document for approval of BA/BE NOC for export purpose as per schedule Y & test license in form 11 of Drugs and Cosmetics rules, 1945
4	Document required for approval of BA-BE center
5	Neutral Code – labelling
6	Revised Checklist for Pre-screening of BA/BE Applications (Draft 2014) effective from 1st Feb 2014
7	Guidance Document for BA/BE NOC Applications for Export Purpose (Draft 2014)

Methods of Enhancement of Bioavailability

The drug exhibits bioavailability problem mainly because of following reasons:

- Poor aqueous solubility and/or slow dissolution rate
- Poor permeability through the biomembrane owing to inadequate partition coefficient.
- Stability issue in biological fluid of choice.

The approaches used for enhancement of bioavailability deals with the problems as discussed above and further correct the problem for enhanced solubility.

A. Methods utilized for enhancement of solubility/dissolution rate

1. Physical methods

(a) Particle size reduction (Micronization and nanonization): The process of size reduction involves the reduction of size of the powder leading to increased effective surface area resulting in enhancement of solubility and dissolution velocity of the drug. Micronization and nanonization techniques are used to improve dissolution rates of drugs into the biological environment, in order to improve the oral bioavailability. Micronization of drugs is done by milling techniques using jet mill, rotor stator, colloid mills or fluid energy mill to reduce the particle size to 1-10 microns. Drugs like spironolactone were 20 times more bioavailable while dose of griesofulvin reduced to half. Different principles used for nanonization are pearl milling (NanoCrystals®), high pressure homogenization (DissoCubes®), solution enhanced dispersion by supercritical fluids (SEDS), rapid expansion from supercritical to aqueous solution (RESAS), spray freezing into liquid (SFL).

(b) **Modification of the crystal habit:** Polymorphs of drugs are chemically identical, but they exhibit different physical properties including solubility, melting point, density, texture, compression characteristics and stability etc. So, if a drug is known to have polymorphs, it is necessary to detect its metastable form as it has higher energy and thus, higher solubility and subsequently higher bioavailability. Melting followed by a rapid cooling or recrystallization from different solvents can produce metastable forms of a drug. Similarly, the amorphous form of drug is always more suitable than crystalline form because of its large surface area and less energy requirement to dissolve into a solvent. Generally, the anhydrous form of a drug has greater solubility than the hydrates. This is because the hydrates are already in interaction with water and therefore have less energy for crystal breakup in comparison to the anhydrates (i.e. thermodynamically higher energy state) for further interaction with water. For e.g. chloramphenicol palmitate exists in three polymeric forms A, B and C, the bioavailability of form B is the best.

(c) **Use of surfactants:** The surfactants enhance dissolution rate of drug as well as permeation. The dissolution rate is increased by increase in wetting of solid and penetration of solvent into the solid drug particles. Non-ionic surfactants are mainly used as they do not have ill effects on the cells or membranes of cells.

(d) **Precipitation:** In this method the poorly aqueous soluble drug is dissolved in an organic solvent like alcohol and deposited on an inert, hydrophilic solid matrix such as starch or microcrystalline cellulose by evaporation of solvent.

(e) **Drug dispersion in carriers:** The term "solid dispersions" refers to the dispersion of one or more active ingredients in an inert carrier or matrix in a solid state. They are generally prepared by solvent or co-precipitation method whereby both the guest solute and the solid carrier solvent are dissolved in a common volatile liquid such as alcohol. The liquid solvent is removed by evaporation under reduced pressure resulting in amorphous precipitation of guest in crystalline carrier. Once the solid dispersion is exposed to aqueous media and the carrier dissolved, the drug is released as very fine, colloidal particles. Because of greatly enhanced surface area obtained in this way, the dissolution rate and the bioavailability of poorly water soluble drugs are expected to be high. Two commercial products, a griesofulvin in polyethylene glycol 8000 solid dispersion (Gris-PEG, Novartis) and a nabilone in povidone solid dispersion (Cesamet, Lilly).

(f) **Inclusion complexation:** Complexation process, an effective tool to increase solubility of poorly soluble drugs, refers to association between two or more molecules to form a non-bonded entity with a well defined stoichiometry. In complexation weak forces such as London forces, hydrogen bonding and hydrophobic interactions occurs between the guest and the host molecule. Inclusion complexes are formed by the insertion of the non-polar molecule or the non-polar region of one molecule (known as guest) into the cavity of another molecule or group of molecules (known as host). Cyclodextrins and their derivatives are best utilized for preparation of inclusion complex to increase water solubility, dissolution rate and bioavailability of lipophilic drugs for oral or parenteral delivery. Cyclodextrins have a hydrophilic exterior and a hydrophobic internal cavity large enough to accommodate the lipophilic drug as guest. This cavity enables cyclodextrins to complex guest drug molecules and hence alters the properties of the drugs such as solubility, stability, bioavailability and toxicity profiles. Barbiturates, diuretics and a number of benzodiazepines are complexed with great improvement in bioavailability.

2. **Chemical methods**

(a) **Salt form of drug:** Drugs which have poor solubility and dissolution are converted into their salt forms having enhanced solubility and dissolution. Acidic drugs are reacted with alkalis to form alkali metal salts of drugs for e.g. diclofenac sodium. Basic drugs like atropine are reacted with acids to form strong acid salts. The size of the counter ion, physical and chemical properties of drugs and route of administration play very important role in salt selection.

(b) **Alteration of pH of microenvironment:** This is done by either in-situ salt formation or by addition of buffers to the formulation. For e.g. buffered aspirin tablets. Under the proper conditions, the solubility of an ionizable drug can increase exponentially by adjusting the pH of the solution. A drug that can be efficiently solubilized by pH control should be either weak acid with a low pKa or a weak base with a high pKa.

3. **Formulation based approaches**

(a) **Co-crystallization:** It is an alternative option to salt formation, particularly for neutral compounds or the compounds which have weak ionizable groups, to modify the chemical and/or physical properties of an active pharmaceutical ingredient (API) without making or breaking covalent bonds. It is also referred as molecular complexes. Three co-crystallizing agents, saccharin, nicotinamide and acetic acid are the most utilized agents for bioavailability improvement.

(b) **Co-solvence:** Weak electrolytes and non-polar molecules frequently have poor water solubility because of polarity difference between the solute and the solvent. The process is usually carries out by the addition of a water miscible solvent in which the drug has good solubility. It is well known that the addition of an organic co-solvent to water can dramatically change the solubility of drugs. This process is known as co-solvency, and the solvents used are known as co-solvents. The mechanism involved in the process of co-solvency is the reduction of interfacial tension between the aqueous solution and the hydrophobic solute, commonly referred to as solvent blending. Currently, the water-soluble organic solvents used are polyethylene glycol 40, ethanol, propylene glycol, sorbitol and glycerin.

(c) **Hydrotrophy:** The term "hydrotropy" indicate the increase in aqueous solubility and dissolution velocity of various poorly water soluble compounds due to the presence of a large amount of additives like concentrated solutions of sodium benzoate, sodium salicylate, urea, nicotinamide, sodium citrate and sodium acetate. The mechanism by which it improves solubility is more closely related to complexation involving a weak interaction between the hydrotropic agents (sodium benzoate, sodium acetate, sodium alginate, and urea) and the solute. Solubilization of theophylline with sodium acetate and sodium alginate is an example of hydrotrophy.

B. Bioavailability enhancement through enhancement of drug stability

1. **Avoidance of degradation in stomach:** An enteric coating is a barrier applied to oral medication that resists the destructive action of the gastric fluid and disintegrates in the intestinal tract thereby releasing the drug in the intestine. Enteric coating is done to prevent destruction of the drug by gastric enzymes or by the acidity of the gastric fluid. It also prevents nausea and vomiting caused by the drug's irritation of the gastric mucosa. Most enteric coatings work by presenting a surface that is stable at the highly acidic pH found in the stomach, but breaks down rapidly at a less acidic (relatively more basic) pH. For example, they will not dissolve in

the acidic juices of the stomach (pH ~3), but will dissolve in the higher pH (above pH 5.5) environment present in the small intestine. Materials used for enteric coatings include fatty acids like stearic acid, hydrogenated castor oil, waxes like carnauba wax, cellulose acetate phthalate and shellac. The enteric materials may be used to coat tablets, capsules or granules to be compressed into tablets or filled into capsules. Enteric coating to certain drugs with azoles groups (esomeprazole, omeprazole, pantoprazole and all grouped azoles), which are acid-unstable, have been found to improve the bioavailability.

2. **Avoidance of degradation in intestine:** There are various drugs that are stable in the acidic environment of stomach but cannot resist the pH and enzymatic conditions of the intestine. An increase in the residence time of such drugs in stomach leads to the enhanced absorption before it reaches the intestine. Enhancement of residence time in stomach can be done by various approaches for e.g. formulation of Gastro Retentive drug delivery system. The systems work on three basic mechanisms: floatation, size expansion and mucoadhesion.

Questions

Multiple Choice Questions

1. If the size of dose to be administered is same, then bioavailability of a drug from its dosage form depends upon:
   (a) Pharmaceutical factors of the drug
   (b) Patient related factors
   (c) Route of administration
   (d) All of the above
2. The term bioavailable fraction refers to the fraction of dose that enters:
   (a) Systemic circulation (b) Tissues
   (c) Systemic circulation and tissues (d) None of the above
3. When systemic availability of a drug after oral administration is compared with that of an oral standard of the same drug it is referred to as:
   (a) Systemic bioavailability (b) Relative bioavailability
   (c) Absolute bioavailability (d) All of the above

4. Select the right one. Drug washout period allowed for between any two studies in the same subject must be a minimum of:
   (a) Eight biological half lives
   (b) Ten biological half lives
   (c) Six biological half lives
   (d) Four biological half lives
5. For bioavailability calculations from urinary excretion studies, the percent drug to be excreted in urine should be at least,
   (a) 5 – 6%
   (b) 5-10%
   (c) 10-20%
   (d) 1-5%
6. In order to affirm that the test formulation is bioequivalent, the relative bioavailability should be in the range of:
   (a) 95-105%
   (b) 80-120%
   (c) 90-110%
   (d) None of the above
7. Generic name means:
   (a) Established, non-proprietary name
   (b) Established, proprietary name
   (c) Commercial name
   (d) None of the above
8. Which of the following result in enhancement of bioavailability?
   (a) Nanonization
   (b) Complexation with beta CD
   (c) Hydrotophy
   (d) All of the above
9. Drug manufacturers must file an ANDA for approval to market a generic drug product
   (a) Generic product
   (b) Branded product
   (c) Both Branded and generic
   (d) All of the above
10. Point to point relationship between *in vitro* dissolution and *in vivo* rate of absorption is seen in case of which IVIVC correlation?
    (a) Level A
    (b) Level B
    (c) Level C
    (d) All of the above

Short Questions

1. Define bioavailability. What are its objectives?
2. Explain how determination of both rate and extent of absorption are important?

3. What is the difference between absolute and relative bioavailability?
4. Name the methods utilized for determination of bioavailability.
5. Explain in detail the parameters used in bioavailability determination by plasma level studies.
6. What is the principle behind assessment of bioavailability using urinary excretion data?
7. What factors should be considered in design of dissolution testing models?

Long Questions

1. What are the various levels of correlation?
2. What are the criteria for assigning biowaiver for *in vivo* bioavailability?
3. The data represents the average findings in antibiotic plasma samples taken from 10 humans (average weight 70 kg), tabulated in a four-way crossover design.

	Plasma concentration (g/ml)			
Time after Dose (hr)	IV Solution (2 mg/kg)	Oral Solution (10 mg/kg)	Oral Tablet (10 mg/kg)	Oral Capsule (10 mg/kg)
0.5	5.94	23.4	13.2	18.7
1.0	5.30	26.6	18.0	21.3
1.5	4.72	25.2	19.0	20.1
2.0	4.21	22.8	18.3	18.2
3.0	3.34	18.2	15.4	14.6
4.0	2.66	14.5	12.5	11.6
6.0	1.68	9.14	7.92	7.31
8.0	1.06	5.77	5.00	4.61
10.0	0.67	3.64	3.16	2.91
12.0	0.42	2.30	1.99	1.83
24.0	29.0	145.0	116.0	116.0

(a) Which of the four drug products would be preferred as a reference standard for the determination of relative bioavailability? Why?

(b) From which oral drug product is the drug absorbed more rapidly?

(c) What is the absolute bioavailability of the drug from the oral solution?

(d) What is the relative bioavailability of the drug from the oral tablet compared to the reference standard?

(e) From the data, determine:

1. Apparent V_D
2. Elimination $t_{1/2}$
3. First-order elimination rate constant K_E
4. Total body clearance

(f) From the data above, graph the cumulative urinary excretion curves that would correspond to the plasma concentration time curves.

4. Define *bioequivalence requirement.* Why does the FDA require a bioequivalence requirement for the manufacture of a generic drug product?

Concepts of Pharmacokinetics

CHAPTER 8

LEARNING OBJECTIVES

- Understanding pharmacokinetics and the need to study it
- Significance of plasma drug concentration profile
- Introduction to pharmacokinetic models
- Basics of compartment and non-compartment models

Rational and optimal drug therapy implies maximum efficacy and minimal toxicity. The therapeutic efficacy, safety and toxicity of a drug depend upon the concentration of drug at the site of action. It is crucial to monitor this concentration, but it is difficult to access the concentration of the drug at the target tissue site, and the drug may also be widely distributed in the body. So, we measure the drug concentration in plasma, urine, saliva, or other easily accessible body fluids and correlate it with the drug concentration at the site of action. This is based on the principle that the drug distributes homogeneously in the body. Often, the information gained about the pharmacokinetics of one drug may help to predict the pharmacokinetic behavior of other drugs. The knowledge of pharmacokinetic behavior of drug coupled with pharmacokinetic parameters like volume of distribution, clearance and therapeutic index can be used for various therapeutic purposes. Pharmacokinetics also finds application in designing dosage regimens, including dose size selection and the number of times it has to be administered to the patient (dosing frequency) within 24 hours. It also helps in determination of dose size for achieving steady state plasma concentration called as "loading dose" and also the dose size for maintaining the concentration in the therapeutic window called as "maintenance dose" in case of i.v infusion. As an important application, it helps in the individualization of the dosage regimen based on age, weight, and disease conditions. Strict monitoring of pharmacokinetic parameters results in therapy that is safe and efficacious.

Pharmacokinetics (PK) is the study of how a drug behaves in the body. In other words, pharmacokinetics is the study of "what the body does to a drug". Some authors describe pharmacokinetics as the study of the kinetics of drug absorption, distribution, metabolism, and excretion (ADME). But overall, the term pharmacokinetics encompasses the fate of a drug after administration to the body, with respect to the drug's (or metabolite's) time course of input into the body, transfer within the body, and elimination from the body. Clinical pharmacokinetics pertains to the application of pharmacokinetic principles to individual patients, in order to safely and effectively manage the drug therapy. Toxicokinetics is an application of pharmacokinetic principles to the design, conduct, and interpretation of drug safety evaluation studies

Why there is a need to study pharmacokinetics?

1. Pharmacokinetic studies try to answer why only a fraction of the total drug dose reaches its target sit
2. It further helps select compounds that have the maximum potential to reach the target site (pre-clinical phase).
3. Selection of appropriate route of administration
4. To develop a relationship between plasma drug level and the efficacy and toxicity of the drug
5. To decide the frequency and duration of dosing to sustain the drug at the target site for disease treatment and management

Plasma Drug Concentration-time Profile

A definite correlation is found between the plasma concentration of a drug and the drug concentration at the site of action responsible for producing a pharmacological effect, which is required for therapeutic goal achievement. Various pharmacokinetic and pharmacodynamic parameters can be obtained from this relationship, which can be depicted by Fig. 8.1, derived from the hypothetical oral data provided.

Table 8.1 Blood concentration and associated data for a hypothetical drug.

Time t_n (hr)	Concentration C_P (µg/mL)	$[AUC]_{tn-1}^{tn}$	$[AUC]_0^t$
0	0.	0.	0.
1	3.13	1.57	1.57
2	4.93	4.03	5.60
3	5.86	5.40	10.99

Contd...

Time t_n (hr)	Concentration C_P (µg/mL)	$[AUC]_{tn-1}^{tn}$	$[AUC]_0^t$
4	6.25	6.06	17.05
5	6.28	6.26	23.31
6	6.11	6.20	29.51
7	5.81	5.96	35.47
8	5.45	5.63	41.10
9	5.06	5.26	46.35
10	4.66	4.86	51.21
12	3.90	8.56	59.77
14	3.24	7.14	66.91
16	2.67	5.92	72.83
18	2.19	4.86	77.69
24	1.20	10.17	87.85
28	0.81	4.02	91.87
32	0.54	2.70	94.57
36	0.36	1.80	96.37
48	0.10	2.76	99.13

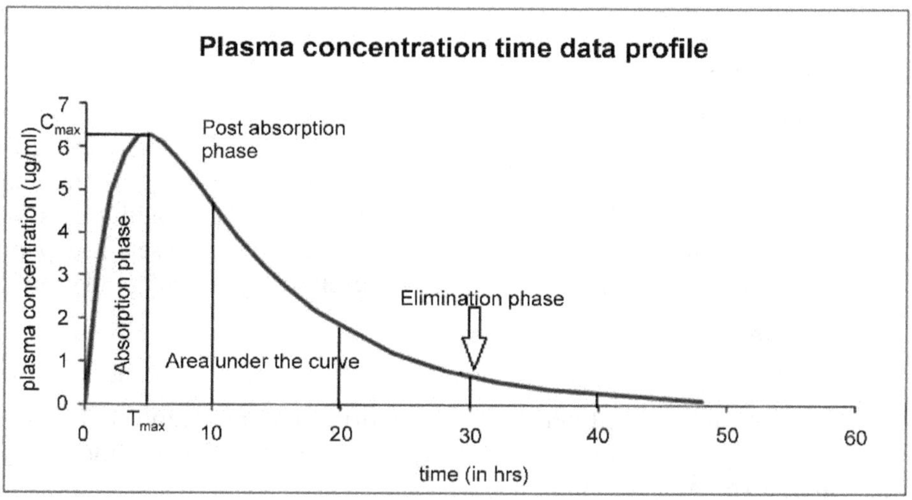

Fig. 8.1 Plasma concentration time profile graph of hypothetical oral drug absorption after single administration.

Pharmacokinetic Parameters

1. **Peak plasma concentration:** The point when the drug concentration is at its highest level in the blood plasma is called the peak plasma concentration (C_{max}). It is also called the maximum plasma concentration, expressed as µg/mL. The peak plasma concentration is achieved at close to zero time in the case of I.V. bolus administration, but in the case of I.V. infusion, it is attained after some time. Extravascular administration of a drug leads to a delay in the attainment of peak concentration as it is dependent on the rate of absorption. It is very important that the peak plasma concentration lies within the therapeutic range; otherwise, toxic effects can be seen if it goes beyond the maximum safe concentration (MSC) and it cannot produce its effect if it lies below the minimum effective concentration (MEC). The value of peak plasma concentration depends upon the size of the administered dose, the rate of absorption of the drug (in the case of extravascular administration), and the rate of elimination."

   Significance

   - It is used to determine the comparative bioavailability and bioequivalence of two products.
   - Comparison of two different routes of administration and different dosage forms with each other.
   - Correlates with the intensity of action of drugs as well as its toxic effects when above MSC.

2. **Time of peak plasma concentration:**

   The time taken by a drug to reach its peak plasma concentration is called T_{max}. It is expressed in hours and is a useful parameter in determining the rate of absorption. If rate of absorption is fast the value of T_{max} is less and vice versa. It is a well-known fact that for I.V. bolus route of administration, the value of Tmax is less than 3 minutes, while in other cases, it depends upon the rate of permeation of the drug to reach the systemic circulation.

   Significance

   - It is used for comparative bioavailability and/or bioequivalence.
   - To determine the preferred route of drug administration and dosage forms, especially in the case of drugs for acute medical conditions (e.g., pain, fever, and vomiting)."

3. **Area under the curve:**

   It is a very important parameter and includes all the area covered under the plasma-concentration time profile curve. "It reflects the actual body exposure to a drug after administration of a dose of the drug and is expressed as mg·h/L. This area under the curve **is** dependent on the rate of elimination of the drug from the body and the dose administered. The AUC should be calculated from zero to a time at which the concentration has returned to its baseline levels." Also, when making comparisons, you should ensure that all AUCs are computed for the same time intervals."

Significance

- "It is used as a means of evaluating the volume of distribution, clearance, and bioavailability of extravascular drug administration."
- To compare the bioavailability of two products or routes of administration."

Pharmacodyanamic Parameters

- "Minimum Effective Concentration (MEC): It is defined as the minimum concentration of unchanged drug in plasma required to produce the therapeutic effect. It bears a correlation with the concentration of the drug at the receptor site, which is needed to elicit the desired pharmacological response." The concentration of a drug below MEC is said to be at the subtherapeutic level and is not able to produce any therapeutic response.
- **"Maximum Safe Concentration (MSC):** It is the concentration of a drug in plasma above which the drug produces its adverse or unwanted effects. A drug concentration above MSC is said to be at the toxic level, and the boundary is termed the minimum toxic concentration."
- **Onset of Action:** The beginning of the desired therapeutic response of a drug is called the onset of action. It occurs when the plasma drug concentration just exceeds the MEC value.
- **"Onset Time:** It is the time required for the drug to start producing its pharmacological response." It corresponds to the time for the plasma concentration to reach MEC after drug administration."
- **Duration of Action:** The time period during which the plasma concentration of a drug is maintained above the MEC level is called the duration of drug action." The concentration of a drug after absorption starts increasing, reaches the MEC value, and goes beyond it. After a certain time, when the rate of elimination >> rate of absorption, the concentration of the drug starts decreasing, and finally, it declines below the MEC value."

- **Duration of Action**: The time period during which the plasma concentration of drug is maintained above the MEC level is called as duration of drug action. The concentration of drug after absorption starts increasing and reaches MEC value and goes beyond it after certain time when rate of elimination >> rate of absorption, the concentration of drug starts decreasing and finally it declines below the value of MEC. So, the duration in between is termed the duration of action."
- **Intensity of Action:** It is the maximum pharmacological response produced by the maximum concentration of the drug, which in turn corresponds to the peak plasma concentration of the drug." It is also called the peak response.
- **Therapeutic Range:** The therapeutic range of a drug is the dosage range or blood plasma or serum concentration usually expected to achieve the desired therapeutic effect. The drug concentration between MEC and MSC represents the therapeutic range. It is also called the therapeutic window."
- **Therapeutic Index:** The ratio of MSC to MEC is called the therapeutic index." "It is also defined as the ratio of the dose required to produce toxic or lethal effects to the dose required to produce the desired therapeutic effect." The larger the therapeutic index (TI), the safer the drug is, and the dose can be varied." In the case of drugs with a very low TI value, the drug must be administered very carefully, as there are chances of toxicity even when increasing the dose very slightly.

Basic Pharmacokinetics and Pharmacokinetic Models

The movement of drugs inside the body is very dynamic, from blood to extracellular fluid to intracellular compartments, and from this state to metabolism and finally excretion. The biologic nature of drug distribution and disposition is complex, and drug events often happen simultaneously. So, it is of utmost importance to consider these important factors when designing drug therapy regimens." This requires a mathematical study regarding the state and rate of different ongoing processes with defined parameters to estimate drug dosing and to predict the time course of drug efficacy for a given dose."

A *model* is a hypothesis using mathematical terms to describe quantitative relationships concisely. "The predictive capability of a model lies in the proper selection and development of mathematical function(s) that parameterize the essential factors governing the kinetic process.

A pharmacokinetic function relates an *independent variable* to a *dependent variable*, often through the use of parameters. "For example, a pharmacokinetic model may predict the drug concentration in the plasma 1 hour after an oral administration of a 20-mg dose. The independent variable is time, and the dependent variable is the drug concentration in the plasma." Based on a set of time-versus-drug concentration data, a model equation is derived to predict the drug concentration with respect to time. In this case, the drug concentration depends on the time after the administration of the dose, where the time-concentration relationship is defined by a pharmacokinetic parameter, k, and the elimination rate constant."

Such mathematical models can be devised to simulate the rate processes of drug absorption, distribution, and elimination to describe and *predict* drug concentrations in the body as a function of time. Pharmacokinetic models find their applications in:

1. Prediction of plasma, tissue, and urine drug levels with any dosage regimen, and relating it to the optimum therapeutic response or dosage regimen.
2. Calculate the optimum dosage regimen for each patient individually, referred to as individualization of dosage regimen.
3. Estimate the possible accumulation of drugs and/or metabolites.
4. Correlate drug concentrations with the pharmacologic or toxicologic activity of the drug.
5. Evaluate differences in the rate and extent of availability between formulations (bioequivalence).
6. Describe the effect of physiological alterations on the pharmacokinetic parameters, finally altering pharmacodynamic parameters.

Compartment Models

If the tissue/organ drug concentrations and protein binding of drugs are known, physiologic pharmacokinetic models, based on actual tissues and their respective blood flow, can easily describe data correlating with the process." Physiologic pharmacokinetic models are frequently used in describing drug distribution in animals, because tissue samples are easily available for assay. On the other hand, tissue samples are often not available for human subjects, and there is vast complexity in the body."

So, drug kinetics in the body is frequently simplified to be represented by one or more tanks, or compartments, that communicate reversibly with each other." A compartment is not a real physiologic or anatomic region but is considered a tissue or group of tissues that have similar blood flow and drug affinity." Within each compartment, the drug is considered to be uniformly distributed. Mixing of the drug within a compartment is rapid and homogeneous and is considered to be "well stirred," so that the drug concentration represents an average concentration, and each drug molecule has an equal probability of leaving the compartment. Rate constants are used to represent the overall rate processes of drug entry into and exit from the compartment. The model is an open system because a drug enters the system and can also be eliminated from the system simultaneously. Compartment models are based on linear assumptions using linear differential equations. Depending upon the arrangement of compartments, compartment modeling is further classified into:

1. Mammillary model
2. Catenary model

1. **Mammillary Model:** A compartmental model provides a simple way of grouping all the tissues into one or more compartments based on some common characteristics (e.g., blood flow)." Drugs move to and from the central or plasma compartment in a reversible manner. The mammillary model is a strongly connected system because one can estimate the amount of drug in any compartment of the system after the drug is introduced into a given compartment. In the one-compartment model, a drug is both added to and eliminated from a central compartment." The central compartment is assigned to represent plasma and highly perfused tissues that rapidly equilibrate with the drug. When an intravenous dose of drug is given, the drug enters directly into the central compartment. Elimination of the drug occurs from the central compartment because the organs involved in drug elimination, primarily the kidney and liver, are well-perfused tissues.

   In a two-compartment model, a drug can move between the central or plasma compartment and the tissue compartment. Although the tissue compartment does not represent a specific tissue, the mass balance accounts for the drug present in all the tissues. In this model, the total amount of drug in the body is simply the sum of the drug present in the central compartment plus the drug present in the tissue compartment.

   The compartmental models are particularly useful when little information is known about the tissues.

   Several types of compartment models are described in Fig. 8.2. The pharmacokinetic rate constants are represented by the letter *k*. Compartment 1 represents the plasma or central compartment, and compartment 2 represents the tissue compartment. The drawing of models has three functions. The model (1) enables one to write differential equations to describe drug concentration changes in each compartment, (2) gives a visual representation of the rate processes, and (3) shows how many pharmacokinetic constants are necessary to describe the process adequately."

Model 1: One compartment open model, intravenous administration

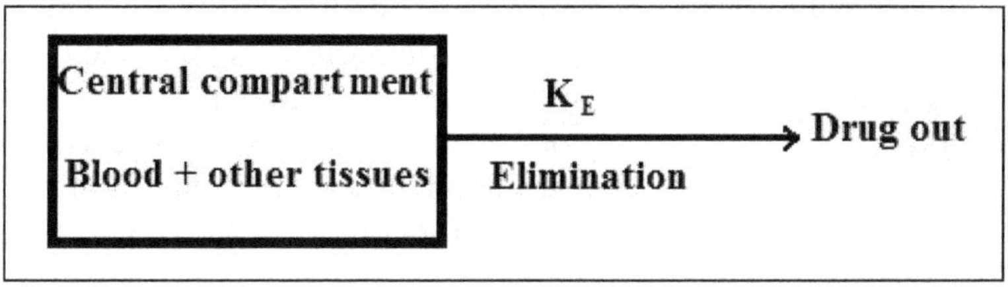

Model 2: One compartment open model, extravascular administration

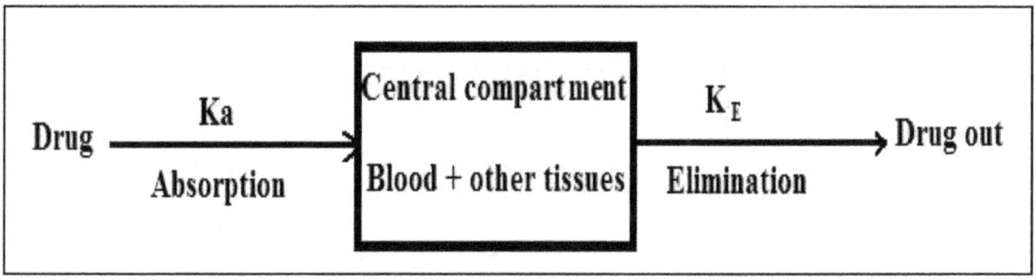

Model 3: Two compartment open model, Intravenous administration

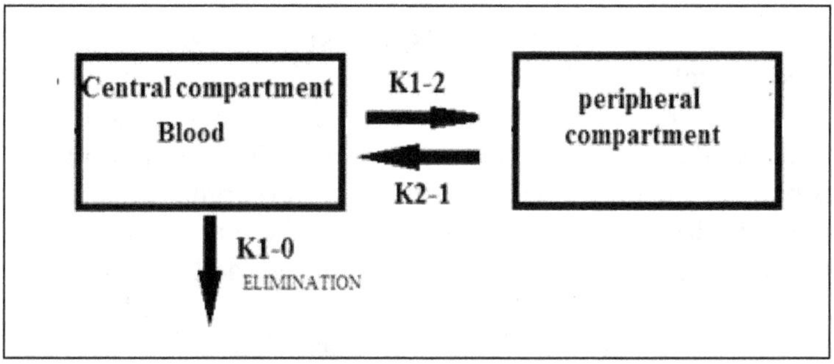

Model 4: Two compartment open model, extravascular administration

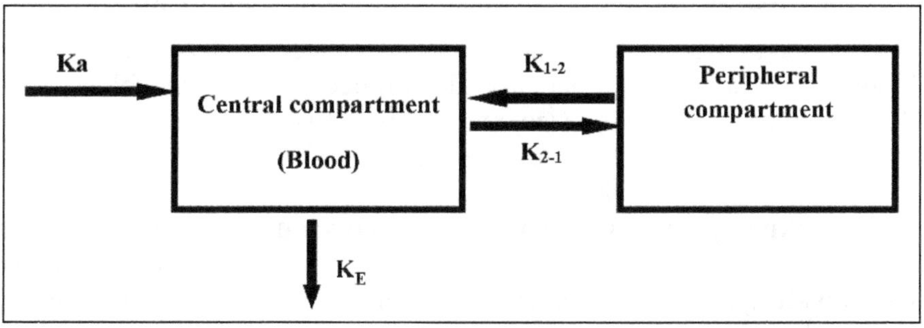

Fig. 8.2 Schematic Diagrams of Compartment models.

2. **Catenary Model:** In pharmacokinetics, the mammillary model must be distinguished from another type of compartmental model called the catenary model. The catenary model consists of compartments joined to one another like the compartments of a train (Fig. 8.3)." In contrast, the mammillary model consists of one or more compartments around a central compartment like satellites. Because the catenary model does not apply to the way most functional organs in the body are directly connected to the plasma, it is not used as often as the mammillary model.

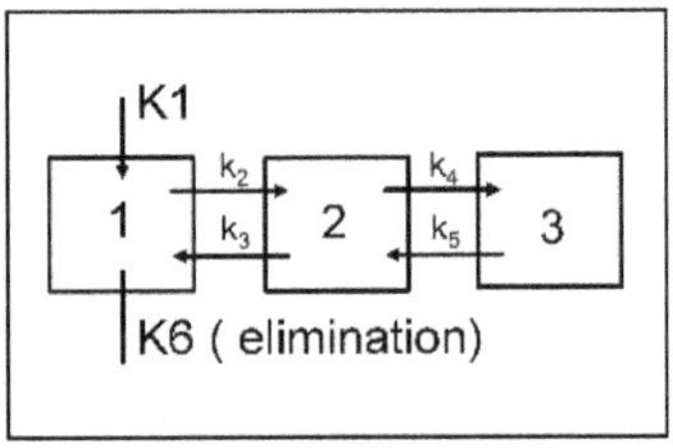

Fig. 8.3 A Catenary model.

Physiologic pharmacokinetic models, also known as blood flow or perfusion rate-based models, are pharmacokinetic models based on known anatomic and physiologic data." The models describe the data kinetically, with the consideration that blood flow is responsible for distributing the drug to various parts of the body." Uptake of a drug into organs is determined by the binding of the drug in these tissues. Because there are many tissue organs in the body, each tissue volume must be obtained, and its drug concentration described. The model shows that adipose tissue accumulates drugs slowly because of low blood supply and is classified as 'slowly equilibrating tissues'." The model would potentially predict realistic tissue drug concentrations, which the two-compartment model fails to do.

Drug concentrations in the various tissues are predicted by organ tissue size, blood flow, and experimentally determined drug tissue–blood ratios. Second, blood flow, tissue size, and the drug tissue–blood ratios may vary due to certain pathophysiologic conditions. Thus, the effect of these variations on drug distribution must be taken into account in physiologic pharmacokinetic models. The model shows that adipose tissue accumulates drugs slowly because of low blood supply and is classified as (**slowly equilibrating tissues**). In contrast, vascular tissues, like the lung, equilibrate rapidly ('rapidly equilibrating tissues') with the blood and start to decline as soon as the drug level in the blood starts to fall." The physiologic pharmacokinetic model provides a realistic means of modeling tissue drug levels. The real significance of the physiologically based model is the potential application of this model in the prediction of human pharmacokinetics from animal data. "Unfortunately, the simulated tissue levels cannot be verified in humans because drug levels in tissues are not available." The common representation of a physiological model is shown in Fig. 8.4. Major tissues/organs are represented by compartments from which blood flow carries a drug into and out of the tissue/organ. The rate of drug presentation to a particular tissue or organ is dependent upon the rate of perfusion of blood to the tissue or organ and the permeability of the drug, which is dependent on its partition coefficient between blood and tissue components."

Compartments such as the lungs, liver, and kidneys get maximum blood inflow and are thus present at the top, followed by other highly perfused organs (termed HPT), and then organs which are poorly perfused by blood (PPT)."

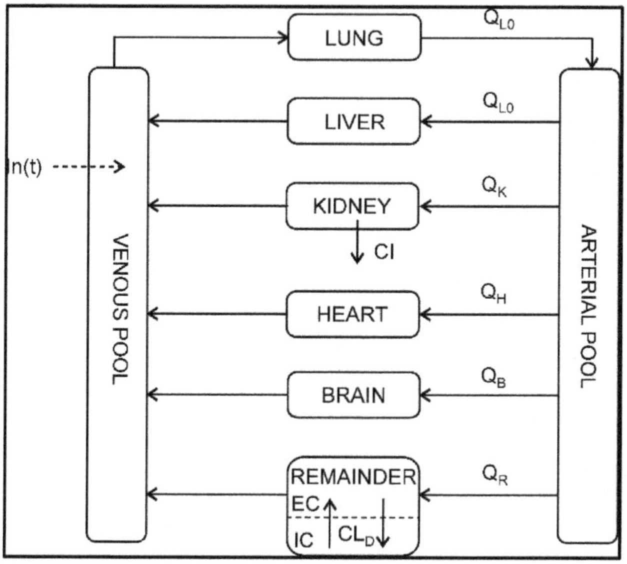

Fig. 8.4 Schematic representation of a physiological pharmacokinetic model.

The physiologic pharmacokinetic model has physiological/anatomical components and biochemical/physicochemical components." The first part includes tissue volumes, blood flow rate, cardiac output, glomerular filtration rate, and alveolar ventilation rate, while biochemical components include tissue-blood partition coefficient, blood-air partition coefficient, and enzymatic rate constants."

The physiologic pharmacokinetic model can be described for a single well-mixed tissue compartment as follows:"

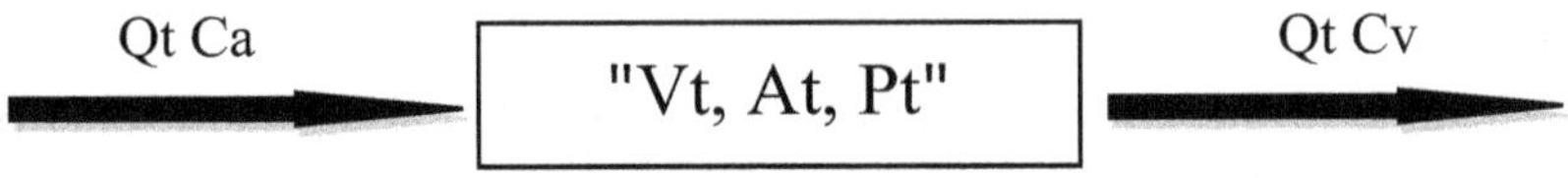

Mass-balance equation: dtdAt = VtdtdC = QtCa – QtCv .....(8.1)

Qt = tissue blood flow, Cv = venous blood concentration, Ca = arterial blood concentration"

Pt = tissue/blood partition coefficient, Vt = volume of tissue, and At = amount of chemical in tissue"

Comparative highlights of Compartment and Physiological pharmacokinetic models

Compartment Model	Physiological Model
1. Hypothetical approach with no relation with real anatomy or physiology.	2. Realistic approach based on physiological and anatomic information
1. Simple and flexible approach.	2. Difficult experimentally.
1. Data fitting is required for predicting drug concentration in a particular compartment	2. Data fitting is not required since drug concentration is practically determined
1. It enables monitoring of drug concentration change with limited amount of data.	2. Exhaustive data is required to monitor time course of drug in body
1. Used when there is little information related to blood flow and tissue characteristics.	2. Used when tissue drug concentration blood flow and binding ability of drug is known.
1. Extrapolation of data to humans is not possible.	2. Extrapolation of data to human is easy.
1. Mechanism cannot be explained	2. ADME mechanism are explained
1. Effect of pathological conditions cannot be predicted	2. Effect of pathophysiological conditions on the drug disposition can be easily predicted
1. It is the most widely used method.	2. Less commonly used owing to its complexity

Non- Compartment Modeling

The noncompartment modeling approach for data analysis does not require any specific compartmental model for the system (body) and can be applied to virtually any pharmacokinetic data." The main purpose of the noncompartmental approach is to estimate various pharmacokinetic parameters such as systemic clearance, volume of distribution, mean residence time, and bioavailability without assuming or understanding any structural or mechanistic properties of the drug in the body." In addition, noncompartmental methods allow the estimation of pharmacokinetic parameters from drug concentration profiles without the complicated process required for compartment models."

Non-compartmental Analysis based on Statistical Moment Theory

The noncompartmental method based on statistical moment theory does not require the assumption of a specific compartment model for either the drug or metabolite. "In fact, this method can be applied to any compartmental model, provided that linear pharmacokinetics is assumed. The time course of drug concentration in plasma can usually be regarded as a statistical distribution curve." The route of drug administration did not affect the process, and the first three (zero to second) statistical moments are defined as follows:"

Zero moment AUC = ∫0∞Cdt .....(8.2)"

First moment MRT = AUCAUMC=∫0∞Cdt∫0∞TCdt .....(8.3)"

Second moment VRT = ∫0∞Cdt∫0∞T2Cdt .....(8.4)"

where MRT stands for mean residence time and VRT stands for variance of the mean residence time of a drug in the body." AUC, MRT, and VRT are termed the zero, first, and second moments, respectively, of the drug concentration-time curve. The area under the curve of a plot of the product of concentration and time versus time from zero to infinity is often referred to as the area under the (first) moment curve, AUMC. The moments defined above can be calculated by numerical integration using the trapezoidal rule from concentration-time data following drug administration. In a single-dose pharmacokinetic study, the calculation of AUC from zero time to infinity is carried out in two steps." The area under the curve from zero to time t is calculated by means of the trapezoidal rule. To this partial area (AUC)0t under the curve, the AUC from t to infinity is added, which is:"

$$\int_t^{\infty} Cdt = \lambda \mathrm{Ct} \quad .....(8.5)$$

where λ is 2.303 times the slope of the terminal exponential phase of a plot of log drug concentration versus time."

"Bioavailability, i.e., a fraction (F) of the oral dose that actually reaches the systemic circulation, can be estimated by statistical moment theory as follows:"

F = Doral·AUCIVDIV·AUCoral .....(8.6)"

"F is simply the ratio of the zero moments after oral and intravenous (I.V.) administration, respectively, and adjusted for differences in the size of the dose."

The first moment of the blood level-time curve, mean residence time, is the statistical moment analog to half-life ($t_{1/2}$)."

It is evident that statistical moment theory permits a wide range of analyses that, in most instances, will be adequate to characterize the pharmacokinetics of the drug, including bioavailability, clearance, and apparent volume of distribution, etc. It is also useful in determining half-life, rate of absorption, and absorption rate constant without the complex procedures of compartment modeling, irrespective of the number of compartments." There are certain problems that are not addressed by this theory:" Non-linear events are not adequately treated by statistical moment theory."

Questions

Multiple Choice Questions

1. Plasma drug concentration versus time graph as shown in the picture, what should be the correct option for the marked place?
   (a) Maximum safe concentration
   (b) Minimum effective concentration
   (c) Therapeutic range
   (d) Onset of action

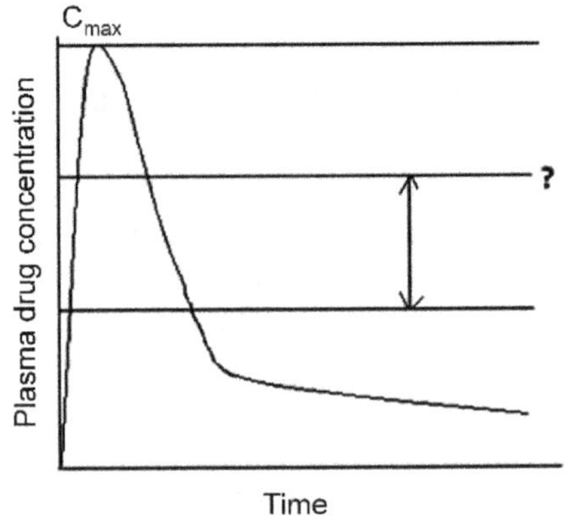

2. In plasma drug concentration versus time graph as shown in the picture, what should be the correct option for the marked place?
   (a) Elimination phase
   (b) Post absorption phase
   (c) Absorption phase
   (d) Duration of action

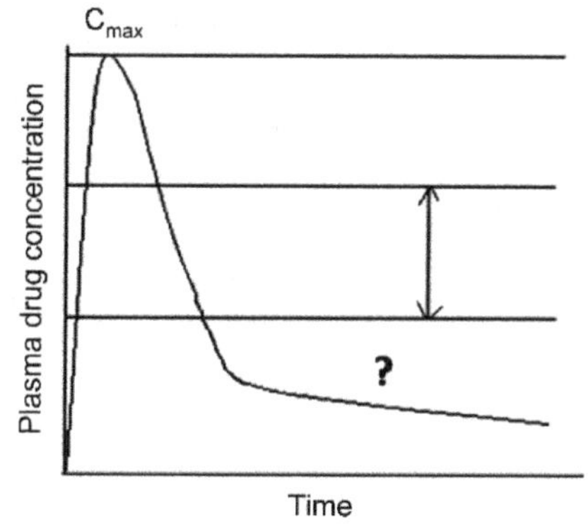

3. In plasma drug concentration versus time graph as shown in the picture, what should be the correct option for the marked place?
   (a) Elimination phase
   (b) Post absorption phase
   (c) Absorption phase
   (d) Duration of action

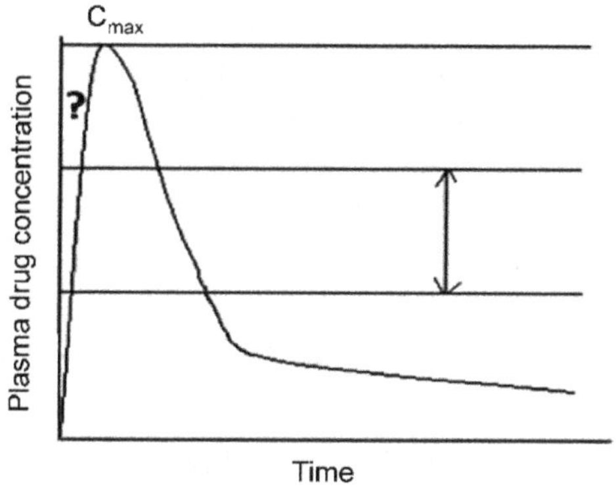

4. In plasma drug concentration versus time graph as shown in the picture, what should be the correct option for the marked place?
   (a) Elimination phase
   (b) Post absorption phase
   (c) Absorption phase
   (d) Duration of action

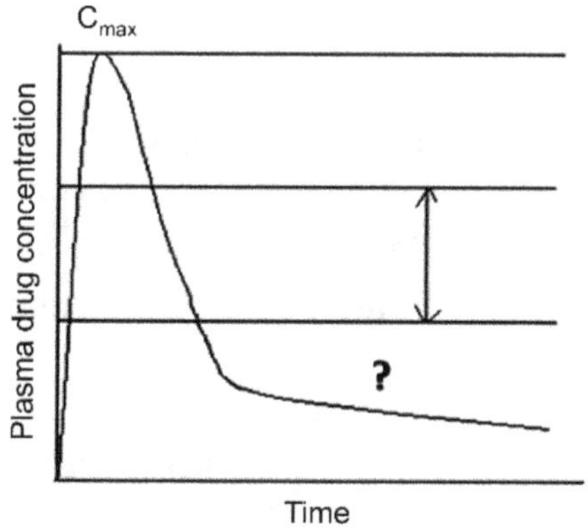

5. In plasma drug concentration versus time graph as shown in the picture, what should be the correct option for the marked place?
   (a) Maximum safe concentration
   (b) Minimum effective concentration
   (c) Therapeutic range
   (d) Onset of action

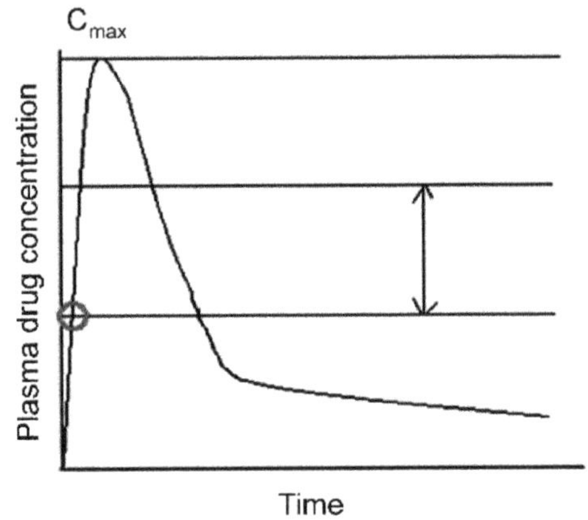

6. In plasma drug concentration versus time graph as shown in the picture, what should be the correct option for the marked place?
   (a) Maximum safe concentrate
   (b) Minimum effective concentration
   (c) Therapeutic range
   (d) Onset of action

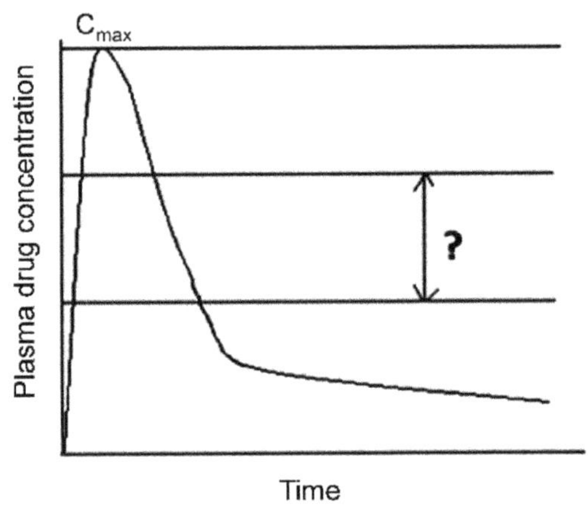

7. The time period for which the plasma concentration of drug remains above minimum effective concentration is known as ____________
   (a) Onset of time
   (b) Onset of action
   (c) Duration of drug of action
   (d) Therapeutic range

State True (T) or False (F)

1. The plasma concentration time profile of a certain drug is not dependent on the dosage form. **T or F**
2. For a zero-order elimination process the half-life is dependent on the plasma concentration at time point 0 (C0). **T or F**

3. Therapeutic drug level monitoring (TDM) can be useful to optimize the dosage regimen for an individual patient. **T or F**
4. Drugs with a low volume of distribution (V_d) have a narrow therapeutic window. **T or F**
5. In the case of permeability limited distribution, the blood flow determines the rate of uptake. **T or F**
6. The concentration time profiles of an oral tablet will be very similar to an i.v bolus injection of the same dose if the absorption is very fast and the oral bioavailability will be close to 100 %. **T or F**
7. Two compartment body model drugs are likely to show pronounced permeability-controlled distribution into at least some tissue components. **T or F**
8. "Linear pharmacokinetics" means that the plasma drug concentration versus time plots are directly related to the dose of the drug. **T or F**

Short Questions

1. Define MEC and MSC.
2. Define onset time and duration of action.
3. What are C_{max}, t_{max}, and AUC?
4. Define MRT.
5. What are AUMC and AUC?
6. What is intensity of action?
7. Define therapeutic range.

Long Questions

1. What is significance of plasma drug concentration time curve? How it is related to pharmacologic activity of drug.
2. Discuss the significance of plasma drug concentration.
3. Explain the purpose and advantages of pharmacokinetic models.
4. Differentiate between mammillary model and caternary model.
5. Explain physiologic model with appropriate diagram.
6. What do you understand by Non-compartmental analysis?
7. List the advantages and disadvantages of non-compartmental analysis.
8. Discuss the applications of pharmacokinetic models.
9. How pharmacokinetic models are useful tool in clinical pharmacy.

Compartment Modelling

CHAPTER
9

LEARNING OBJECTIVES

- Understanding the concept of compartment
- One compartment open model concept
- Pharmacokinetic treatment of plasma concentration data
- Pharmacokinetic treatment of urinary excretion data

The journey of a drug starts from administration to a patient followed by absorption of drug from site of absorption to reach systemic circulation (central compartment) followed by distribution and finally elimination. Compartmental modeling of pharmacokinetics considers the body as single or set of compartments interconnected to each other. Movements of drug from one compartment to another can be characterized by transfer rate constants: in linear kinetics, the rate of transfer is assumed to be directly proportional to the amount of drug available for transfer. In each compartment, characterized by its own volume, the drug concentrations are proportional to the amount. The compartments considered here do not have any realistic anatomical or physiological existence but are considered to mathematically characterize and explain the process and kinetics involved into it. A compartment involves several organs or tissues and is kinetically homogenous.

One Compartment Open Model

Oral route of drug administration is the most common and most desirable route of drug administration using tablets, capsules, or oral solutions. In developing pharmacokinetic models to describe and predict drug disposition kinetically, the model must account for both the route of administration and the kinetic behavior of the drug in the body. One compartment model (Fig. 9.1) is based on following assumptions:

- The body is considered to be a single compartment and it is assumed that is homogeneous in nature and the drug moves freely in the entire compartment.
- The distribution of drugs is very rapid throughout the compartment.
- Drug moves freely in and out of the compartment at defined rate.
- Elimination of drug always proceeds with first order kinetics.
- Rate of input is greater than rate of output.
- Plasma compartment is the single compartment considered here and represents all tissues and organs and any change in plasma profile reflects change in drug concentration in all over body.

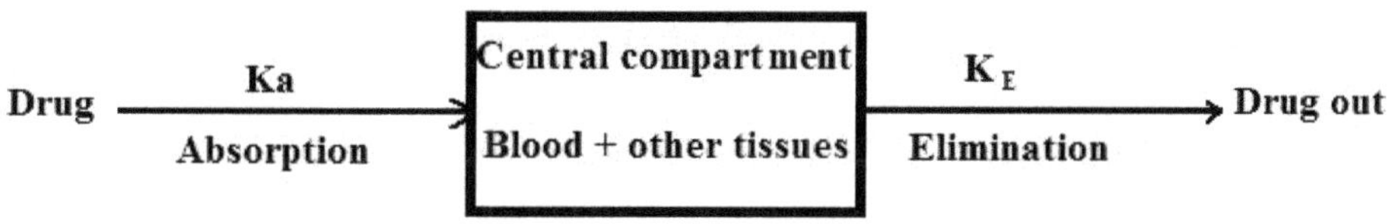

Fig. 9.1 Diagrammatic representation of one compartment open model.

One Compartment Open Model - Intravenous (i.v.) Bolus Administration

In the body, when a drug is given in the form of an i.v. bolus, the entire dose of drug enters the bloodstream immediately, and the drug absorption process is considered to be instantaneous and the rate of absorption is considered negligible. In most cases, the drug distributes via the circulatory system to potentially all the tissues in the body. Uptake of drugs by various tissues/ organs will occur at varying rates, depending on the blood flow to the tissue, the lipophilicity of the drug, the molecular weight of the drug, and the binding affinity of the drug for the tissue mass. Most drugs are eliminated from the body either through the kidney and/or by being metabolized in the liver. Because of rapid drug equilibration between the blood and tissue, drug elimination occurs as if the dose is all dissolved in a tank of uniform fluid (a single compartment) from which the drug is eliminated. The representation can be shown as :

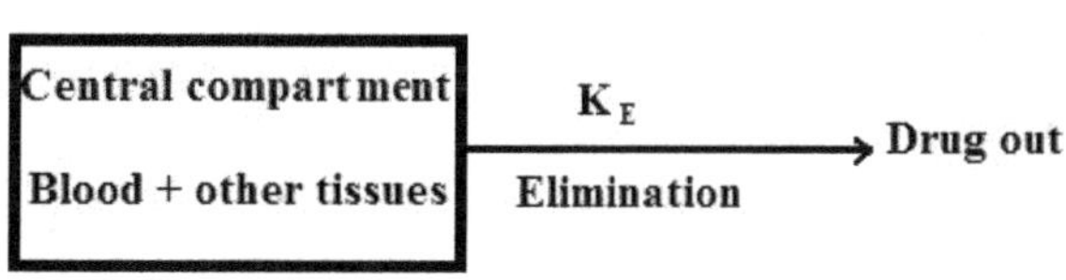

Fig. 9.2 Schematic representation of one compartment open model I.v. bolus administration.

The system can be represented mathematically as

$$dX/dt = \text{absorption rate} - \text{elimination rate} \quad .....(9.1)$$

Since absorption rate is negligible in case of i.v. bolus, the eq. 9.1 becomes:

$$dX/dt = -\text{ elimination rate} \quad .....(9.2)$$

Based on the assumption that elimination rate follows first order kinetics, the rate of decrease of the amount of drug in the body will only be dependent on the amount of drug present in the body at any time. Thus,

$$dX/dt = -K_E X \quad .....(9.3)$$

where dX/dt = rate of change of drug amount,

K_E = Elimination rate constant (negative sign indicates that the drug is being lost) and

X = amount of drug in the body at any time t.

Determination of Pharmacokinetic Parameters – i.v. Bolus

The one compartment open model does not predict actual drug levels in the tissues. However, the model assumes that changes in the plasma levels of a drug will result in proportional changes in tissue drug levels, since their kinetic profile is consistent with inclusion within the vascular compartment and the various drug concentrations within the compartment are in equilibrium. The drug in the body, X, cannot be measured directly; however, accessible body fluids (such as blood) can be sampled to determine drug concentrations. The drug concentration data is plotted against time and the curve is used to determine various pharmacokinetic parameters.

(i) **Elimination rate constant:** The rate of elimination for most drugs from a tissue or from the body is a first-order process, in which the rate of elimination is dependent on the amount or concentration of drug present and can be represented as:

$$\int_0^t dx/dt = \int_0^t -K_E\, dt \quad .....(9.4)$$

$$[\ln X]_0^{\,t} = -K_E\,[t]_0^{t} \quad .....(9.5)$$

$$\ln X = \ln Xo - K_E\, t \quad .....(9.6)$$

It can further be written as by applying logarithm values

$$\log X = \log Xo - K_E \frac{t}{2.303} \quad .....(9.7)$$

where X = drug in the body at time t and Xo = drug in the body at t = 0.

Since it is difficult to measure the amount of drug in the body, the concentration of drug in plasma is a measurable quantity which is directly related to amount of drug as ($X = V_d \times C$).

So we get a new equation.

$$\log C = \log Co - K_E \frac{t}{2.303} \quad \text{.....(9.8)}$$

When log C is plotted against t for this equation, a straight line is obtained. In practice, instead of transforming values of C to their corresponding logarithms, each value of C is placed at logarithmic intervals on semilog paper.

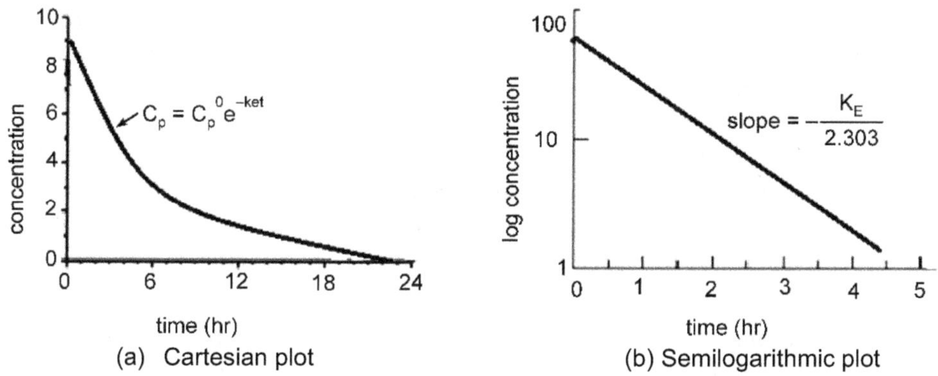

Fig. 9.3 (a) Cartesian plot of plasma concentration versus time for one compartment model following i.v. bolus injection and (b) semilogarithmic plot of plasma concentration versus time.

Rearranging equation 9.8 we can get

$$K_E \frac{t}{2.303} = \log \frac{Co}{C} = \log Co - \log C \quad \text{.....(9.9)}$$

$$K_E = \frac{2.303\,[\log Co - \log C]}{t} \quad \text{.....(9.10)}$$

Therefore, if log C is plotted against time (Fig. 9.3), the plot will be a straight line with an intercept of log Co and the slope of the line will be K_E/ 2.303. The elimination rate constant has dimensions of reciprocal of time and is represented as hr^{-1} or min^{-1}.

(ii) Elimination half life: Elimination half life is also called as biological half-life. It is defined as the time in which the amount of drug in the body as well as plasma concentration reduces to one-half or 50% its initial value. It is expressed in hours or minutes. For e.g. After giving a shot of i.v. bolus injection the plasma concentration was found to be 10 mg/ml, therefore the time required for the concentration to reach 5 mg/ml is termed as elimination half life or biological half life ($t_{1/2}$). Half-life is related to elimination rate constant by the following equation:

$$t_{1/2} = \frac{0.693}{K_E} \quad .....(9.11)$$

It can be seen clearly from the equation that elimination half life is constant and is not dependent upon the concentration or amount of drug present in the plasma.

(iii) Apparent volume of distribution: As per one compartment model, a drug equilibrates rapidly in the body and achieves a homogeneous state. When plasma or any other biologic compartment is sampled and analyzed for drug content, the results are usually reported in units of concentration instead of amount. The volume of distribution represents a volume that must be considered in estimating the amount of drug in the body from the concentration of drug found in the sampling compartment. The volume of distribution is also the apparent volume in which the drug is dissolved. Because the value of the volume of distribution does not have a true physiologic meaning in terms of an anatomic space, the term apparent volume of distribution is used.

The amount of drug in the body is not determined directly. Instead, a blood sample is removed at periodic intervals and analyzed for its concentration of drug. The V_d relates the concentration of drug in plasma (C_p) and the amount of drug in the body (Xo), as in the following equation:

$$V_d = \frac{Xo}{C_p} = \frac{\text{i.v. bolus dose}}{\text{plasma concentration}} \quad .....(9.12)$$

Substitute $X = V_d$ Co in equation 9.3, and rearrange it. We get

$$dX = K_E V_d Co\, dt \quad .....(9.13)$$

Integrating the equation on both sides (K_E and V_d are constants),

$$\int_{x0}^{x} dx = K_E V_d \int_{0}^{C\infty} Cp\, dt \quad .....(9.14)$$

At initial time t = 0 , Xo = 0 and summation of $\int_{0}^{C\infty} Cp\, dt$ = [AUC], so we have

$$X = K_E V_d [AUC] \quad .....(9.15)$$

For drugs given by i.v. bolus by model independent method we have;

$$V_d = \frac{X}{K_E[AUC]}$$

Significance of the Apparent Volume of Distribution

Most drugs have an apparent volume of distribution smaller than, or equal to, the body mass. The value of volume of distribution depends upon the plasma concentration of drug. Drugs which are lipophilic in nature distribute more in fat and adipose tissues and have large V_d as the concentration of drug in plasma is very low. While, if a drug is highly bound to plasma proteins or remains in the vascular region, then Cp will be higher, resulting in a smaller V_d. From the value of apparent volume of distribution we get very important and useful information regarding the nature of drug as well as its pharmacokinetic journey in the body.

Clearance

Clearance is a measure of drug elimination from the body without identifying the mechanism or process. Clearance (drug clearance, systemic clearance, total body clearance, Cl_T) considers the entire body as a drug-eliminating system. Clearance is a very important parameter and very useful in clinical drug applications from evaluation of mechanism from different organs of body, the rate of elimination and finally using this data to calculate dosage regimen of a drug. Drug elimination from the body is an ongoing process due to both metabolism (biotransformation) and drug excretion through the kidney and other routes. Drug clearance refers to the volume of body fluid (i.e. that fraction of apparent volume of distribution) that is cleared of drug per unit time. The rate of drug elimination may be expressed in several ways, each of which essentially describes the same process, but with different levels of insight and application in pharmacokinetics.

Drug Clearance in the One-Compartment Model

Drug elimination expressed as amount per unit time

The expression of drug elimination from the body in terms of mass per unit time (e.g., mg/min, or mg/hr) is simple, absolute, and unambiguous. For a zero-order elimination process, expressing the rate of drug elimination as mass per unit time is convenient because the rate is constant. In contrast, the rate of drug elimination for a first-order elimination process is not constant and changes with respect to the drug concentration in the body. For first-order elimination, drug clearance is expressed as volume per unit time (e.g., L/hr or mL/min) is convenient because it is a constant.

Drug elimination expressed as volume per time unit

The concept of expressing a rate in terms of volume per unit time is common in pharmacy. For example, a patient may be dosed at the rate of 2 teaspoonful (10 mL) of a liquid medicine (10 mg/mL) daily, or alternatively, a dose (weight) of 100 mg of the drug daily.

Clearance is a concept that expresses "the rate of drug removal" in terms of volume of drug solution removed per unit time (at whatever drug concentration in the body prevailing at that time. In contrast to a solution in a bottle, the drug concentration in the body will gradually decline by a first-order process such that the mass of drug removed over time is not constant. The plasma volume in the healthy state is relatively constant because water lost through the kidney is rapidly replaced with fluid absorbed from the gastrointestinal tract.

Since a constant volume of plasma (about 120 mL/min in humans) is filtered through the glomeruli of the kidneys, the rate of drug removal is dependent on the plasma drug concentration at all times. This observation is based on a first-order process governing drug elimination. For many drugs, the rate of drug elimination is dependent on the plasma drug concentration, multiplied by a constant factor (dC/dt = kC). When the plasma drug concentration is high, the rate of drug removal is high, and vice versa.

Determination of Clearance

The rate of elimination of drug is directly proportional to the plasma concentration of drug.

$$\text{Rate of elimination } \left({}^{dX}\!/_{dt}\right) = Cl_T \times Cp \qquad .....(9.15)$$

where Cl_T is proportionality constant known as total body clearance.

Integrating the equation we get

$$\int_0^{\infty} dX = Cl \int_0^{\infty} Cp\, dt \qquad .....(9.16)$$

$$X = Cl_T\, [AUC]_0^{\infty} \qquad .....(9.17)$$

$$\text{Thus, total body clearance } (Cl_T) = Xo\, /\, [AUC]_0^{\infty} \qquad .....(9.18)$$

On substituting $Xo = Co \times V_d$, in equation 9.18 we have

$$Cl_T = \frac{Co\ V_d}{[AUC]_0^{\infty}} \qquad .....(9.19)$$

One Compartment Open Model i.v. Infusion

Drugs may be administered to the patients by variety of routes ranging from oral to topical to parenteral. Examples of parenteral routes of administration include intravenous, subcutaneous, and intramuscular. Intravenous (i.v.) drug solutions may be given either as a bolus dose (injected all at once) or infused slowly through a vein into the plasma at a constant or zero-order rate. The positive outcomes associated with intravenous infusion are as follows :

- It allows precise control of plasma drug concentrations to fit the individual needs of the patient. This is especially useful for drugs with a narrow therapeutic window (e.g., heparin).
- Intravenous infusion maintains an effective constant plasma drug concentration by eliminating wide fluctuations between the peak (maximum) and trough (minimum) plasma drug concentration.
- In critically ill patients, intravenous infusion of drugs, such as antibiotics, may be given with intravenous fluids that include electrolytes and nutrients.
- Furthermore, the duration of drug therapy may be maintained or terminated as needed using intravenous infusion.

During intravenous infusion the drug concentration slowly increases as the time proceeds and reaches a steady state concentration or plateau level. The rate of drug infusion is a zero order process and it is equal to rate of elimination at the steady state.

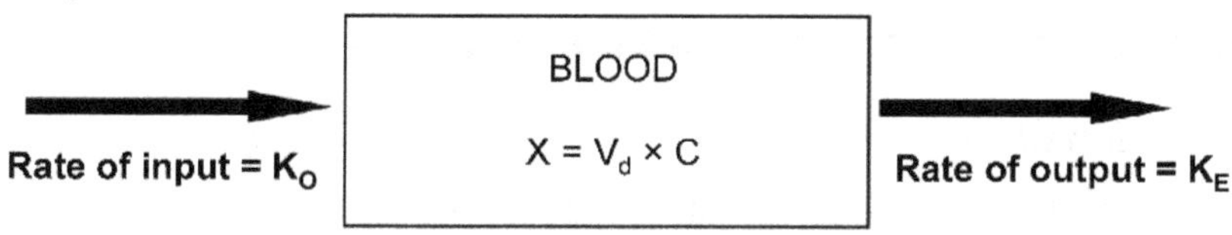

Fig. 9.4 Schematic representation of one compartment open model for intravenous infusion.

The change in amount of the drug in the body at any time (t) is the rate of input minus rate of output.

$$\frac{dX}{dt} = K_o - K_E X \qquad .....(9.20)$$

Dividing the entire equation by V_d, we get

$$\frac{dX / V_d}{dt} = \frac{K_o}{V} - \frac{K_E X}{V_d} \qquad .....(9.21)$$

$$\frac{dC}{dt} = \frac{K_o}{V_d} - K_E C \qquad .....(9.22)$$

Rearranging the equation and multiplying it with e^{-kt}, we get

$$\frac{dC}{dt} e^{kt} + K_E C e^{-kt} = \frac{Ko}{Vd} e^{-kt}$$

Integrating and rearranging this equation we get

$$C = \frac{K_o}{V_d K_E}\left(1 - e^{-kt}\right) \qquad .....(9.23)$$

$$X = \frac{Ko}{K_E} (1 - e^{-kt}) \qquad .....(9.24)$$

At steady state, the rate of change of concentration or the amount of drug is zero and hence the equation becomes

$$K_o = K_E X_{ss} \qquad .....(9.25)$$

$$X_{ss} = \frac{Ko}{K_E} \qquad .....(9.26)$$

$$C_{ss} = \frac{K_o}{K_E V_d} \qquad .....(9.27)$$

Thus C_{ss} is dependent on infusion rate and clearance ($Cl_T = K_E V_d$).

Calculation of Pharmacokinetic Parameters

Elimination half-life

The Cp versus time relationship that occurs during an IV infusion may be used to calculate K_E, and the elimination half-life of the drug in a patient. Some information about the elimination half-life of the drug in the population must be known, and one or two plasma samples must be taken at a known time after infusion. Knowing the half-life in the general population helps to determine if the sample has been taken at steady state in the patient. To simplify calculation, Equation (9.27) is arranged to solve for K_E.

Putting the value of Ko/Cl $= C_{ss}$ from equation (9.27) in equation (9.23), we have

$$C = C_{ss} (1 - e - K_E t) \qquad .....(9.28)$$

Rearranging this equation gives

$$\frac{C_{ss} - C}{C_{ss}} = e - K_E t \qquad .....(9.29)$$

Taking log of both sides

$$\log\left(\frac{C_{ss}-C}{C}\right) = \frac{-K_E\, t}{2.303} \quad .....(9.30)$$

On plotting a graph for equation 9.30, on a semilog graph paper we get an equation for straight line as can be seen as in Figure 9.5.

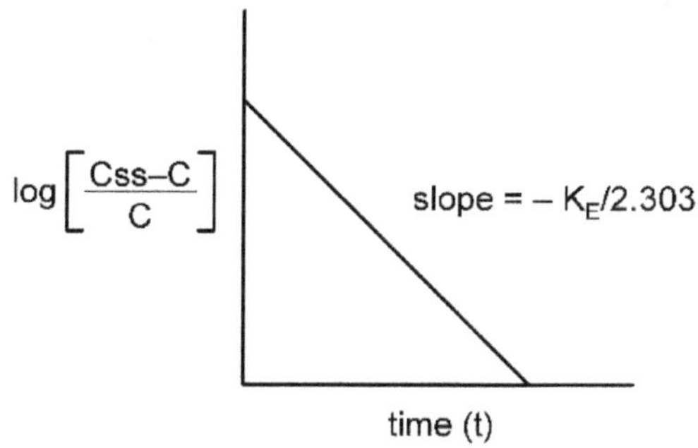

Fig. 9.5 Semilog plot to compute K_E from infusion data beyond steady state.

The rate with which the steady state is achieved is independent of rate of drug infusion; instead the time to reach it depends upon the elimination half life of the drug. If the rate of infusion is increased there will be no change in time to reach C_{ss} but it will increase the value of C_{ss} by the same factor by which the rate is increased.

Infusion plus loading dose

For the drugs given by intravenous infusion,

- Dose rate = mg/hr = dose divided by dosing interval
- Maintenance dose = mg/hr = desired peak concentration x clearance

  $= C_{ss} \times K_E \times V_d$
- Loading dose = desired peak concentration x volume of distribution $= C_{ss} \times V_d$

When the drug is given by continuous infusion the drug accumulates gradually. The steady state concentration is determined primarily by two major factors, the dose rate and the clearance rate. Steady state is achieved when clearance rate and dose rate are equal and the time taken to achieve the steady state in continuous infusion is 3-5 biological half lives.

In case of drugs required for critical conditions and in case of drugs having long half lives it is very important to reach C_{ss} as early as possible. This is where the loading dose plays an important role to achieve C_{ss} immediately upon injection prior to starting the infusion.

Loading dose rapidly achieves the peak plasma concentration necessary to compete with clearance, so that the desired effect is achieved and maintained sooner.

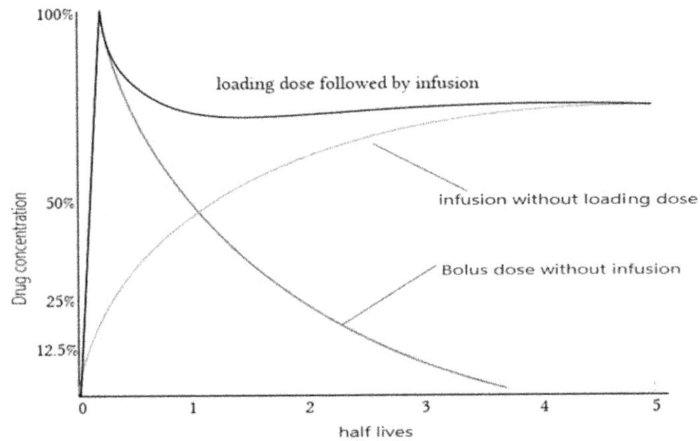

Fig. 9.6 Intravenous infusion with loading dose.

Loading dose (X_o,L) is calculated by multiplying the desired peak concentration by volume of distribution

$$X_{o,L} = V_d \text{ x } C_{ss} \quad \text{.....(9.31)}$$

Substitution of $C_{ss} = K_o/K_E\ V_d$ from equation 9.27, we have loading dose in terms of infusion rate

$$X_{o.L} = K_o/K_E \quad \text{.....(9.32)}$$

The equation describing the plasma concentration time profile following simultaneous i.v. loading dose followed by constant rate of i.v. infusion is the sum of the following two equations respectively

$$C = Co\ e^{-KEt} + Co\ (1 - e^{-KEt}) \quad \text{.....(9.33)}$$

$$C = X_o\ e^{-KEt}/V_d + Ko\ (1 - e^{-KEt})\ /K_E V_d \quad \text{.....(9.34)}$$

The first order elimination rate constant and elimination half life can be calculated by a semilog plot of post infusion concentration time data. Total drug that reaches the systemic circulation is equal to C_{ss} x T. where T is infusion time.

One Compartment Open Model (Extravascular Administration)

The pharmacokinetics of drugs following intravenous drug administration is simpler to model compared to extravascular delivery. Extravascular delivery routes, especially oral route are important and popular means of drug administration. In case of extravascular administration a drug undergoes the phenomenon of absorption from the lung, the gut, etc., before it reaches the systemic circulation. The delivery route is very complicated and there are various variables which further complicate the process of absorption including variability in absorption site, drug interactions, drug degradation and inter patient variability. The variability in systemic drug absorption can be minimized to some extent by proper biopharmaceutical design of the dosage form to provide predictable and reliable drug therapy.

The systemic drug absorption from the gastrointestinal tract or from any other extravascular site is dependent on (1) the physicochemical properties of the drug, (2) the dosage form used, and (3) the anatomy and physiology of the absorption site. Oral route is discussed in this chapter that can be representative of other extravascular routes. For oral dosing, factors such as surface area of the gastrointestinal tract, stomach emptying rate, gastrointestinal mobility, and blood flow to the absorption site affect the rate and the extent of drug absorption. In pharmacokinetics, the overall rate of drug absorption may be described as either a first-order or zero-order input process. Most pharmacokinetic models assume first-order absorption unless an assumption of zero-order absorption improves the model significantly or has been verified experimentally.

The rate of change of the amount of the drug in the body following extravascular administration is equal to the difference between the rate of absorption and the rate of elimination (Eq. 9.31).

$$\frac{dX}{dt} = \frac{dXa}{dt} - \frac{dX_E}{dt} \quad .....(9.35)$$

As can be seen in Fig. 9.7, plasma concentration time profile for single oral dose, the curve is divided into various phases on the relative magnitude of the rate of absorption and rate of elimination at different time points.

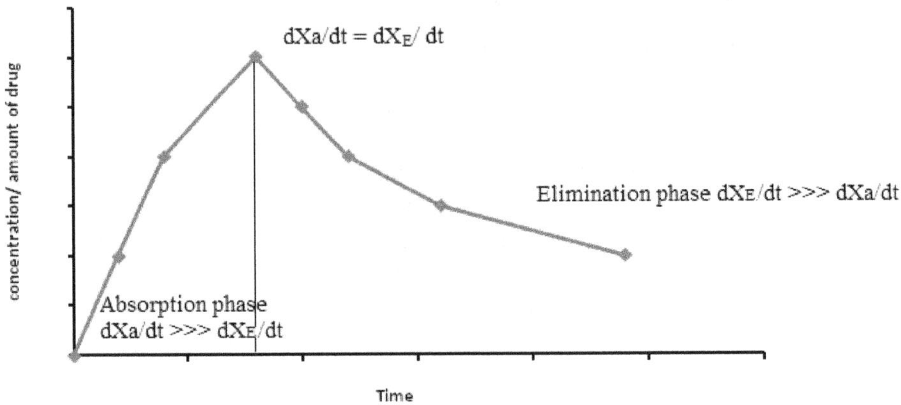

Fig. 9.7 Various phases of a drug plasma level versus time curve for single oral dose.

Absorption phase: After the oral administration of dosage form the drug released from the dosage form is available for absorption through the gastrointestinal tract. At zero time the whole drug is available for the absorption and as the time precedes the amount of drug at the absorption site declines and the rate of absorption follows the same pattern. The rate of absorption is greater than the rate of elimination ($dX_a/dt >> dX_E/dt$).

Plateau phase: Absorption of drug into the systemic circulation gradually increases the plasma concentration of drug as long as rate of absorption is greater than the elimination rate. The gradual increase in drug concentration in plasma also increases the rate of elimination of drug from plasma. It means rate of absorption gradually decrease with time but rate of elimination increases with time. Eventually a stage is reached where rate of absorption becomes equal to rate of elimination of drug. The concentration of drug achieved at this point is highest and is called as peak plasma concentration and the time at which this occurs is called as time of peak plasma concentration ($dX_a/dt = dX_E/dt$).

Post absorption phase: Immediately after the plateau phase the rate of elimination of drug is faster than the rate of absorption as represented in the figure. During this phase the plasma concentration declines slowly as the elimination phase is little bit greater than absorption rate. ($dX_a/dt <<< dX_E/dt$).

Elimination phase: When the drug at the absorption site is exhausted, the rate of drug absorption approaches zero but the elimination continues from the body by first order kinetics ($dX_e/dt = - K_E\, X$).

First order absorption model – Extravascular administration

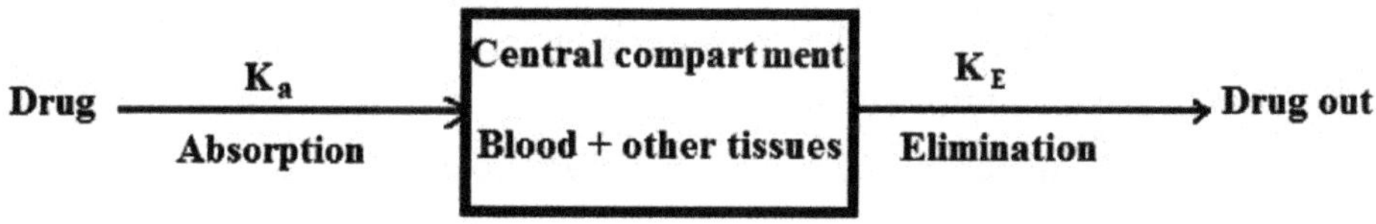

Fig. 9.8 Schematic representation of one compartment extravascular model.

The rate of change of amount of drug

$$\left(\frac{dX}{dt}\right) = Ka\ Xa - K_E\ X \qquad .....(9.36)$$

where, Xa is the amount of drug available at the absorption site at any given time, and X is the amount of drug in the blood at the same time.

Let us assume that "F" is the fraction of the oral dose (Xo) that will be absorbed ultimately. At time zero, FXo is the amount available for absorption and it declines as a function of time. Therefore, Xa = FXo. The rate of disappearance of drug from gastrointestinal tract is described by the equation

$$\frac{dXa}{dt} = -Ka\ Xa \qquad .....(9.37)$$

Integrate equation 9.36 between time limits t = 0 to t = t , yields the equation

$$\int_0^t \frac{dXa}{Xa} = -Ka \int_0^t dt$$

Thus, $$[\ln Xa]_o^t = -Ka\ [t]_o^t \qquad .....(9.38)$$

$$\ln Xa - \ln Xa^o = -Kat$$

$$\ln Xa = \ln Xa^o - Kat \qquad .....(9.39)$$

but we know that $Xa^o = FX_o$

so we have, $$\ln Xa = \ln F\ Xo - Kat \qquad .....(9.40)$$

Putting this value in equation ($dX/dt = Ka\ Xa - K_E X$), we have

$$dX/dt = Ka\ F\ Xo\ e^{-Kat} - K_E\ X \qquad .....(9.41)$$

$$dX/dt + K_E\ X = Ka\ FXo\ e^{-Kat} \qquad .....(9.42)$$

Multiplying equation 9.42 by $e^{K_E t}$ we get

$$\frac{dX}{dt} e^{K_E t} + K_E X e^{K_E t} = Ka\ F\ Xo\ e^{-Kat}\ e^{K_E t} \qquad .....(9.43)$$

Rearranging the above equation we have

$$dX\ e^{K_E t} + Ke\ X\ e^{K_E t}\ dt = Ka\ FXo\ e^{-(Ka-K_E)t}\ dt \qquad .....(9.44)$$

Integrating this equation between limit t = 0 to t = t and arranging it we finally get

$$X = \frac{Ka\ F\ Xo[\ e^{-KEt} - e^{Kat}]}{Ka - K_E} \qquad .....(9.45)$$

As X= C/V_d the equation can be written as

$$C = \frac{Ka\ F\ Xo[\ e^{-K_E t} - e^{Kat}]}{Vd(Ka - K_E)} \qquad .....(9.46)$$

Pharmacokinetic Parameters

Elimination Rate Constant

This parameter can be calculated from the elimination phase of the plasma level time profile. For most drugs administered by extravascular absorption rate is significantly higher as compared to elimination rate. At such a stage when absorption is complete, the change in plasma concentration is dependent only on elimination rate and the eq. 9.46 reduces to

$$\log C = (\log Ka\ F\ Xo - K_E t/2.303])/(V_d(Ka - K_E) \qquad .....(9.47)$$

A plot of log C versus time yields a straight line with slope $-K_E/2.303$. Half life can be calculated from K_E.

Absorption Rate Constant

Absorption rate constant can be determined by two methods namely, (i) Method of residuals, and (ii) Wagner – Nelson method.

(i) **Method of residuals:** The value of Ka is determined by following procedure:

- Plot the graph between drug concentration versus time on a semilog graph paper with the plasma concentration values on log axis (Fig. 9.9).
- Calculate the slope of the terminal linear portion of the graph. Calculate K_E from the slope and also elimination half life.

- Extend the terminal linear portion of the graph backward to meet the Y axis. The intercept is equals to $= \frac{logKa\ F\ Xo}{Vd(Ka-KE)}$
- Subtract the true plasma concentration values from the extrapolated plasma concentration values to yield a series of residual concentration values (Cr).

A plot of log Cr versus time yields a straight line with slope –Ka/2.303 and intercept log A.

Absorption half life can be calculated using the equation t1/2 = 0.693/Ka.

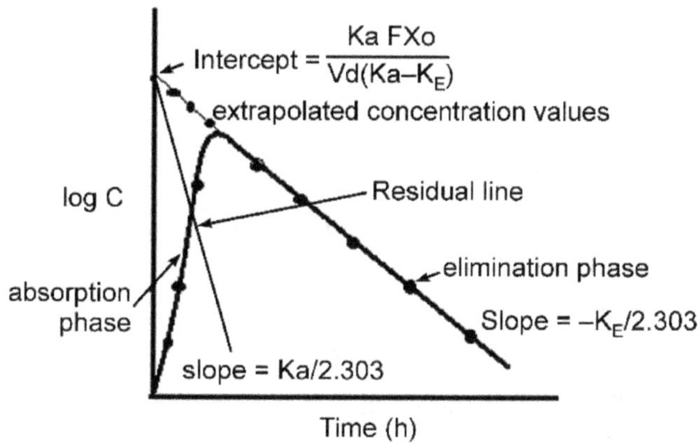

Fig. 9.9 Semi logarithmic plot for calculation of absorption rate constant.

(ii) Wagner-Nelson Method: In the method of residuals the absorption process is assumed to be of first order. It is true for conventional tablet and capsule dosage forms but cannot be used for modified release dosage forms where release of the drug is not rapid and is rate controlled. It may be zero order or first order or pseudo zero order. It is based on the assumptions that the body behaves as a single homogeneous compartment and the elimination of drug follows first order kinetics. After oral administration of a single dose of a drug, at any given time, the amount of drug absorbed into the systemic circulation Xa is the sum of amount of drug in the body X and the amount of drug eliminated from the body (Xe). This method requires collection blood samples at regular intervals until entire amount of blood is eliminated from the body.

Thus, $$Xa = X + Xe \quad .....(9.48)$$

The amount of drug in the body X = V_d C. The amount of drug eliminated at any time t can be calculated as

$$Xe = K_E V_d [AUC]_o^t \quad .....(9.49)$$

Substitute the values of X and Xe

$$Xa = V_d C + K_E V_d [AUC]_o^t \quad .....(9.50)$$

The total amount of drug absorbed into the systemic circulation from time zero to infinity X_a^∞ can be written as:

$$X_a^\infty = V_d C^\infty + K_E V_d [AUC]_o^\infty \quad .....(9.51)$$

Since at infinite time the concentration of drug in plasma will be minimal that is almost equal to zero. Thus C^∞ equals to 0, and the above equation reduces to

$$X_a^\infty = K_E V_d [AUC]_o^\infty \quad .....(9.52)$$

The fraction of drug absorbed at any time t is given as

$$\frac{X_a}{X_a^\infty} = \frac{V_d C + K_E V_d [AUC]_0^t}{K_E V_d [AUC]_0^\infty} \quad .....(9.53)$$

$$\frac{Xa}{Xa^\infty} = \frac{C + K_E [AUC]_0^t}{K_E [AUC]_0^\infty} \quad .....(9.54)$$

Fraction of drug unabsorbed at any time t is calculated as:

$$[1 - \frac{Xa}{Xa^\infty}] = [1 - \frac{C + K_E [AUC]_0^t}{K_E [AUC]_0^\infty}] \quad .....(9.55)$$

Percentage of drug unabsorbed (or amount remaining to be absorbed, (ARA) at any time t is expressed as $[1 - \frac{C + K_E [AUC]_0^t}{K_E [AUC]_0^\infty}] \times 100$

Plot a grp between ARA ad time (Fig. 9.10 and deduce K_a)

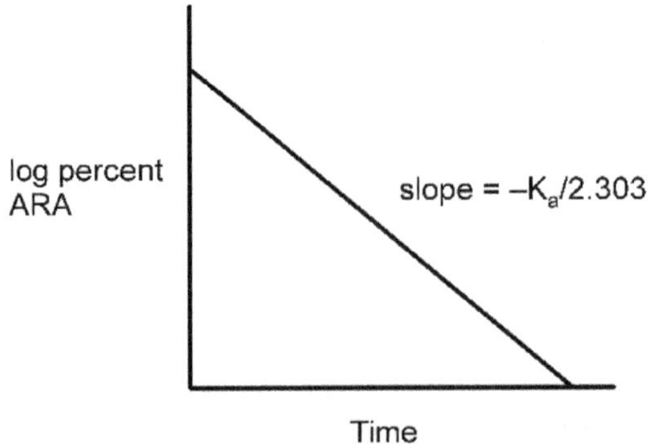

Fig. 9.10 Semilog plot of percent amount of drug remaining to be absorbed versus time.

The major limitation of Wagner Nelson method is that it applies only to drugs following one compartment characteristics. Ka can also be estimated from urinary excretion data.

Urinary Excretion Method

In certain cases the plasma concentration time data is not available due to various reasons. In such cases the useful information and parameters are obtained from the urinary data. This method has several positive features:

- It is very useful when there is lack of sufficient analytical techniques to measure plasma concentration of drug.
- The method is non-invasive in nature so is patient compliant.
- The method requires less sophisticated and less sensitive techniques to quantify the amount of drug.
- Direct measurement of bioavailability, both absolute and relative can be done without the need of fitting the data to a mathematical model.
- It can also be used to calculate clearance when combined with plasma level time data.

Limitations include:

- Calculation of V_d and CI_T from urine data alone is not possible.
- It is not a substitute for plasma level time studies.
- It only provides a rough estimate of pharmacokinetic parameters and lacks accuracy.

Determination of elimination rate constant

The first order elimination rate constants can be computed from urinary data by two methods: (i) Rate of excretion method, and (ii) Sigma minus method.

Rate of excretion method

The rate of urinary drug excretion dXu/dt is proportional to the amount of drug present in the plasma (X) and written as:

$$\frac{dX_u}{dt} = K_E\,X \qquad .....(9.56)$$

where Ke is first order urinary excretion rate constant.

According to first order disposition kinetics $X = Xo\ e^{-K_E t}$, where Xo is the dose administered as IV bolus. Substituting the value in equation 9.56, we have,

$$\frac{dX_u}{dt} = Ke\ Xo\ e^{-K_E t} \quad .....(9.57)$$

Transform the equation to log form to get

$$\log \frac{dX_u}{dt} = \log K_E Xo - \frac{K_E t}{2.303} \quad .....(9.58)$$

The above equation is an expression of straight line and a semilog plot of rate of excretion versus time will yield a straight line with slope $-K_E/2.303$. Thus, the slope gives elimination rate constant. The excretion rate constant can be calculated from the Y intercept ($\log K_E\ Xo$). Elimination half life and non-renal elimination rate constant can be computed from K_E and K_e.

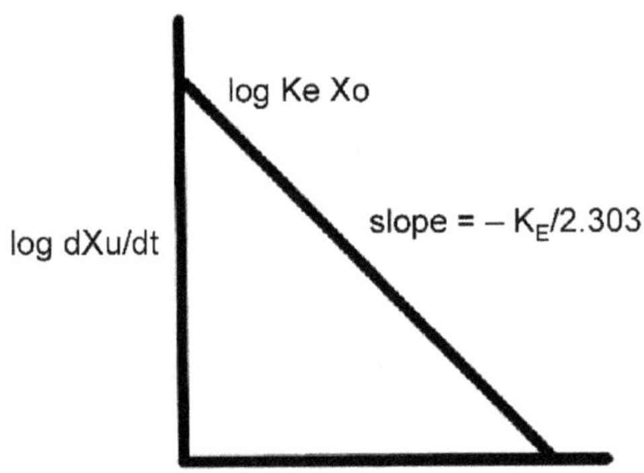

Fig. 9.11 Semilog plot of excretion rate versus midpoint time of urine collection period.

Sigma minus method

A disadvantage of rate of excretion method in estimating K_E is that fluctuations in the rate of drug elimination are observed to a higher degree. This problem can be minimized by sigma minus method.

We already have the equation, $\frac{dX_u}{dt} = K_E\ Xo\ e^{-K_E t}$ and its integration yields

$$Xu = \frac{K_E\ Xo}{K_E} (1 - e^{-K_E t}) \quad .....(9.59)$$

where Xu is the cumulative amount of drug excreted unchanged in urine at any time t. As time approaches infinity after 6 to 7 half lives the value of $e^{-K_E t}$

becomes zero. Therefore, the cumulative amount of drug excreted at infinite time (X_u^{∞}) can be given as:

$$X_u^{\infty} = \frac{K_E\,Xo}{K_E} \qquad .....(9.60)$$

Substitute eq. 9.56 in 9.55 to get

$$Xu = X_u^{\infty}\,(1 - e^{-K_E t}) \qquad .....(9.61)$$

Rearrange and take its log form to get:

$$\log\,(X_u^{\infty} - Xu) = \log X_u^{\infty} - \frac{K_E t}{2.303} \qquad .....(9.62)$$

where, (Xu^{∞} – Xu) = amount remaining to be excreted (ARE) at any given time. A semilog plot of ARE versus time yields a straight line with slope $-K_E/2.303$. The method is also called as ARE plot method.

There are certain limitations of this method which includes collection of urine sample up to seven half-lives until no unchanged drug is detected in urine sample which may be tedious for drugs having long $t_{1/2}$. The urinary excretion method can be used only when at least 10 % of unchanged drug is excreted in urine and the samples must be collected for at least 7 biological half lives in order to ensure collection of more than 99% of excreted drug.

Questions

Multiple Choice Questions

1. What does the word "open" mean in the one compartment open model?
   (a) The drug easily enters
   (b) The drug readily mixes with the blood
   (c) Unidirectional input and output
   (d) Easy absorption
2. How much time does an intravenously administered drug take to complete a complete circulation?
   (a) 5-8 min (b) 7-10 min
   (c) 1-3 min (d) 1 min
3. In the equation log C = log Co – $K_E t/2.303$, what does Co stand for ________
   (a) Plasma drug concentration after 60 min of i.v. injection

(b) Plasma drug concentration after 15 min of i.v. injection

(c) Plasma drug concentration after 30 min of i.v. injection

(d) Plasma drug concentration immediately after i.v. injection.

4. What is meant by elimination half-life?

(a) Time taken for half of the amount of drug to get completely eliminated from only the organs

(b) Time taken for half of the amount of drug to get completely eliminated from only blood

(c) Time taken for half of the amount of drug to get completely eliminated from only plasma

(d) Time taken for half of the amount of drug to get completely eliminated from the body as well as plasma

5. What is the equation to find out the apparent volume of distribution?

(a) Amount of drug in the body/plasma drug concentration

(b) Plasma drug concentration/amount of drug in the body

(c) 1 / plasma drug concentration

(d) 1 / Amount of drug in the body

6. The i.v. bolus dosage is 500 mg and the plasma drug concentration is 0.8 mg/ml. What should be the volume of distribution?

(a) 625 mg/ml (b) 625 litres

(c) 625 ml (d) 0.0016 mg/ml

7. To have a plasma distribution value of 900 ml and plasma drug concentration to be 1.2 mg/ml what should be the amount of drug that should be given to the patient?

(a) 1080 ml (b) 1080 g

(c) 1080 mg (d) 1 g/ml

8. A 60-kg patient is to be started on a continuous intravenous infusion. From a previous regimen of the same drug, you estimate the patient's Ke is 0.07 h-1 and the V_d is 40 L. Assume that none of this drug has been administered this month. If the Css is to be 30 mg/L, what would be the loading dose (mg) given as intravenous bolus injection?

(a) 120 mg (b) 240 mg

(c) 1200 mg (d) 1220 mg

(e) 2400 mg

Short Questions

1. What is the difference between a rate and a rate constant?
2. Why does k always have the unit 1/time (eg, hr–1), regardless of what concentration unit is plotted?
3. If a drug is distributed in the one-compartment model, does it mean that there is no drug in the tissue?
4. How is clearance related to the volume of distribution and k?
5. Define the term apparent volume of distribution. What criteria are necessary for the measurement of the apparent volume of distribution to be useful in pharmacokinetic calculations?
6. What are the practical problems in obtaining valid urinary drug excretion data for the determination of the drug elimination half-life?

Multicompartment Modelling

CHAPTER 10

LEARNING OBJECTIVES

- Understanding multicompartment (two) model
- Pharmacokinetic treatment of two compartment model
- Two compartment model after iv bolus
- Two compartment model after iv infusion
- Two compartment model after extravascular administration

One compartment open model adequately describes pharmacokinetics of various drugs but it is based on certain assumptions like instant distribution of drug to all the tissues and that the decline in concentration of drug is monoexponential. But instantaneous distribution of drug is not possible as body is composed of different types of tissues each with different degree of blood flow and affinity for drug and therefore different rate of equilibration.

Multicompartment models have been proposed on certain assumptions:

1. There are different types of tissues based on their **perfusion rate.** Brain, heart, lungs and kidneys are highly perfused tissues and along with blood/plasma constitute **central compartment.**
2. Tissues having similar distribution characteristics are categorized together to constitute a **peripheral compartment.**
3. Intravenously administered drugs are considered to directly enter the central compartment and establish equilibrium rapidly.
4. Irreversible loss of drug from the body in the form of metabolism or excretion always occurs from the central compartment.
5. Reversible transfer of drugs also takes place between the central compartment and peripheral compartments until equilibrium is achieved.

6. All rate processes involving passage of drug in and out of individual compartment are first order processes and plasma level time curve is best described by sum of series of exponents.
7. The peripheral compartments normally are considered inaccessible as it is very difficult to directly measure the amount of drug and it is not a site of drug elimination.

Two Compartment Open Model

The two compartment model is the most common of all multicompartment models. In this study the body is divided into two compartments, a central compartment comprising of blood and highly perfused tissues for rapid equilibration and a peripheral compartment that is constituted of poorly perfused and slow equilibrating tissues such as muscles, skin or adipose tissues. The plasma concentration of a drug, that follows a two compartment model declines biexponentially as the sum of two first order processes, namely, distribution and elimination.

Two compartment model (i.v. bolus administration)

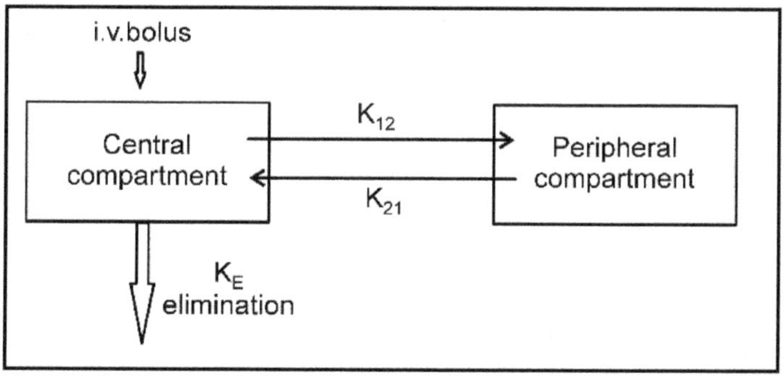

Fig. 10.1 Schematic representation of a drug following two compartment open model after i.v. bolus administration.

In case of intravenous bolus administration the drug plasma level time curve represents an initial distributive phase during which the drug is diffused into peripheral compartments till equilibrium is achieved followed by elimination phase.

The rate constants K_{12} and K_{21} represent the first order rate constants for the movement of drug from compartment 1 to compartment 2 and vice versa. K_E is elimination rate constant. The equation that describes the time course of drug concentration in the central compartment and peripheral (tissue) compartment following intravenous bolus administration can be seen as below. According to mass balance equation:

$$X_o = X_c + X_t + X_E \qquad \text{.....(10.1)}$$

where, Xo = total amount of drug given as i.v. dose, X_c = amount of drug in central compartment, X_t = amount of drug in peripheral (tissue) compartment and X_E = amount of drug eliminated.

The rate of change of amount of drug in central compartment is the net balance of rate of input – rate of output.

$$dX_c/d_t = K_{21}\,X_t - (K_{12}\,X_c + K_E\,X_c) \qquad \text{.....(10.2)}$$

The differential equation for rate of change of drug levels in tissue compartment is given by

$$dX_t/\,dt = K_{12}\,X_c - K_{21}\,X_t \qquad \text{.....(10.3)}$$

The rate of elimination from central compartment is given by:

$$dX_E/dt = K_E\;X_c \qquad \text{.....(10.4)}$$

On integrating equation 10.4 between t = 0 to t = t, we get the following equation.

$$X_E = K_E \int_0^t Xc\,dt \qquad \text{.....(10.5)}$$

Substituting the value of X_E in equation 10.1 and differentiating it we have,

$$d^2Xc\,/dt^2 + (\alpha + \beta)\frac{dXc}{dt} + \alpha\beta Xc = 0 \qquad \text{.....(10.6)}$$

This equation can be written in simple form as

$$(\alpha + \beta) = K_{12} + K_{21} + K_E \qquad \text{.....(10.7)}$$

$$\alpha\beta = K_{21}\,X_E \qquad \text{.....(10.8)}$$

$$Xc = \frac{Xo(\alpha - K_{21})}{\alpha - \beta}\,e^{-\alpha t} + \frac{Xo(K_{21} - \beta)}{\alpha - \beta}\,e^{-\beta t} \qquad \text{.....(10.9)}$$

Dividing Eq. 10.9 by V_c we get the following equation in terms of concentration

$$C = \frac{Xo(\alpha - K_{21})}{Vc(\alpha - \beta)}\,e^{-\alpha t} + \frac{Xo(K_{21} - \beta)}{Vc(\alpha - \beta)}\,e^{-\beta t} \qquad \text{.....(10.10)}$$

In simpler form this biexponential equation can be written as

$$C = A\,e^{-\alpha t} + B\,e^{-\beta t} \qquad .....(10.11)$$

Thus, C equals to distribution exponent + elimination exponent. A and B are hybrid constants for the two exponents and can be resolved graphically by the method of residuals.

$$A = \frac{Xo\,(\alpha - K_{21})}{Vc(\alpha-\beta)} = Co\,\frac{(K_{21}-\alpha)}{(\beta-\alpha)} \qquad .....(10.12)$$

$$B = \frac{Xo\,(K_{21}-\beta)}{Vc(\alpha-\beta)} = Co\,\frac{(K_{21}-\beta)}{(\alpha-\beta)} \qquad .....(10.13)$$

A plot of the logarithm of plasma drug concentration versus time according to equation 10.11 will yield a biexponential curve. It can be resolved into individual components by method of residuals. Rewriting equation 10.11

$$C = A\,e^{-\alpha t} + B\,e^{-\beta t}$$

As evident from the curve (Fig. 10.2) there is an initial decline due to distribution which is very rapid and the slope is very steep while there is a phase of terminal decline due to elimination which is not so steep. The rate constant $\alpha >>> \beta$, hence the term $e^{-\alpha t}$ approaches zero very fast as compared to $e^{-\beta t}$ reducing the equation to

$$\overleftarrow{C} = B\,e^{-\beta t} \qquad .....(10.14)$$

In the log form the equation becomes:

$$\log \overleftarrow{C} = \log B - \frac{\beta t}{2.303} \qquad .....(10.15)$$

where $\overleftarrow{C}$ = back extrapolated plasma concentration values. A semilog graph plotted between log C versus time yields the terminal linear phase with a slope equal to $-\frac{\beta}{2.303}$ that yields β. When it is back extrapolated to time zero to intercept Y axis log B is determined. Assuming first order elimination, the half life is calculated by the equation 10.16.

$$t_{1/2} = 0.693/\beta \qquad .....(10.16)$$

Further, the extrapolated concentration values of elimination phase are subtracted from corresponding real plasma concentration values to yield a series of residual concentration

$$\overleftarrow{C_r} = C - C = A^{e-\alpha t} + B^{e-\beta t} - B^{e-\beta t} = A^{e-\alpha t} \qquad .....(10.17)$$

In the log form the equation becomes:

$$\log C_r = \log A - \frac{\alpha t}{2.303} \qquad .....(10.18)$$

A semilog plot of C_r versus t yields a straight line with slope $-\frac{\alpha}{2.303}$ and the y intercept is log A.

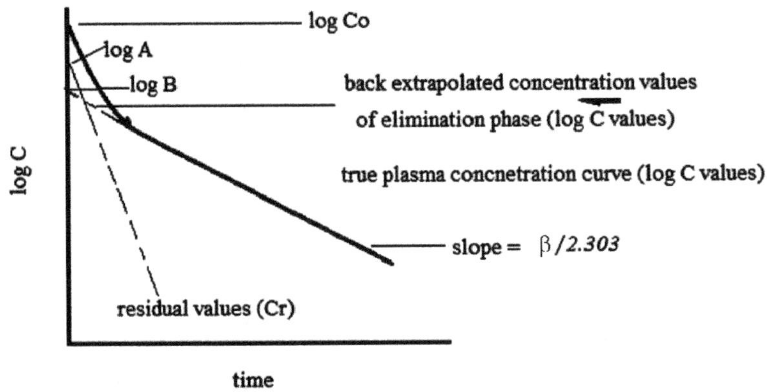

Fig. 10.2 Resolution of biexponential plasma concentration by the method of residuals for two compartment i.v. bolus administration.

Various pharmacokinetic parameters can be derived by following tabulated equations:

S.No	Parameter	Equation
1	Concentration of drug in plasma at t = 0	$Co = A + B$
2	Elimination rate constant	$K_E = \frac{\alpha \beta Co}{A\beta + B\alpha}$
3	Microconstant/ transfer constant 12	$K_{12} = \frac{A B (\beta - \alpha)^2}{C_o(A\beta + B\alpha)}$
4	Microconstant/ transfer constant 21	$K_{21} = \frac{A\beta + B\alpha}{C_o}$
5	Area under the plasma concentration versus time curve	$AUC = \frac{A}{\alpha} + \frac{B}{\beta}$
6	Apparent volume of central compartment	$Vc = \frac{X_o}{C_o} = \frac{X_o}{K_E\, AUC}$
7	Apparent volume of peripheral compartment	$Vp = \frac{V_c K_{12}}{K_{21}}$
8	Total systemic clearance	$Cl_T = \beta V_d$

Two Compartment Open Model-Intravenous Infusion

The model can be depicted Fig. 10.3 with elimination from central compartment.

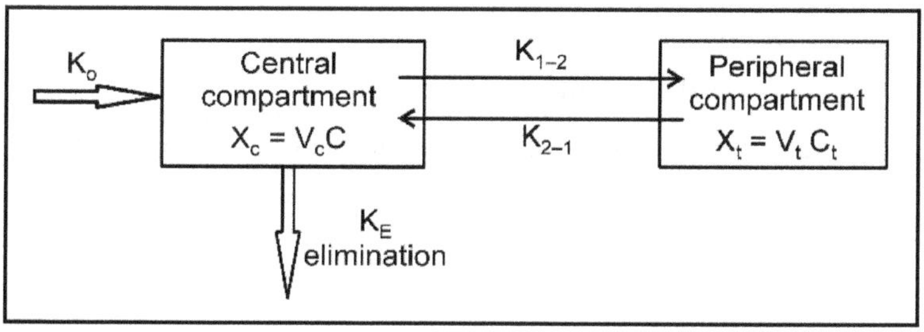

Fig. 10.3 Schematic representation of a drug administered by intravenous infusion for two compartment open model.

where Ko is the constant infusion rate (mg/hr). The rate of input is a zero order process. Three important processes are to be considered in deriving an equation that describes the plasma drug level – time profile following intravenous infusion.

1. **Input**: Drug is infused at constant rate Ko. The zero order kinetics governs this process.
2. **Distribution of drug:** The drug entering the central compartment is distributed to the tissue compartment till the steady state is ready.
3. **Elimination of drug:** Drug in the central compartment is eliminated by an apparent first order process.

The net result of the above processes is that the drug level builds up slowly in the body till a steady level is reached. The rate of change of the drug level in the central compartment is given by:

$$dC/dt = Ko + K_{21}C_t - (K_{12} + K_{13})C \qquad \text{.....(10.19)}$$

Solving equation 10.19 for drug concentration in blood, we get

$$C = \frac{Ko}{Vc\,K_E}\left[1 + \left(\frac{K_E - \beta}{\beta - \alpha}\right)e^{-\alpha t} + \left(\frac{K_E - \alpha}{\alpha - \beta}\right)e^{-\beta t}\right] \qquad \text{.....(10.20)}$$

The above equation describes the time course of drug concentration in plasma on i.v infusion. At steady state, after infinite time, the second and third term becomes negligible and the equation reduces to:

$$C_{SS} = \frac{Ko}{Vc\,K_E} \quad .....(10.21)$$

On rearrangement it becomes

$$Ko = C_{ss}\ Vc\ K_E \quad .....(10.22)$$

Replace $K_E Vc$ by Vd β. Thus, Ko = C_{ss} Vd β .....(10.23)

After the attainment of steady state plasma concentration when the infusion is stopped the drug plasma levels can be described by monoexponential equation:

$$C = C_{SS}.\ e^{-\beta t} \quad .....(10.24)$$

Two Compartment Open Model – Extravascular Administration

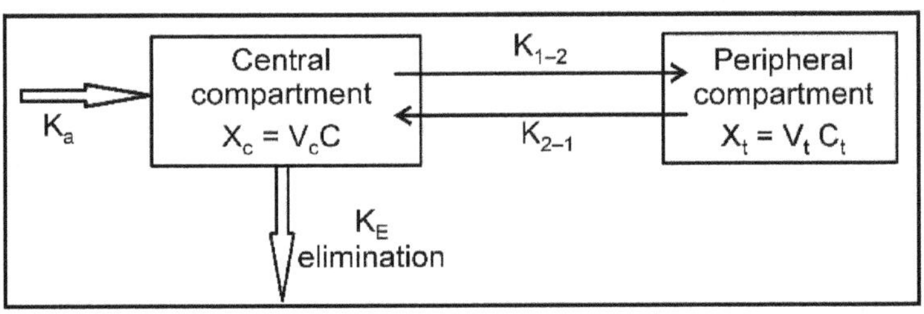

Fig.10.4 Schematic representation of extravascular administration of a drug following two compartment open model.

where Ka is first order absorption rate constant, Xc is the amount of drug in central compartment. Vc and C are the volume of fluid in central compartment and concentration of drug respectively. While Vt and Ct are volume of distribution in tissue compartment and concentration of drug in tissue compartment respectively. As long as the drug enters the central compartment by absorption process distribution and elimination is also taking place simultaneously. When absorption is ceased distribution occurs until equilibrium is reached and after that only elimination takes place. It simply means that plasma drug concentration depends initially on three process (three exponential), then on two processes (biexponential) and finally on elimination only (monoexponential).

The equation that describes time course of drug in central compartment can be written as:

$$C = Le^{-\alpha t} + M\,e^{-\beta t} - N\,e^{-Kat} \quad .....(10.25)$$

At time zero (t = 0), C is 0. Thus the equation becomes

$$0 = Le^{0} + Me^{0} - N e^{0} \qquad .....(10.26)$$

$$L + M = Co \qquad .....(10.27)$$

where, $L = \frac{Xo}{V_c} \frac{(\alpha - K_{21})}{(\alpha - \beta)}$ and $M = \frac{Xo}{V_t} \frac{(K_{21} - \beta)}{(\alpha - \beta)}$

According to equation 10.27 if a graph is plotted between log plasma concentration versus time we will get a complex curve which is triexponential initially, becomes biexponential after some time and finally gives a straight line (after distribution phase) with a slope = $-\beta/2.303$. then finally the parameters are calculated and the absorption rate constant is calculated by the method of residuals (Figure 10.6).

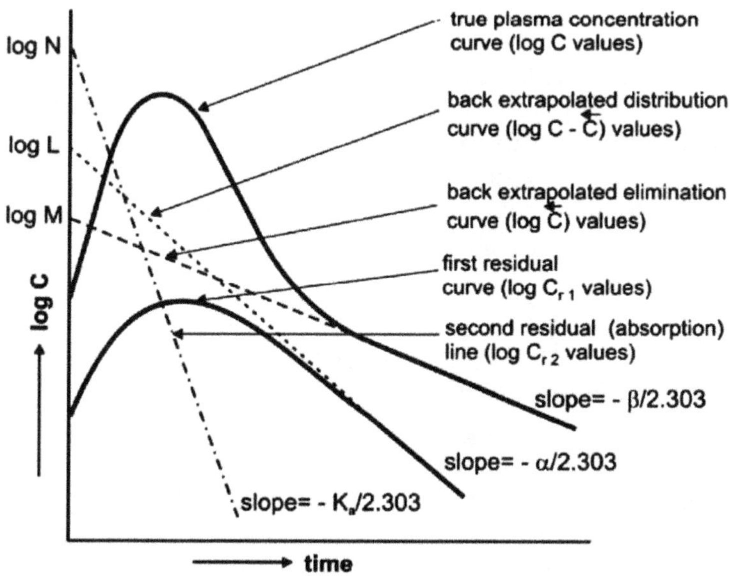

Fig. 10.5 Resolution of biexponential plasma concentration by the method of residuals for two compartment open model after extravascular bolus administration.

Besides the method of residuals, Ka can also be found by Loo-Riegelman method for drug that follows two compartment characteristics. The Loo-Riegelman method is a classical method for obtaining the ka of the 2-compartment model, which has few restrictions on the order processes and compartment model characteristics of the absorption process. This method requires plasma drug concentration- time data both after oral and i.v. administration of the drug to the same subject at different times in order to obtain all the necessary kinetic constants. Despite its complexity, the method can be applied to drugs that distribute in any number of compartments. The Loo-Reigelman absorption method provides the correct rate constant ka (if absorption is first order), whether metabolism occurs in compartment 1 only, compartment 2 only, or both compartments 1 and 2 of the two-compartment open models. The primary limitation of this method for calculation of Ka by this method is that the drug must be given iv to allow evaluation of the distribution and the elimination rate constants. For the drugs that cannot be given i/v, K_a cannot be calculated by Loo-Reiegelman Method. So for those drugs, Wagner-Nelson method may be used that assumes ka in one-compartment model.

Three Compartment Model

Three compartment model consist of (i) Central compartment, (ii) Tissue compartment, and (iii) Deep tissue compartment. In this compartment model drug distributes most rapidly in to first or central compartment, less rapidly in to second or tissue compartment and very slowly to the third or deep tissue compartment. The third compartment is poor in tissue such as bone and fat. Each compartment is independently connected to the central compartment.

Questions

Multiple Choice Questions

1. An antibiotic is given to a 70 kg individual by constant rate intravenous infusion. It is known that the drug follows a linear one-compartment model. The drug has a volume of distribution of 10 L and a first-order elimination rate constant of 0.2 h^{-1}. What is the infusion rate needed to achieve the desired plasma drug concentration of 20 μg/mL?
   (a) 200 mg/h (b) 2 mg/h
   (c) 40 μg/min (d) 40 mg/h
2. A drug is given intravenously to a patient at a constant dose rate of 10 mg/h. The drug follows a linear one-compartment model. The volume of distribution is 10 L and the first-order elimination rate constant is

$0.2\ h^{-1}$. The desired plasma drug concentration is 5 μg/mL. The time to reach 95% steady-state plasma drug concentration is:

(a) 15 h (b) 23 h
(c) 3.5 h (d) 12 h

3. What does the word "open" mean in the two compartment open model?
   (a) The drug easily enters
   (b) The drug readily mixes with the blood
   (c) Unidirectional input and output
   (d) Easy absorption
4. Which of the following organs, comprises the central compartment in a two compartment model?
   (a) Muscles (b) Skin
   (c) Adipose (d) Liver
5. Which organ comprises the peripheral compartment in a two compartment model?
   (a) Liver (b) Lungs
   (c) Kidneys (d) Muscles
6. Which of the following is not a category of 2 compartment model?
   (a) Two compartment model with elimination from the central compartment
   (b) Two compartment model with elimination from the peripheral compartment
   (c) Two compartment model with elimination from only plasma and blood
   (d) Two compartment model with elimination from both the compartments
7. In the given picture, the marking "?" represents the drug concentration of which compartment?

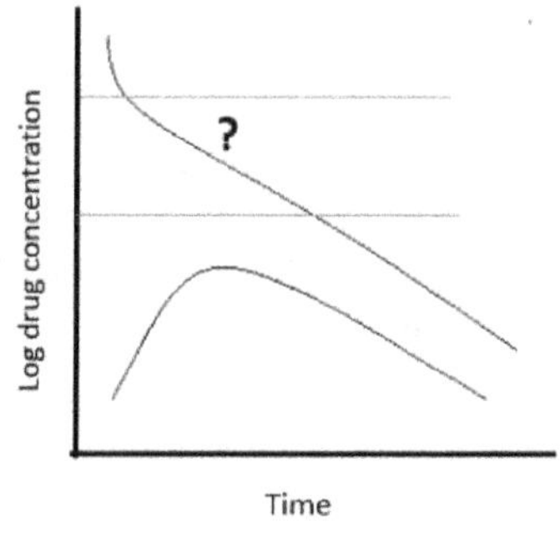

   (a) The central compartment in a two compartment model
   (b) The peripheral compartment in a two compartment model
   (c) The central compartment in a one compartment model
   (d) Drug concentration of the plasma

Short Questions

1. Depict the plasma concentration versus profiles of a drug following two compartment model after extravascular administration for central and peripheral comapartments.
2. Give an account of Loo Reigelman method for determination of Ka.
3. Give the schematic representation of two compartment open model after i.v. infusion and explain the pharmacokinetic characteristics.

Long Questions

1. What are the steps to be followed to resolve various components by method of residuals for a drug following two compartment model after extravascular administration?
2. A drug that follows a multicompartment pharmacokinetic model is given to a patient by rapid intravenous injection. Would the drug concentration in each tissue be the same after the drug equilibrates with the plasma and all the tissues in the body? Explain
3. An antibiotic is given by I.V bolus to patient of 65 kg. A dose of 650 mg is injected and plasma samples were collected at different time periods. The drug concentrations were determined after taking samples and analyzing them. The following data was obtained:

Time (hr)	C_p (g/mL)	Time (hr)	C_p (g/mL)
0.00	70.0	2.5	14.3
0.25	53.8	3.0	12.6
0.50	43.3	4.0	10.5
0.75	35.0	5.0	9.0
1.00	29.1	6.0	8.0
1.50	21.2	7.0	7.0
2.00	17.0		

Calculate the values for intercepts A and B and slopes A, B, K, K_{12} and K_{21}.

Non-Linear Pharmacokinetics

CHAPTER 11

LEARNING OBJECTIVES

- Concept of non- linear pharmacokinetics
- Causes of non-linearity
- Michaelis-Menten equation
- One compartment model with Michaelis-Menten elimination (IV BOLUS)

In previous chapters, we have studied the rate and course of drug disposition and action and it was said that the process follow first order kinetics. These linear models assumed that the pharmacokinetic parameters for a drug would not change when different doses or multiple doses of a drug were given. But there are certain exceptions there, where the increased doses or chronic medication can cause deviations from the linear pharmacokinetic profile previously observed with single low doses of the same drug. This *non-linear* pharmacokinetic behavior is also termed *dose-dependent pharmacokinetics.* The differences between linear and non-linear pharmacokinetics are summarized in Table 11.1.

Table 11.1 Differences between linear and non-linear pharmacokinetics.

Linear Pharmacokinetics	Non-linear Pharmacokinetics
Pharmacokinetic parameters for a drug would not change with dose	Pharmacokinetic parameters for a drug can change with change in dose
Dose independent	Dose dependent
Called as first order kinetics	Also called as mixed order, saturated kinetics, capacity limited
All semilog plots of C versus t for different doses are superimposable	Not superimposible

Generally five pharmacokinetic parameters fraction absorbed (F), absorption rate constant (Ka), elimination rate constant (Ke), volume of distribution (V_d), and clearance (Cl) define and summarize the time course of drug in the body and are generally linear or dose dependent. However, for some drugs, the principle of linearity may not hold good. For example when the dose of phenytoin is increased by 50 percent in a patient from 300 mg/day to 450 mg/day, the average steady state concentration may increase by almost ten times. This can only be explained by the phenomenon of non-linearity. In order to determine whether a drug is following dose dependent kinetics or not, the drug is given at various doses levels and a plasma concentration time curve is plotted for each dose. The curves should exhibit parallel slopes if the drug follows dose dependent kinetics. Thus the definition of Non-linear pharmacokinetics is : *Kinetics resulting from saturable drug transfer, leading to variation of the standard kinetic parameters with drug concentration.* Non-linear kinetics is usually due to saturation occurring in one of the pharmacokinetic mechanisms: protein binding, hepatic metabolism, or active renal transport of the drug.

1. **Saturable elimination:** The elimination rate tends to reach a maximal value above a certain drug concentration. Beyond this no further increase in the elimination rate occurs even when plasma drug concentration increases. Therefore, in non-linear elimination kinetics, the drug clearance decreases with increasing drug concentration.
2. **Saturable binding or reabsorption:** The drug protein binding or drug reabsorption in kidney tubules tends to reach maximal capacity above a certain drug concentration. This leads to a disproportionate increase in the rate of elimination with increasing drug concentrations (e.g. with high doses of vitamin).
3. **Saturable absorption:** Above a certain drug concentration at the absorption site, there is no further increase in the absorption rate. Thus absorption rate becomes constant and the bioavailability decreases with doses leading to concentrations at the absorption site above the maximal absorption capacity.

Non-linear pharmacokinetics can arise from factors associated with absorption, first-pass metabolism, binding, excretion and biotransformation. Non-linearities in absorption and bioavailability can cause increases in drug concentrations that are disproportionately high or low relative to the change in dose. One of the more important sources of non-linearity is the partial saturation of presystemic metabolism exhibited by such drugs as verapamil, propranolol and hydralazine. Only a few of the many hundreds of drugs in use exhibit non-linear behaviour that leads to clinical implications. Table 11.2 summarizes the reasons for non-linear pharmacokinetics.

Table 11.2 Causes of non-linear pharmacokinetics.

Cause	Example	Parameter Affected	Result
Gastrointestinal absorption			
Saturable transport in gut wall.	Amoxicillin	F	Decrease
Saturable hepatic metabolism on first pass	Nicardipine	F	Decrease
Saturable GI decomposition.	Penicillins	F	Increase
Distribution			
Saturable protein binding	Naproxen, lidocaine, salicylic acid	V_d	Increase
Saturable tissue binding	Naproxen, imipramine	V_d	Decrease
Renal excretion			
Active secretion saturable	Penicillin	Cl_R	Decrease
Active reabsorption saturable	Ascorbic acid	Cl_R	Increase
Change in urine pH	Salicylic acid	Cl_R	Decrease
Nephrotoxicity	Amino-glycosides	Cl_R	Decrease
Increase in urine flow	Theophyllines	Cl_R	Increase
Hepatic metabolism			
Enzyme induction	Carbamazepine	Cl_H	Increase
Hepatotoxicity	Acetaminophen	Cl_H	Decrease
Decreased hepatic blood flow	Propranalol	Cl_H	Decrease
Inhibition by metabolite	Lidocaine, diazepam	Cl_H	Decrease

A number of drugs demonstrate *saturation* or *capacity-limited metabolism* in humans. Examples of these saturable metabolic processes include glycine conjugation of salicylate, sulfate conjugation of salicylamide, acetylation of *p*-aminobenzoic acid, and the elimination of phenytoin. Drugs that demonstrate saturation kinetics usually show the following characteristics.

1. Elimination of drug does not follow simple first-order kinetics – that is, elimination kinetics is non-linear.

2. The elimination half-life changes as dose is increased. Usually, the elimination half-life increases with increased dose due to saturation of an enzyme system. However, the elimination half-life might decrease due to "self"-induction of liver biotransformation enzymes, as is observed for carbamazepine.
3. The area under the curve (AUC) is not proportional to the amount of bioavailable drug.
4. The saturation of capacity-limited processes may be affected by other drugs that require the same enzyme or carrier-mediated system (i.e. competition effects).
5. The composition and/or ratio of the metabolites of a drug may be affected by a change in the dose.

For drugs with saturable elimination, an increase in dosage or dosage frequency can lead to a disproportionate increase in plasma drug concentration when the rate of elimination tends to reach its maximum capacity. Therefore, changing dose is difficult and unpredictable. Special caution should be taken when deciding to change the dosage regimen of such drugs, particularly if elevated plasma concentrations are associated with toxicity. On the other hand, for drugs with saturable absorption or tubular reabsorption, a change in dosage may lead to a less than proportional change in plasma concentration. This is important in evaluating the efficiency of a drug dosage regimen. Partial saturation of elimination pathways can result in the well known behaviour typical of Michaelis-Menten pharmacokinetics.

Michaelis-Menten Equations

The elimination of a drug by a saturable enzymatic process is described by Michaelis-Menten kinetics. If C is the concentration of drug in plasma then

$$\text{Elimination rate} = -\frac{dC}{dt} = \frac{Vm\ C}{Km + C} \qquad .....(11.1)$$

where C is the plasma concentration, Vm is the maximum rate of process and Km is the Michaelis-Menten constant.

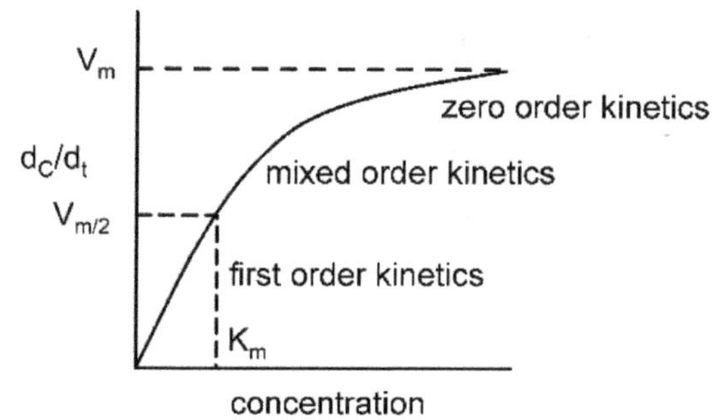

Fig. 11.1 A plot of Michaelis-Menten equation (elimination rate versus concentration).

It is important to note that Km is not an elimination constant, but is a hybrid rate constant in enzyme kinetics, representing both the forward and backward reaction rates and equal to the drug concentration or amount of drug in the body at 0.5 Vm. The values for Km and Vm are dependent on the nature of the drug and the enzymatic process involved.

The elimination rate of a hypothetical drug with a Km of 0.1 g/mL and a Vm of 0.5 g/mL per hour is calculated in by means of Equation 11.1. Because the ratio of the elimination rate to drug concentration changes as the drug concentration changes (i.e. dC/dt is not constant, Eq.11.1), the rate of drug elimination also changes and is not a first-order or linear process. In contrast, a first-order elimination process would yield the same elimination rate constant at all plasma drug concentrations. At drug concentrations of 0.4-10 g/mL, the enzyme system is not saturated and the rate of elimination is a mixed or nonlinear process. At higher drug concentrations, 11.2 g/mL and above, the elimination rate approaches the maximum velocity (Vm) of approximately 0.5 g/mL per hour. At Vm, the elimination rate is a constant and is considered a zero-order process.

The Michaelis-Menten equation is commonly used to describe the kinetics *in vitro, in situ* and certain *in vivo* conditions that are known to be controlled by enzymes.

At very low concentration, where Km >>> C, Km+ C is approximately equal to Km,

$$\frac{dC}{dt} = \frac{Vm\ C}{Km} \qquad .....(11.2)$$

As Vmax/Km is a constant term the rate of elimination is described as first order equation as it is directly proportional to concentration.

In case of higher doses where C >> Km, we have Km + C = C

$$\frac{dC}{dt} = \frac{Vm\ C}{C} = Vm \qquad .....(11.3)$$

The above equation describes zero order kinetics as rate of elimination is not dependent on concentration.

One Compartment Model with Michaelis-Menten Elimination (IV BOLUS)

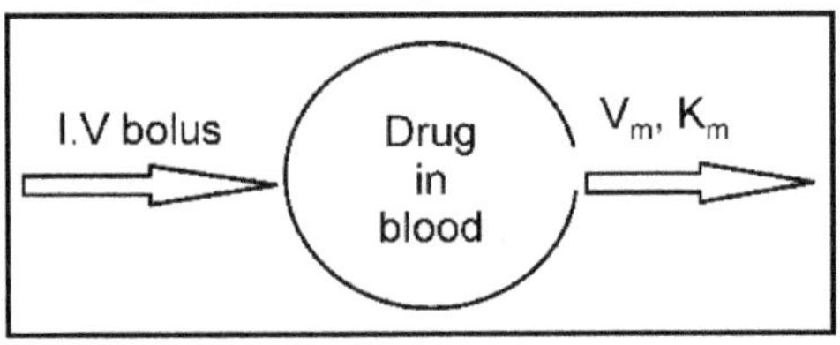

Fig. 11.2 Schematic diagram of one compartment model following Michaelis-Menten kinetics.

The rate of elimination of a drug that follows a capacity limited or saturable process can be determined using Michaelis-Menten equation

$$\frac{dC}{dt} = \frac{Vm\ C}{Km+C}$$

Integration of the above equation with respect to time gives,

$$\frac{C_o - C}{t} = Vm - \frac{Km}{t}\ ln\ \frac{Co}{C} \qquad .....(11.4)$$

where, C_o is the zero time concentration of the drug in plasma following an iv bolus injection of dose Xo and C is the concentration of drug in plasma at time t. Alternatively the amount of the drug in the body after an iv bolus injection may be calculated by the following equation.

$$\frac{Do - D}{t} = Vm - \frac{Km}{t}\ ln\ \frac{Do}{Dt} \qquad .....(11.5)$$

where, Do is the iv bolus dose and Dt is the amount of the drug in the body at any time, t. Equation 11.5 may be used to simulate the decline of the drug in the body after various sixe doses are given, provided the Km and V_m of the drug are known. In order to calculate the time for the dose of the drug to decline to a certain amount of the drug in the body. Equation 5 must be rearranged and solved for time t.

$$t = \frac{1}{V_m}(Do - Dt) + Km \log\frac{Do}{Dt} \quad .....(11.6)$$

Thus according to equation 11.6 there is an inverse relationship between the time for the dose to decline to a certain amount of the drug in the body and Vm. An increase in the Km value will increase the time for the drug to be eliminated from the body. The Km is a hybrid constant in kinetics representing both the forward and backward reaction rates and is equal to the drug concentration or amount of drug in the body at Vm/2.

Estimation of Km and Vm

Method I

Equation 11.7 relates the rate of drug transformation to the concentration of the drug in the body.

$$V = \frac{Vm\ C}{Km + C} \quad .....(11.7)$$

On rearrangement, equation 11.7 yields

$$1/V = \frac{Km}{Vm}\frac{1}{C} + \frac{1}{Vm} \quad .....(11.8)$$

Equation 11.8 can be plotted on a graph as 1/V versus 1/C. the intercept of the line is 1/Vm and the slope is Km/Vm.

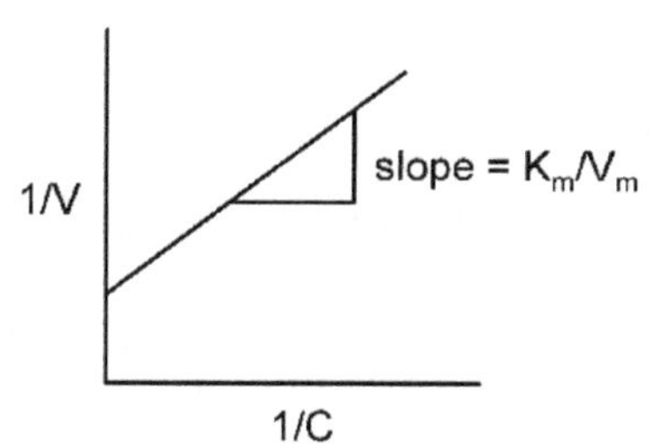

Fig. 11.3 Plot of 1/V versus 1/C for determining Km and Vm.

Method II

On rearranging equation 11.8, we have

$$\frac{C}{V} = \frac{1 \times C}{Vm} + \frac{Km}{Vm} \quad .....(11.9)$$

A plot of C/V versus C could yield a straight line with $1/V_m$ as slope and Km/V_m as intercept.

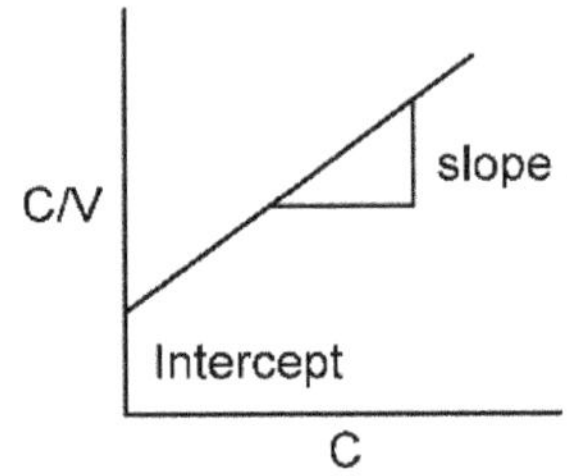

Fig.11.4 Plot of C/V versus C for determining Km and Vm.

Method III

On further rearranging equation 11.9 we get,

$$V = -Km\ V/C + Vm \qquad .....(11.10)$$

A plot of V versus V/C would yield a slope of –Km and an intercept of V_m.

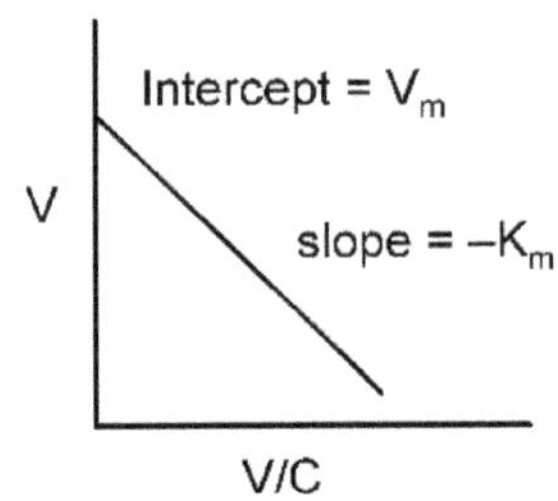

Fig. 11.5 Plot of V/C versus C for determining Km and V_m.

Determination of Km and V_m for One Compartment Steady State Concentration

When a drug is administered at a constant rate by i.v infusion or in a multiple dosage regimen, the steady state concentration C_{ss} is given by the equation:

$$DR = C_{ss}\ Cl_T \qquad .....(11.11)$$

where DR= Ko when administered as iv infusion and it is equal to F Xo/ τ when administered as multiple oral dosage regimen. Where F= fraction bioavailable, Xo is the oral dose and τ is the dosing interval.

At steady state the dosing rate equals the decline in plasma drug concentration and if the decline is capacity rate limited then,

$$DR = \frac{Vm\ Css}{Km+C} \qquad .....(11.12)$$

A plot of C_{ss} versus DR yields a typical curve shape graph as shown in Fig. 11.6.

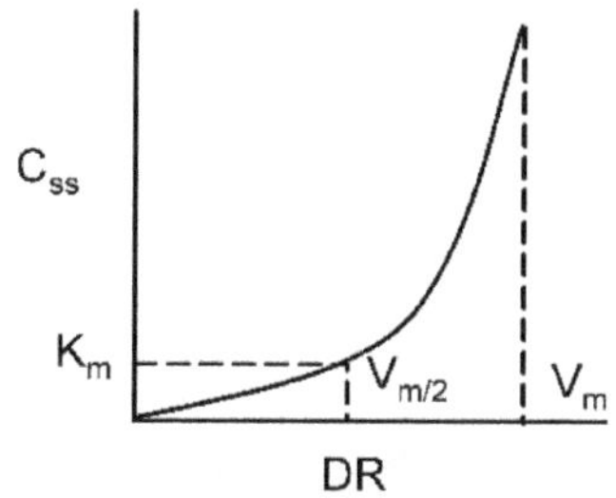

Fig. 11.6 Curve for a drug with non-linear kinetics between Css and dosing rates.

To determine the value of Km and V_m practically and graphically we have, Lineweaver-Burker plot. Equation 11.12 can be reversed and arranged as,

$$1/DR = \frac{K_m}{V_{max} \times C_{ss}} + \frac{1}{V_{max}} \qquad .....(11.13)$$

A plot of 1/DR versus $1/C_{ss}$ yields a straight line with slope Km/V_{max} and intercept of $1/V_{max}$ as seen in Fig 11.7.

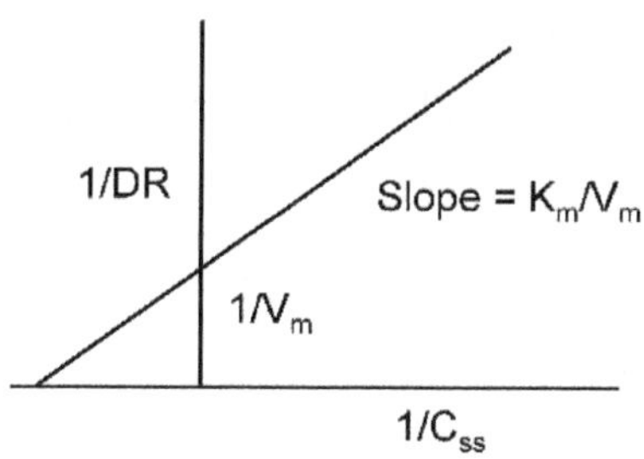

Fig. 11.7 Lineweaver-Burker plot for estimation of K_m and V_m at steady state concentration of drug.

Determination of Km and V_m by direct method

Km and V_m may be calculated by solving two simultaneous equations formed by substituting C_{ss} and R with C_{ss1}. R_1 and C_{ss2}.R_2 in equation 11.12.

$$R_1 = \frac{Vm\ Css_1}{Km+Css_1} \qquad .....(11.14)$$

$$R_2 = \frac{Vm\ Css_2}{Km+Css_2} \qquad .....(11.15)$$

Combining equations 11.14 and 11.15 we have

$$Km = \frac{R_2 - R_1}{\frac{R_1}{Css_1} - \frac{R_2}{Css_2}} \qquad .....(11.16)$$

where C_{ss1} is the steady state plasma drug concentration after dose 1 and C_{ss2} is steady state plasma concentration after dose 2. R_1 is first dosing rate and R_2 is second dosing rate.

There are several limitations of Km and V_{max} estimated by one compartment system and single capacity limited process. More complex equations and results will be generated if the drug is eliminated by more than one capacity limited process and if the drug follows multi compartmental kinetics. So it is essential to closely monitor the drugs that follow non-linear kinetics in the therapeutic regimen. E.g. phenytoin where toxic effects may precipitate.

Questions

Multiple Choice Questions

1. Michaelis-Menten elimination kinetics is due to
   (a) Saturation of metabolic sites
   (b) Due to partial saturation of these sites.
   (c) Both are true
   (d) Both are false
2. When a drug is administered as i.v. infusion the steady state concentration in terms of dosing rate can be written as
   (a) $DR = C_{ss}\ Cl_T$ (b) $C_{ss} = DR\ Cl_T$
3. The non-linear kinetics is governed by which equation
   (a) Michalis-Menten (b) Noyes Whitney.
   (c) Ficks law (d) Hixon crowell
4. Km is defined as
   (a) $V_{max}/2$ (b) $1/V_{max}$
   (c) $1/C_{ss}$ (d) $V_{max}\ C/\ Km + C$

5. What is the reason for non-linear pharmacokinetics
   (a) Carrier saturated transport
   (b) Enzyme saturation
   (c) Saturation of protein binding sites
   (d) All of the above
6. Michaelis-Menten equation is written as
   (a) $\frac{-dC}{dt} = \frac{V_{max}C}{K_{m+C}}$
   (b) $\frac{-dC}{dt} = \frac{V_{max}C}{V_{max}+C}$
   (c) $\frac{-dC}{dt} = \frac{K_{m+C}}{V_{max}+C}$
   (d) $\frac{-dC}{dt} = \frac{V_{max}C}{K_m C}$

Short Questions

1. Define non-linear pharmacokinetics.
2. Give mathematical expression for Michaelis-Menten equation.
3. Give plasma level times curve for drug which follows non-linear pharmacokinetics.
4. Give a plot of Michaelis-Menten equation.
5. Drugs showing capacity limited elimination follow ....
6. The value of Km is equal to ....
7. What are the units of V_{max} and KM?
8. What is the linearized form of the Michaelis-Menten equation?

Long Questions

1. List the causes of non-linear pharmacokinetics.
2. What is the difference between linear (dose-independent) and nonlinear (dose-dependent) kinetics?
3. Briefly explain the estimation of K_m and V_m.

4. Explain in detail the estimation of kinetic parameters for a process following one compartment non linear pharmacokinetics.
5. Discuss briefly the significance of non linear pharmacokinetics in governing the fate of drugs in body. Discuss different methods of estimation of Km.
6. Theophylline was administered to a patient at a dosing rate of 600 mg/day and 1200 mg/day and the respective steady state plasma concentration was found to be 9.8 mg/l and 28.6 mg/litre. Find the value of Km and V_m. Determine the dosing rate to achieve a C_{ss} of 15 mg/litre.
7. How does the clearance, plasma half life, or the time to reach steady state of a drug exhibiting capacity limited metabolism change in response to a change in dose?